I0103957

Shifting Borders, Negotiating Places

Cultural Studies and the Mutation of Value(s)

BORDIGHERA

Library of Congress Cataloging-in-Publication Data
Shifting borders, negotiating places : cultural studies and the mutation of value(s) / contributors Brent Adkins ... [et al.].
p. cm. -- (Via folios ; 42.)
Papers presented at the international conference held in Italy at the University of Rome "La Sapienza" Feb. 21-23, 2000.
Includes index.
ISBN 1-884419-82-8 (alk. paper)
1. Culture--Study and teaching--Congresses. 2. Social values--Congresses. I. Adkins, Brent.

HM623.S55 2006
306.01--dc22 2006047583

Proceedings of an Interdisciplinary Conference sponsored by LOYOLA UNIVERSITY CHICAGO in conjunction with the UNIVERSITY OF ROME "LA SAPIENZA"

21-23 February 2000
University of Rome "La Sapienza"
Rome, Italy

Organizing Committee and Editors

Loyola University Chicago
BRENT ADKINS
ANTHONY ELLIS
DAVID JESUIT
KEVIN MCCRUDEN
RACHEL POULSEN
JENNIFER WOZNIAK

University of Rome
DAVIDE BENNATO
FRANCESCO D'AMATO
DONATELLA DELLA RATTA

@ 2006 by Contributors

All rights reserved. Parts of this book may be reprinted only by written permission from the authors, and may not be reproduced for publication in book, magazine, or electronic media of any kind, except in quotations for purposes of literary reviews by critics.

Printed in the United States.

Published by
BORDIGHERA PRESS
Languages and Literatures
Florida Atlantic University
Boca Raton, FL 33431

VIA FOLIOS 42
ISBN 1-884419-82-8

Table of Contents

Acknowledgments

General Introduction (1)
Anthony Ellis and Rachel Poulsen

Border Disputes: Philosophy and Interdisciplinarity (9)
Brent Adkins

KEYNOTE ADDRESS

The Third Regime of Art (15)
Mario Perniola

PART I - ON THE BORDERS OF THEORY

Culture visuali: Una introduzione etnografica alla pixel zone (31)
Massimo Canevacci

Work (and Resistance) in Progress: Towards the Many Speeds of the Present (45)
Laura Hengehold

Theory on Borderlines: A Collective Experience and a Free Market (65)
Zeynep Mennan

Transiti di scrittura (87)
Isabella Vincentini

PART II - CONSTRUCTING NATIONAL & INTERNATIONAL IDENTITIES

Un approccio di Antropologia del Diritto al problema dell'armonizzazione europea: l'esempio nordamericano (99)
Barbara Faedda

Transidioma/Transidiomatic Practices (113)
Marco Jacquemet

Subsidiarized Places, Reimagined Communities: Stateless Regions in a United Europe (119)
Kyriaki Papageorgiou

Sexual Harassment in the Context of a Gender-Egalitarian Culture: The Example of the Philippines (131)
Patrocinio P. Schweickart

"La Massa è Donna": La Giornata della "fede" and Remembering Fascist Italy (145)
Anne Wingenter

PART III – LANGUAGE & TEXT

Linguaggio mutazione net-pidgin (161)
Franco Berardi

Un teatro per l'estetica: Edipo contro Freud (167)
Carlo Ferrucci

1789-1989: Romanticism, Liberalism, and the End of History? (181)
Gary Kelly

Capital Flows Through Language: Market English and the World Bank (191)
J. Paul Narkunas

Il muro di Gutenberg (211)
Grazia Sotis

CLOSING ADDRESS

Una notte a Internet (225)
Paola Colaiacomo

CONTRIBUTORS

Acknowledgments

We wish to express our deepest gratitude to James Brennan, Dean of the Graduate School at Loyola University Chicago at the time of the Shifting Borders conference, for all his support and encouragement. We would also like to acknowledge the hospitality of the University of Rome "La Sapienza," especially Paolo De Nardis, Mario Morcellini, and Alberto Abruzzese of the Department of Sociology. Sincere thanks go out to all those who traveled from near and far to participate in this event. We appreciate the cooperation of the faculty and staff of the Loyola University Rome Center and its Director, George Hostert. A debt is owed to John Casey and Wiley Feinstein for the editorial assistance they provided in the latter stages of this book's preparation. Finally, the American editors remain profoundly indebted to Anna Camaiti Hostert for her leadership and kindness during their stay in Rome as Loyola University Graduate Fellows. The extent of her contribution—to this book and to the wonderful experience of six visiting American scholars—is inestimable.

General Introduction

Anthony Ellis & Rachel Poulsen

In recent years, two important books have treated the subject of the practice of cultural studies in Italy. The first, *Italian Cultural Studies: An Introduction* (1996), edited by David Forgacs and Robert Lumley, begins by declaring that cultural studies as it has been variously practiced, first in Britain and then in North America, has experienced "no equivalent boom" in Italy (8). According to the editors, the combination of an entrenched humanist intellectual tradition in Italy and limited access to higher educational opportunities for many Italian citizens worked to delay the national impact of this fast-growing interdisciplinary movement, which features among its aims the leveling of time-honored distinctions between high and low culture. The "delayed reception" in Italy of the theoretical and methodological innovations of cultural studies practitioners frustrated "the development of an alternative definition of culture" (3), one that might have been more inclusive as well as more likely to stimulate inquiry into the relationships of Italian cultural products with areas like politics, economics and technology—that is, the mutual influence of text and social context that is a major concern of cultural studies. Forgacs and Lumley assert that despite this delay in the Italian adoption of cultural studies (with some notable exceptions, it should be noted, e.g., the work of Umberto Eco), its influence can be perceived in the 1990s in the growing number of Italian Studies scholars who began to apply their critical acumen to areas outside the domain of high culture. The essays included in their volume illustrate this new focus, as do the interventions in *Italian Cultural Studies* (2001), the product of a conference on this subject held at Dartmouth College in October 1999. Maria Galli Stampino, in her contribution to Parati and

Lawton's collection, suggests the type of difference cultural studies makes in the world of scholarship, and thus what advantages it promises to teachers and students of *l'italianistica.* In cultural studies

> [n]ot only is the concept and tradition of the canon challenged, but its intellectual basis is undermined: the idea of a "pure" literature that is born and read (and hence can be subsequently studied) in full isolation from culture at large. In this respect, Gramsci's intuitions linked to his historical analysis of the juxtaposition between "intellettuali" and "popolo" can prove fundamental and prescient. If we understand Gramsci's groundbreaking role, then, another distinctive feature of Cultural Studies has to be acknowledged: a pervasive, deeply rooted sense of class consciousness that general cultural analyses of other sorts are typically missing. (43)

When cultural studies investigates the complex relationship between a society's cultural practices and its manifestations of political power, it can shed light on that society's more insidious economic and ideological substructures, on the ways the class system referred to by Galli Stampino gets maintained and justified. The most politically committed work associated with cultural studies, beginning with the likes of Raymond Williams, Stuart Hall and Richard Hoggart in the 1960s and 70s, has concentrated on probing the dynamics of capitalism, in the interest of eventually, as much as possible, subverting it. It is true that as the breadth of subjects addressed by cultural studies practitioners has increased—and the number of theoretical and methodological approaches has likewise proliferated—the dedication of its adherents to promoting political change has been questioned, particularly in American circles, where many scholars have been faulted for relying too much on an apolitical (and ahistorical) "cultural populism" (Kellner 142). Yet still the political rootedness of cultural studies remains the best reason to be excited about the new directions this admittedly diffuse sphere of intellectual inquiry is taking, in Italy and elsewhere.

As we prepared to host an international conference on cultural studies in Rome in February 2000, the heterogeneity of our chosen topic, coupled with the emergent nature of cultural studies in Italy, produced an air of excitement as well as curiosity about the proposals we would receive. In addition, we suspected that the ongoing process of European political and economic unification would encourage speculation on issues related to globalization and the place of cultural studies in apprehending and theoretizing transnational change. The phrases "Shifting Borders" and "Mutation of Value(s)" were included in the conference title precisely to invite consideration of the heightened political and cultural stakes both in a newly unified Europe and in a rapidly shrinking world. The conference was held at the Università di Roma "La Sapienza" on 21-23 February, 2000 and was free and open to the public.

Although a diversity of nationalities and types of institutional affiliations were noticeably evident at the Shifting Borders conference, it would be inaccurate to speak of stark division along geographic lines, of, for example, an incipient Italian conception of cultural studies versus a somewhat more established American tradition of applying postmodern theory to the scrutiny of popular culture. Rather, the participating speakers from all parts of Europe and North America demonstrated a range of interests and methods in which one could observe the component parts of the three-dimensional "multiperspectivist approach" advocated by Douglas Kellner in a recent essay on the relationships among philosophy, social theory, and cultural studies. Kellner's three dimensions—what he sees as the three metatheoretical avenues into cultural studies—include "(1) the production and political economy of culture; (2) textual analysis and critique of its artifacts; and (3) study of audience reception and the uses of media / cultural products" (143). While noting that these three realms of inquiry can and should overlap, he proposes this division in the belief that attempts at clarifying the aims and means of cultural studies are necessary if practitioners are to restore the "normative critical standpoint" and "activist political thrust" that have been sacrificed in cultural studies' postmodern turn (144). In this context, it is interesting to discern these three approaches, variously undertaken (and with or without a postmodern perspective), in the papers published in this volume.

Several authors in this collection concern themselves with Kellner's first dimension, that is, with political economy and production, as they consider the distribution and consumption of valuable commodities in times of rapid and often turbulent globalization. For example, J. Paul Narkunas' "Capital Flows Through Language: Market English and the World Bank" argues that throughout the world the English language functions increasingly as a commodity, as a form of what Michel Foucault refers to as "bio-power." As a powerful entity offering wealth to underdeveloped nations under strict conditions, the World Bank uses education (in English) as part of its "human capital" development program. Narkunas contends that as the Bank's global hegemony grows, those states dependent on it as a source of wealth risk compromising both their political sovereignty and their cultural individuality. Also focusing on the fragility of a localized people's identity in the face of global and national forces, Kiki Papageorgiou's "Subsidiarized Places, Reimagined Communities: Stateless Regions in a United Europe" examines the experience of the Bretons, a group formerly subordinated in the process of French nation-state construction, now newly validated with the emergence of the idea of a "Europe of the Regions." According to Papageorgiou, the European Union's formation of the Committee of the Regions has legitimized the efforts of "substate groups" such as the Bretons to resist "supranational authorities" where those groups have managed to reclaim their cultural origins. Similarly to how Narkunas reveals language as a commodity, Papageorgiou shows how culture itself "connotes a commodity that has the ability to unite people and to give them a sense of shared belonging" as it provides a form of resistance against large-scale political and economic forces. Barbara Faedda's "Un approccio di Antropologia del Diritto al problema dell'armonizzazione europea: l'esempio nordamericano" takes up a similar theme as it explores the precarious social and legal position of various Canadian substate groups: aborigines, immigrants and refugees. Faedda believes that Europe can use Canada as a model as it tries to harmonize state, national and federal law with the traditional legal structures of these populations. Like France with the Bretons, Canada first adopted a misguided policy of assimilation but has since adopted the path of harmonization.

Other papers perform the textual analysis and consideration of cultural artifacts identified by Kellner as the second dimension of a theoretically informed cultural studies. For example, in *"Il muro di Gutenberg,"* Grazia Sotis interprets Giuseppe Cassieri's novel of the same title both within its contemporary political and historical framework and in the context of Cassieri's previous writings. She maintains that the novel's interdisciplinary scope enables an impressive historic and cultural synthesis, as Cassieri chronicles the nature and mutation of values in a world experiencing globalization. Isabella Vincentini, with "Transiti di scrittura," speculates more broadly on artistic movements as the author discusses how and why we are in a period featuring the shifting of borders and negotiation of places. After describing trends in philosophy and art over the past thirty years, Vincentini concludes that due in part to the influences of postmodernism and French poststructuralism we find ourselves at the end of the "grandi narrazioni." What is needed at this point? Vincentini calls for the return of the truly anarchic element in art, which she describes as "perturbante," as opposed to that which is only "provocatorio"; the latter is a characteristic of art produced in intellectual and emotional isolation, whereas the former can assist us to find our "luogo di transito." Gary Kelly, in "1789-1989: Romanticism, Liberalism, and the End of History?" examines the role of Romanticism in the construction of the modern liberal state. Kelly begins by asserting that the ascendancy of the Romantic movement during the Enlightenment led to the establishment of the sovereign subject as we know it and moves on to hypothesize the decline of this figure as a consequence of globalization. In the course of his paper, Kelly points to several literary texts as examples of how Romanticism has affected national politics. Although this paradigm may be shifting, the formal study of literature as developed "in the Romantic discursive revolution" remains a precondition for an individual's professional advancement.

In the papers that concentrate on issues of mixed media and audience reception, many contributors share a curiosity about the power of the Internet to alter our conceptions of the effects of technological advancement on both individuals and communities. As many of our most fascinating papers contend, the Internet acts not only as a storehouse of information, but as an agent of change in the very ways that information is apprehended and put to use. The Internet's increasing availability around the world especially seems to intrigue linguists, who wonder what consequences our on-line interconnectedness will have on linguistic diversity. Will the World Wide Web prove to solidify the place of English as a truly global language, or will the end result be a flourishing of dialects and/or hybridized languages? On this subject, Franco Berardi, in "Linguaggio mutazione net-pidgin," argues that human society is undergoing a period of deterritorialization in which English occupies a dominant position as world language. Berardi attributes this dominance to the plasticity of English, and the hegemony of the English-speaking world to its considerable "cultural plasticity." When we visit cyberspace, we enter a region in which the relationship between English and various "pidgins" is played out. Massimo Canevacci introduces "Culture visuali: Una introduzione etnografica alla pixel zone" by discussing recent developments in anthropology, notably its departure from the Geertzian model, and the significant implications of this shift for cultural studies. He writes of a "dissolution" of society, or at least of the State, as the old binaries give way to the tryptych "culture-communication-consumption." The triumph of visual culture promotes the crossing and shifting of borders. In his provocative study, Canevacci discusses the nature of e-space, the pixellated environment, digital collage, mediagenic reality, and avant-pop, among other colorful manifestations of the electronic age.

The conference's closing address, Paola Colaiacomo's "Una notte a Internet," revisits this subject, as the author's "night on the Internet" leads her to contemplate the loss of established concepts of distance and perspective. But as her nocturnal trip causes her to perceive profound change around her, she also pays homage to some remote literary precursors of the contemporary impulse to call into question "homologized notions of perspective," among them Shakespeare's Caliban, Montaigne's cannibals, and Spenser's "Castle of Alma" episode from *The Fairie Queene*.

These and the other papers included here indicate some of the directions scholars working in cultural studies have been taking. If cultural studies took hold in Italy later than it did in Great Britain and North America, Italian academia now includes both many enthusiastic practitioners and a committed audience, as the diverse proceedings of this intellectual satisfying conference indicate.

WORKS CITED

Forgacs, David, and Robert Lumley, ed. *Italian Cultural Studies: An Introduction*. Oxford: Oxford UP, 1996.

Kellner, Douglas. "Cultural Studies and Philosophy: An Intervention." *A Companion to Cultural Studies.* Ed. Toby Miller. Oxford: Blackwell, 2001. 139-53.

Stampino, Maria Galli. "What We Talk About When We Talk About [Italian] Cultural Studies, and Why (with Apologies to Raymond Carver)." *Italian Cultural Studies*. Ed. Graziella Parati and Ben Lawton. Boca Raton, FL: Bordighera, 2001. 27-51.

BORDER DISPUTES
Philosophy and Interdisciplinarity

Brent Adkins

Discussion of and indeed the very possibility of interdisciplinarity is a relatively recent phenomenon. The ancient Roman curriculum of logic, rhetoric, and grammar, the trivium, was adapted *in toto* from the Greeks, and remained relatively unchanged throughout the entire Middle Ages. Beginning in the modern period, however, the rise of the experimental sciences through the application of the scientific method to an ever-increasing array of topics began to show the limitations of classical pedagogy. The expansion of the experimental sciences, nevertheless, remained housed comfortably under the aegis of philosophy through the eighteenth century. One could easily call a chemist as well as a metaphysician a philosopher. A further distinction might be made between a natural philosopher and a speculative philosopher, but this distinction was not necessary. The comfort of the experimental sciences as a mode of philosophy did not survive the nineteenth century, however. The increasing gap between the experimental sciences and philosophy was accompanied by the genesis of the social sciences during this same period. The disciplines of psychology, sociology, anthropology, economics, linguistics, and historical-critical methods of textual analysis began to distinguish themselves throughout the nineteenth century. These new sciences modeled their methodology explicitly on the experimental sciences and hoped to emulate the progress of the experimental sciences. Thus, by the end of the nineteenth century philosophy is no longer the most foundational science of which other sciences are merely a mode, but simply one discipline among others, each with its own subject matter and methodology. The questions that Kant poses and believes he has answered at the end of the *Critique of Pure Reason* in 1781— "What can I know? What ought I to do? What can I hope?"—can no longer be answered within the confines of philosophy, but now require a vast array of disciplines.

The disciplinary model that arises in the nineteenth century has many benefits. It allows a much greater depth of analysis as practitioners of a discipline are trained within that discipline. Investigative techniques are codified. A jargon is developed that allows for an economy of explanation. One may take for granted the foundational concepts of a discipline in order to pursue ever-finer distinctions within that discipline. This allows the discipline to grow very rapidly. The difficulty, of course, is that the specialization that is required of each discipline makes it very difficult for the disciplines to communicate effectively with one another. The specialization required for each discipline also makes it difficult for someone to gain an appropriate level of expertise in order to mediate among multiple disciplines. At the same time, however, the desire and even the need to use the best knowledge available from multiple disciplines may be required to solve particular problems or account for particular phenomena. How is it possible to adjudicate the demands of multiple disciplines simultaneously? The answer to this question is the difficulty and the promise of cultural studies.

Now that the complex phenomenon of culture has presented itself as an object of study, no discipline by itself seems fully adequate to the task of analysis. The experimental sciences and the social sciences have spent the last two centuries defining themselves as self-contained disciplines sometimes in explicit opposition to philosophy. The carefully constructed boundaries between disciplines that for so long facilitated the growth of the disciplines are now an obstacle to a clear understanding of culture. The essays in this collection solve the problem of relating disparate disciplines in surprising and fruitful ways. Some use the interpretation of empirical data to challenge longstanding concepts in the social sciences, such as the nature of cultural identity. Other essays develop new concepts in order to account for new political phenomena, such as the recent turmoil in the Balkans. I would like to suggest that whatever form this adjudication takes, it represents the return of a certain type of philosophical theorizing that is demanded anytime one must ask conceptual or foundational questions. Philosophy can no longer relate to other disciplines as that which grounds the legitimacy of their project, as was the case throughout the eighteenth century. Philosophy can no longer provide an encyclopedia of the sciences as Hegel dreamed. What philosophy can do, however, is mediate between the disciplines and provide a means for analyzing their conceptual foundations.

Keynote Address

THE THIRD REGIME OF ART

Mario Perniola

1. *Art without aura, critique without theory.* Common among young art critics today is the opinion that art can do without theory. The art critic should no longer deal with questions of aesthetics, poetics, and art history but rather should limit his task to a type of chronicle reporting and publicity of the artists he likes. This opinion is a comprehensible reaction to the inconsistency and the inconclusive verbosity of much of the art criticism—with which many young art critics are in bitter polemics—of the second half of the twentieth century. But it roots its more profound intuitions in those tendencies of the art of the nineties, which, like the *Posthuman,* define themselves by a complete reduction to the existent object, by an ultra-naturalism alien from every type, even merely theoretical, of transcendence, and by a sensibility permeated with disgust and abjection. So it seems that young art critics, instead of explaining the artists of the *Posthuman* to the public, want to compete with them. They draw from their message not the extremism of provocation and transgression, but the flatness, the banality, and the "idiocy" of their works. In aligning themselves with this anti-theoretical orientation, these young art critics unfortunately follow young music, film and literary critics. But the most paradoxical aspect of this orientation consists in the fact that the reduction to the existent object does not at all exempt these young critics from expressing their judgment on artists; rather, their work abounds in evaluations, appraisals, and unmotivated and superficial rejections. This does not depend so much on the fact that the critic claims the liberty of the artist for himself, as much as on the dilettantish attitude of expressing a judgment of personal and private taste: "I like this," "I don't like this." For the most part it does not go beyond this.

2. *On the credibility of art and the singularity of the artist.* Benjamin's 1936 essay "The Work of Art in the Age of Mechanical Reproduction" constitutes a very significant point of reference for the examination of the question of the importance of theory in the plastic arts today. As is well known, Benjamin's essay works on the opposition between two regimes of the work of art. On the one hand, the *aura* characterizes the traditional regime of the work of art. This *aura* is the cultural value attributed to a unique and lasting object, which solicits an aesthetic experience based on a relationship of *distance* from the viewer. On the other hand, the mechanical reproduction of the work of art, which confers a merely expositive value on the work of art, inaugurates a completely secularized and disenchanted regime, founded on a relationship of *nearness* to the public. Benjamin does not discuss the role of theoretical mediation in the constitution of the artistic value of the two regimes. He would in any case have erred had he deduced that the second regime, on account of this implicit mass reproducibility, no longer needs theory. Indeed, Benjamin is certainly a stranger to any kind of populism, which he in fact considers to be rather close to fascism, in that it "sees its salvation in giving these masses not their right, but instead a chance to express themselves" (Epilogue). In the era of mechanical reproducibility, it seems that the fundamental task of theory is to consider art from a secularized and disenchanted point of view. So for this reason, theory can neither go back to the *aura*, nor suppress itself and allow the public to establish, immediately and empirically, what is art and what is not.

It seems, however, that the history of the plastic arts from the Sixties forward has followed a rather different path from that delineated by Benjamin. As a matter of fact, Benjamin connects the disappearance of the *aura* with the dissolution of the criteria of authenticity of the work of art and the transformation of the author into a kind of technician. But nowadays these three elements of art—*aura*, work, and author—have undergone unexpected transformations. As far as the presence of a quasi-religious transcendent dimension in the experience of art is concerned, it is doubtful that any kind of secularization has effectively taken place. Indeed, some have considered the religious paradigm articulated by the three figures of the prophet, the faithful, and the priest pertinent for explaining the artistic paradigm as articulated by the figure of the artist, the public and the specialist (Bourdieu). Besides, the very survival of the artistic object seems to depend on an attitude of "belief" which allows us to affirm the difference of the artistic object from objects of daily life (Didi-Huberman). It is nevertheless beyond question that the principle of the authenticity of the work of art has been extraordinarily reinforced: in fact, the more the artistic object is indistinguishable from the useful object—as in the "ready-made"—the more it has to be certified and guaranteed as unique, unrepeatable and endowed with cultural authority. In the end, the artist is involved in an unprecedented process of singularization that has even broken those principles of universality on which aesthetic experience from the eighteenth century forward has been founded: singularity and its most transgressive manifestations have ended up constituting the only criterion of value of art today.

3. *Beyond the aura and mechanical reproducibility.* The opposition between the regime of the *aura* and the regime of mechanical reproducibility does not do justice to Benjamin's essay; it ignores its most important theoretical contribution: the determination of a *third regime of art and aesthetic experience.* Reification, fetishism, and, more generally, the phenomenon that Benjamin himself defined as "the sex appeal of the inorganic" characterize this regime. It is from the perspective of this third dimension, irreducible to and different from the other two, that we can finally under-

stand the dynamics of contemporary art. Neither religious in a traditional sense nor technological in the functional sense of the term, the dynamics of contemporary art participate as much in the pathology of religious experience, in the form of fetishism, as in technological imagination, in the form of the animation of the inanimate. It is to this third dimension that Benjamin refers when he underscores the confusion, implicit in cinematography, between actor and instrument, between human being and thing; or when, in the work of the film actor, he sees a reification not only of his labor power, but also of his body, of his skin and hair, of his heart and kidneys. This mixing of materiality and abstraction finds its most extreme manifestations in contemporary art: in it, in fact, the personality of the artist becomes a trademark that guarantees the value of the artistic product. The formal characteristics of the artistic product lose their importance and can, as for example happens in conceptual art, be in fact substituted for by an idea.

A truly singular aspect of contemporary art consists in the fact that no matter how radical its demystification—that is, the unveiling of its supporting economic and institutional mechanisms—has been, its cultural credibility has been compromised very little, while its commercial and social credibility has not been compromised at all. But revolutionary thinkers (from Benjamin to Debord, from Castoriadis to Baudrillard) are not the only ones to have taken the *aura* away from art; the artists themselves (from Duchamp to Warhol, from Fontana to Boltanski, from Christo to Beuys)—authors of work not any less radical than that of the thinkers—have participated in even greater measure in this process of unveiling.

4. *Modern paradigm and contemporary paradigm.* As the French sociologist of art Nathalie Heinich has recently demonstrated in her ample volume *Le triple jeu de l'art contemporain* (1998), the entire history of contemporary art can

be interpreted as a transgression of frontiers and as an immense territorial expansion. Such crossing of limits should not be thought of as an absence of norms, but rather as a complex strategy of challenge and of scandal, which has more to do with the economy of communication and information than with artistic products understood as objects of collection. Pertinent in this regard is Heinich's distinction between the modern paradigm (for which artistic value resides in the work of art and all of that which is outside of it is added to its intrinsic value) and the contemporary paradigm (for which artistic value resides in the combination of connections—discourses, actions, networks, situations and sense effects—established around or coming from an object, which is only an occasion or pretext or point of passage). While there is no doubt that the modern paradigm corresponds perfectly to that which I indicated in the introduction as "art of the works of art," the identification of the contemporary paradigm with media vitalism is much more uncertain. By "contemporary paradigm" Nathalie Heinich means rather an intermediate situation—between "art of the work of art" and artistic communication—in which public artistic institutions (that is, large museums and international expositions) have a fundamental role by playing on two territories: the valorization of works of art and the media event. In fact, unlike past years, institutions and the media-transgressive artist have come to an accord at the expense of the third term of "the game of contemporary art," the public. That is to say, while in the past the institution shared the point of view of the public and condemned the transgressive activities of the avant-garde, today the institution considers it more appropriate to sustain and favor the transgressive artist, since it draws from scandal a benefit in terms of publicity and media resonance much greater than that which it could have attained in adhering to the traditional tastes of the public. So an art of the avant-garde with direct ties to institutions was born. And it has been able to attain market values higher than art that relies on private galleries and collectors; the privileged buyer of the new transgressive artist is no longer the merchant or the far-sighted collector (as in the modern paradigm) but rather the institution! The fracture between artistic innovation and the public has grown to the point of becoming a real and proper irresolvable disagreement. The public is like a spectator of a chess match who completely ignores the rules of the game; he sees two people who move at turns statuettes placed on a chessboard. At the same time, however, the institution's acceptance of this situation annuls the transgressive effect of artistic innovation and transforms the entire system of art into a game for the initiated from which—as Nathalie Heinich rightly observes—precisely those who could still be unsettled are absent! This ends up generating a profound malaise not only in the public, but also in the greater part of artists and mediators (critics, curators, art theorists). How to get out of it?

In the first place, we need to abandon the idea that transgression constitutes in itself a type of efficacious opposition. If transgression characterizes the movement of modern art from the second half of the nineteenth century until today, it has completely exhausted its polemical function. An opposition that determines itself on the base of that which it denies had already appeared to Nietzsche as a merely reactive attitude, incapable of affirming the autonomy of its own difference: he defined it in the last aphorism of the second part of *Human, All Too Human* as "the sickness of the chains." Art today still suffers from this sickness. These chains are "Those heavy and pregnant errors contained in the conceptions of morality, religion and metaphysics" (Nietzsche 350). It is not enough to demythologize art by stripping it of its *aura*—that which in fact constitutes the metaphysical, moral, and religious way in which the difference of the work of art from the world has been conceived—since this demythologization, which Benjamin connected with the advent of mechanical reproducibility, ends up by flattening art onto the most insignificant reality, reducing it to an instrument of recreation and edification. For this reason Gianni Vattimo has very eloquently underscored the importance of completing the process of demystification by means of an "unmasking of the unmasking": in fact, the demythologization shows itself to be functional with respect to the needs of a society which no longer needs to maintain its relative autonomy from symbolic activities, such as art, philosophy, and the humanities in general. For this reason, it tends to transform the bearers of symbolic activities into "functionaries of a productive system, by reducing them to a link of unmediated reference to the needs of production and of social organization" (Vattimo 141). In this sense, the art without *aura* of the *Posthuman* and the critique without theory that promotes it would constitute a notable acceleration of this process. The transgression of the frontiers of art would not therefore be in any sense a progressivist movement. It would aim instead at taking any sort of autonomy away from the artist, the critic and curator, bringing them down to the plane of reality, that is to say, to the direct dependence on economic imperatives. In this sense, the vindication of the *aura* of works of art and of the autonomy of symbolic worlds would signify social contestation, because it would constitute the last line of defense against the total and direct domination of capital. Paradoxically, however, whoever works against cultural mediation in favor of communicative and expositive spontaneity, notwithstanding his progressivist intentions, would not do anything other than accelerate the process of the liquidation of symbolic worlds.

The fact is that the "contemporary paradigm" described by Heinich, to which the greater part of the large institutions of art today conform, does not at all follow the route of demythologization and of unmasking. Rather, it promotes a hypermystfication. On the one hand, it exaggerates the singularity of the artist, and on the other, it dissolves all of the contents of his personality; it still proposes works of art for public appraisal, while at the same time it proceeds according to open-minded strategies of promoting an image of its own that no longer has anything to do with art. In other words, the artist, the critic, and the art theorist find that they have to deal with very muddy situations, in which the mix of cynicism, market interests, and personal rivalries impedes proper professional practices. In the face of such situations, the traditionalist defense of the *aura*, as well as the way of unmasking and of extreme transgression, end up losing; in fact, the "contemporary paradigm" does not deny the *aura*, but mystifies it by means of the hyperbolic economic evaluation of the signature of certain artists, promoted by means of strategies that belong more to the market of information than to that of art; since it appropriates transgression by turning it in its own favor, it does not so much deny it as render it inoperative.

5. *The heroic-ironic role of art and philosophy.* Notwithstanding all of that, the "contemporary paradigm" of art must be placed among the most exciting aspects of contemporary culture, precisely because of its rather incongruous mixture of economic, aesthetic and communicative aspects. Reflection on such a phenomenon benefits not only sociology—as Nathalie Heinich sustains in her brilliant pamphlet, *Ce que l'art fait à la sociologie* (1988)—but also, and perhaps even more so, philosophy. In fact, while for sociology art is (at least according to Heinich) only an object of study that constrains it to refine its investigative tools, for philosophy art is something much closer; philosophy itself participates in that regime of singularity—based on the unicity, irreducibility, originality, and the transgression of the canons—on which the world of art stands. It is difficult, for example, to consider a philosophical work as "good" only because it meets a certain "standard"; in fact, to attribute such a qualification to it means to discredit it,

that is, to consider it devoid of those requirements of innovation and creativity essential for philosophical production. So the expression "philosophical career" sounds no less reductive than "artistic career," since it implies a standardization of that which by definition is modeled on the imperative of being exceptional. As Heinich acutely observes, the exercise of art is precisely the opposite of a bureaucratic career: while the latter pursues personal ends (promotion) by means of impersonal means (the application of rules), the artist (like the philosopher) pursues impersonal ends (the opening of horizons of experience characterized by a pretext of universality) by personal means (the tutelage and development of his own singularity).

The idea of an artist or organic thinker—that is, of a producer of innovation—who draws his own credibility uniquely from the fact of expressing his ideas and collective feeling is no longer viable. In fact, such an idea presupposes in its turn that there exists today such a thing as collectivity, endowed with a unique identity, founded on nation or religion, on class or gender, or on some other datum. It is interesting to observe that also inside so-called Cultural Studies the same notions of culture and value collide with each other. The concept of culture (or of subculture) seems in fact bound to a normative presupposition of the traditional and conservative type which, in the final analysis, appeals to principles of social purity, integrity and vitality (Frow 10-11); instead, valorization in the field of art and philosophy would imply, with regard to the canons, the promotion of transgressive choices and strategies which can be grasped only by those who have the knowledge and instruments to understand them, and who would in any case tend to constitute an autonomous social group endowed with specific interests (Frow 131ff).

On the other hand, the products of art and philosophy have always required universal recognition, however potential or virtual; therefore, innovation with respect to precedent models can never be too great, at the expense of falling into extravagance and inaccessibility. The artist and the philosopher consequently tend to see themselves in a "heroic-ironic" role (Vattimo 140) that, on the one hand, contains an element of challenge towards that which is socially dominant, and on the other, cannot exhaust itself in transgression, at the expense of remaining in that state of subordination to the past that Nietzsche defined as "the sickness of the chains."

The question that is difficult to answer here is whether this "heroic-ironic" role is more consonant today with the philosopher or the artist. The latter seems in fact too entangled in the ambiguities and incongruence of the "contemporary paradigm" to be able to attain that *third regime of art and aesthetic experience* that lies beyond the traditional *aura* and mechanical disenchantment. Paradoxically, therefore, the philosopher of art seems today better equipped than the artist to valorize without remaining captive of the cult of works of art, and to communicate without being a victim of realistic crudeness of immediate transmission.

6. *Grandeur, justification, compromise.* It is certain today that art and philosophy need to be *put to the test,* that is, they need to face situations external to the artistic microenvironment and the philosophical institution. The possibility of attaining new forms of grandeur that heal them from the "sickness of the chains," i.e., from restorations and transgressions, depends on this test. That which characterizes this putting to the test is the comparison with things: as Luc Boltanski and Laurent Thévenot observe in *De la justification: Les économies de la grandeur* (1991), the values of people, of objects, and of actions are strictly bound up with each other and it is precisely from the discovery of such an interrelation that the *third regime of art,* in which appraisal is not focused exclusively on singularity, the work, or communication, is born. According to Boltanski and Thévenot, a comprehensive rethinking of the notion of grandeur is a very important contribution. In the

first place, the metaphysical idea of grandeur, based as it is uniquely on the intrinsic property of a person, an object, or an action, must be put aside: the theory of *aura* is comprised precisely in this first conception of grandeur, which prescinds from existence of common worlds. On the contrary, the notion of grandeur must be considered in reference to the plurality of political contexts determined in historical experience: therefore, while an absolute form of grandeur does not exist, there do exist various *political forms of grandeur*. Boltanski and Thévenot individuate six political forms of grandeur that correspond to six worlds. They examine their characteristics by means of a study of authors who theorized them first: the inspired city (Augustine), the domestic city (Bossuet), the city of opinion (Hobbes), the civic city (Rousseau), the mercantile city (Smith), the industrial city (Saint-Simon). This anchoring of the notion of grandeur in specific worlds and concrete situations allows metaphysics to avoid the opposite danger, that is to say, the nihilistic relativism that beyond every grandeur sees misery and beyond misery sees a will to power. Such a perspective, no matter how often it returns to the notion of "interest," does not in any case belong to the economic sphere, which, in view of a general idea of grandeur, implies the sacrifice of the impulses of the individual. Secularization and disenchantment pushed to the extreme—according to Boltanski and Thévenot—destroy themselves: they break every political bond and regress to the search for "a self-satisfaction that is no longer worried with establishing an accord with others" (414), that is, towards an infantilism that they define as the "rejoicing in the happiness of being little" (413). Nihilism would therefore be a form of infantilism: it is, after all, children who do not have access to any type of generality, that is, to "a universe subjected to the obligation of justification," in which "rationality of conduct can be put to the test" (290).

It is important that Boltanski and Thévenot recognize

in the world of inspiration (which comprises the practice of art and philosophy) a *political* significance that cannot be subordinated to the other worlds: in other words, the practice of art and of philosophy are not private affairs: "in the world in which beings are appraised for their *singularity* and in which the most general is the most *original*, the greats are unique and universal at the same time" (201-202). This aspect has found further development in Heinich. In her opinion, until now the social sciences have not recognized the importance of singularity and uniqueness as factors of production and action; they have adopted reductivist criteria that take as a given the superiority of the social over the singular. But the reduction to the social is not a judgment of fact, but a judgment of value. It is absurd that disciplines which pretend, like sociology, to be descriptive and not normative, remain victims of such prejudices (Heinich, *Le triple jeu* 17). It is not at all a question of reevaluating the ontological significance of singularity, but of taking seriously the motivations provided by the actors and "installing oneself in the observation of the construction of values" (21). Instead of imposing the primacy of the social in an authoritative and dogmatic fashion, one needs to "highlight the plurality of the regimes of action and axiology" (24), and move from an analysis of essences to one of representations. In other words, what is relevant is not knowing whether originality really exists or whether it is an illusion, but knowing by means of which operations it is constructed, maintained, and dissolved.

The conception of society as something organic and unitary is a sociological myth: the various worlds individuated by Boltanski and Thévenot are profoundly different from each another. The task of the theorist is not to propose models of total harmonization and synthesis. These models, in whose invention aesthetics has exercised its imagination, hide concrete situations in which human beings interact. Nonetheless, nor do we have to join indissolubly any specific group: "every person must confront, be able to recognize and adapt to daily situations that depend on distinct worlds" (266). But this adaptation can occur in two ways: by means of *arrangement* or by means of a *compromise*. Only in the second case is the search for a common good made present. *Arrangement* is instead a contingent agreement related to the convenience of the two parties, devoid of legitimacy and not universalizable. The reciprocal concessions on which an *arrangement* is based aim at arresting dissension without going back to motivations on which different evaluations concerning the grandeur of people, of things and actions in play stand. Only in *compromise* does the search for an agreement obligate the rival parties to elevate themselves above contingencies and formulate a *justification* for their own words, behavior, and actions. Without *justification*, therefore, no type of grandeur, no type of agreement, is possible.

If in light of this ambitious sociological theory one reflects on the case of the "contemporary paradigm" of art, one realizes at once that for the most part it stands on *arrangements* and not on *compromises*. Petitions from the world of inspiration, from the mercantile world, and from the world of opinion all converge in agreements whose sustaining principles are oftentimes not manifest. All of this creates a feeling of disorientation not only in the public, but also in many artists, art critics, and experts and ends up by putting art outside of any possible grandeur. Nonetheless, the sociological works to which we have referred retain the possibility of *mystifications* and boasts; in fact, they pose the problem of the so-called "artistic values" in a way that is both concrete and attentive to specific situations. The trend inside of which they are posited tends to study the dynamics of valorization and devalorization from up close. It overcomes the limits of an approach which is overly abstracted from values (typical of philosophy of art) or one which is too superficial and extrinsic (typical of the sociology of art). This tendency also involves a profound theoretical renewal, manifested in a meaningful conceptual innovation in traditional aesthetics: justification takes the place of judgment, competence takes the place of genius, admiration for grandeur supplants taste. In the third regime of art, many artful oppositions tend to fall: the conditions are given for which artists and critics, curators and theorists find themselves joined in a single common struggle.

(translated by John Casey)

Works Cited

Benjamin, Walter. "The Work of Art in the Age of Mechanical Reproduction." *Illuminations*. Trans. Harry Zohn. Ed. Hannah Arendt. New York: Harcourt, Brace & World, 1968. 217-51.

Boltanski, Luc and Laurent Thévenot. *De la justification: les économies de la grandeur*. Paris: Gallimard, 1991.

Bourdieu, Pierre. "Une interprétation de la théorie de la religion selon Max Weber." *Archives européennes de sociologie* 12 (1971): 3-21.

Didi-Huberman, Georges. *Ce que nous voyons, ce qui nous regarde*. Paris: Minuit, 1992.

Frow, John. *Cultural Studies and Cultural Value*. Oxford: Clarendon, 1995.

Heinich, Nathalie. *Ce que l'art fait à la sociologie*. Paris: Minuit, 1998.

_______. *Le triple jeu de l'art contemporain: sociologie des arts plastiques*. Paris: Minuit, 1998.

Nietzsche, Friedrich. *Human, All Too Human*. Trans. R. J. Hollingdale. London: Cambridge University Press, 1986.

Vattimo, Gianni. *Il soggetto e la maschera: Nietzsche e il problema della liberazione*. Milano: Bompiani, 1974.

Part I On the Borders Of Theory

Culture visuali: Una introduzione etnografica alla pixel zone

Massimo Canevacci

1. Etnografia

Vi è uno scambio profondo – e vorrei dire anche privilegiato – tra studi culturali e antropologia: l'antropologia culturale, infatti, si configura come disciplina solo in quanto fa etnografia. Il fare etnografia è cioè l'elemento distintivo, caratterizzante e anche differenziante questa disciplina. Etnografia come ricerca micrologica sul campo, dentro la quale e nella quale non hanno diritto metodi oggettivistici, questionari quantitativistici, rappresentazioni esterne – quasi rubate – di un qualcosa che sarà per sempre un "oggetto" di ricerca per l'unica soggettività ammessa: quella del ricercatore e della sua obsoleta autorità.

Le nuove caratteristiche della ricerca etnografica si sono affermate a partire dalla critica culturale riaffiorata nella metà degli anni '80.

Estrema intersoggettività: ciò vuol dire che l'interprete di un determinato tratto culturale singolo o anche di visioni generali è in primo luogo il soggetto che vive dentro il suo ambiente culturale. Non solo: vuol dire anche che non solo il ricercatore – etnografo o altro – interpreta il suo informatore, ma che anche quest'ultimo – l'informatore – interpreta il suo interprete. Lo scambio è quindi duplice. Il significato è un risultato *parziale* e *conflittuale* – e quindi non solo *contrattato* – dato dalla tensione intersoggettiva tra due soggetti che, insieme, lo producono e lo trasformano. Lo *muovono*.

Strappare il significato dalla sola scrittura dell'osservatore: questo un compito decisivo della nuova antropologia.

Questo approccio va contro e oltre due caratteristiche della antropologia interpretativa di impostazione geertziana:[1]

- a) *contro la contrattazione dei significati.* Le diverse narrazioni non sono solo il risultato di una "umanistica" interazione tra due soggetti paritari (l'etnografo e l'informatore); esse si possono anche tra loro contrapporre senza trovare soluzioni ordinate e tautologiche (i balinesi costretti a interpretare per sempre se stessi tramite l'interpretazione dell'antropologo). Il conflitto irriducibile tra punti di vista diversi sta dentro il disordine delle nuove etnografie.
- b) *contro il significato pubblico.* Che la cultura sia pubblica perchè è pubblico il significato è un'altra affermazione obsoleta, palesemente tale nelle culture visuali. Qui il significato non può essere stabile, solido, identitario: per l'appunto *pubblico;* al contrario, i significati sono liquidi, mobili, plurali. I codici che nascono e si muovono tra le culture visuali non possono essere pubblici nè riconoscibili, ma costantemente estranianti, innovativi, decodificabili solo tra alcune interzone linguistiche per essere subito dopo modificate nel segno.

La de-classificazione è il tratto caratteristico della danza dei codici visuali.

In questo modo, le nuove sensibilità cognitive vanno oltre la pura osservazione partecipante. L'osservazione non appartiene più solo all'osservatore (antropologo o chi sia). L'osservazione dell'altro—di quello che una volta era considerato un oggetto di ricerca e che ora sempre più si è affermato come soggetto che è parte costruttiva della ricerca—è anche l'altro-che-osserva: questi deve essere inserito all'interno del *frame* costitutivo della intrepretazione. Inoltre, l'osservatore si osserva nel corso della ricerca: l'osservatore è anche riflessivo, è un "farsi sensibilità visiva" che *si* osserva mentre osserva.

Questa è la prospettiva polifonica che si basa su una corrente intersoggettiva della nuova dialogica. La trascrizione della ricerca deve contenere al suo interno le voci

[1] C. Geertz, *Interpretazione di culture* (Bologna: Il Mulino, 1987).

altre dei soggetti che hanno contribuito alla costruzione, alla contrattazione e alla "conflittazione" del significato.

Dissolvere il monologismo è, quindi, un altro scopo esplicito di questo approccio.

In questa direzione va Renato Rosaldo, secondo cui:

> social analysis should look beyond the dichotomy of order versus chaos toward the less explored realm of "nonorder"[...]. A focus on nonorder directs attention to how people's actions alter the conditions of their existence, often in ways they neither intend nor foresee.[2]

È uno spostamento decisivo dei punti di osservazione, per uscire fuori dalle trappole dicotomiche e fluidificarle. L'elaborazione del concetto liquido di non-ordine contribuisce a considerare l'esistenza individuale non come un destino ascritto, bensì da scrivere e riscrivere; esso serve ad alterare l'esistenza e non a riprodurla. Le conseguenze fluidificano il metodo:

> Social analysis must attend to improvisation, muddling through, and contingent events. Furthermore, from a processual perspective, change rather than structure becomes society's enduring state.[3]

È condizione stabile il mutamento piuttosto che la struttura: una vera e propria rivoluzione, perché in tal modo l'improvvisazione e la spontaneità—viste sempre come dannose, superficiali e irrequiete dalle scienze sociali solide—divengono aspetti mobili e decisivi che si innestano e sconvolgono nel corso stesso della ricerca o della sua rielaborazione.

Il metodo non sta più nel paradigma unificato e nei suoi "domatori": il metodo sta anche nell'improvvisazione, come tanta arte contemporanea sperimentale. Ogni interpretazione, per Rosaldo, non è diretta a oggettivare l'altro, elaborare regole spaziali, leggi universali, modelli culturali

---

[2] R. Rosaldo, *Culture and Truth: The Remaking of Social Analysis* (Boston: Beacon Press, 1989), 102.

[3] R. Rosaldo, *Culture and Truth: The Remaking of Social Analysis*, 102.

ecc.: essa non assume un unico punto di vista, bensì "[it] involves the irreducible perceptions of both analysts and their subjects."[4]

Ogni aspetto della conoscenza è relazionale, cioè dialogico e sincretico. Per Rosaldo:

> borderlands should be regarded not as analytically empty transitional zones but as sites of creative cultural production that require investigation.[5]

Attraverso confini—linee che separano e uniscono—si conclude per sempre l'estrazione di "cristalli puri di significato" con cui inquadrare l'intera cultura dentro uno schema, ma si ricercano "the blurred zones in between."

La sua prospettiva di chicano—che scorre *in between* tra i confini e contro i confini, sedotto dall'improvvisazione e alla ricerca di *nonorder*—si conclude con una immagine liquida per eccellenza:

> Creative processes of transculturation center themselves along literal and figurative borders where the "person" is crisscrossed by multiple identities.[6]

2. Rimpatrio

Rimpatrio dell'antropologia: con questo termine, la svolta degli anni '80 si riallaccia a una forte tradizione dell'antropologia, affermando l'istanza di svolgere la funzione di critica culturale all'interno della cultura dell'antropologo.[7] Ma, a differenza del passato, dove ad es. Margaret Mead aveva pionieristicamente quanto parzialmente anticipato questo approccio, il rimpatrio attuale non applica solo i risultati delle ricerche etnografiche svolte in contesti classici (tra i cosiddetti nativi) al proprio interno, bensì imposta su basi nuove proprio la ricerca etnografica su

---

[4] R. Rosaldo, *Culture and Truth: The Remaking of Social Analysis*, 102.
[5] R. Rosaldo, *Culture and Truth: The Remaking of Social Analysis*, 208.
[6] R. Rosaldo, *Culture and Truth: The Remaking of Social Analysis*, 209.
[7] G. Marcus, M. Fischer, *Anthropology as Cultural Critique: An Experimental Moment in the Human Sciences* (Chicago: University of Chicago Press, 1986).

specifici e determinati settori. Da qui la svolta e gli infiniti intrecci possibili con i *cultural studies* . . .

Il nuovo rimpatrio svolge ricerche etnografiche nei settori non più tradizionali della cultura dell'antropologo (il folklore che resiste, il marginale che commuove, la memoria che svanisce), al contrario: dentro le correnti delle innovazioni sorprendenti, delle sperimentazioni sconfinanti, dei conflitti dislocanti. È troppo semplicistico—come conclude James Clifford[8] affermare che una etnografia surrealista aspetta ancora una sua applicazione: il contesto attuale della comunicazione esplora modificazioni corporali, configurazioni mutoidi, techno-performance.

In questo intreccio di rimpatrio, multivocalità, intersoggettività, pluritestualità si diffonde la critica culturale. Sperimentazione e conflitto sono dentro i *cultural studies,* ben oltre le pur significative prospettive surrealiste.

3. Il dissolvimento della società

> Il trittico cultura-comunicazione-consumo sta subentrando al tradizionale (moderno) concetto di società. La metropoli immateriale (net-metropoli) post-industriale, post-dualista, post-urbana si articola tra i panorami fluidi di net-scape : e-space : x-scape.[9]

I *cultural studies* non possono essere rinchiusi dentro il paradigma dominato dal concetto ottocentesco di società (e di conseguenza di produzione, politica ecc) che, come tutti i concetti, è storicamente determinato e non riesce più a afferrare il mutamento. La politica (se ancora vogliamo utilizzare questo nome) non emerge dal contesto della società, così unitario, identitario, dualista, ma dai flussi della cultura visuale, del consumo performativo, del nonorder

---

[8] J. Clifford, *The Predicament of Culture: Twentieth-Century Ethnography, Literature, and Art* (Cambridge: Harvard University Press, 1986).

[9] Cfr. M. Canevacci, *Culture extreme: mutazioni giovanili tra i corpi delle metropoli* (Roma: Meltemi, 1999).

metropolitano: frammentari, plurali, decentrati, disordinati.

Ciò che si è diffuso e proliferato, spezzando ogni progetto unitario di tipo sociale, è la *metropoli comunicazionale – una net-metropoli* – che non ha più un centro (es. la struttura), bensì è policentrico e polifonico. Finisce per sempre l'incerta dialettica struttura-sovrastruttura. Il conflitto, la competizione, l'innovazione si plasmano sulla capacità di rimodellare i nuovi flussi *techno*-comunicativi.

L'intreccio disordinato e immateriale tra gli interstizi fluidi della metropoli – tra cultura-comunicazione-consumo – dissolve la società civile, come distinzione classica della modernità, e le forme dualiste del pensiero ad essa connesse "dialetticamente" (natura-cultura; organico-inorganico, maschio-femmina; stato-società civile, pubblico-privato, corpo-mente ecc.). La società come l'abbiamo conosciuta in Occidente è stata il risultato di una forma storicamente determinata della città, della città come luogo della modernità, che ha prodotto la rivoluzione industriale, i conflitti di classe, la dialettica tra Stato e società civile. Ora così come quella forma di Stato si sta dissolvendo sotto i segni della globalizzazione e delle aperture senza frontiere dei mercati, allo stesso modo si dissolve la struttura di una società dualista, divisa in classi ben determinate dentro un sistema produttivo industrialista.

Se l'intero concetto di società diventa archeologia concettuale simmetrica alle archeologie industriali, allora si deve saper leggere la sintesi (come atto filosofico per eccellenza prodotto dalla *polis*) come un'archeologia politica, industrialista, epistemologica. È anche codice autoritario e unitario del dominio.

La nuova metropoli è senza società: per questo è senza luoghi; produce anomie, amnesie, aporie e per questo confligge con i custodi (ipocriti) della memoria, del diritto, dell'identità; viaggia nelle diaspore e per questo strappa attraverso i suoi traslochi concettuali e comunicativi ogni radice sedimentata.

4. La cultura visuale

Qui si seleziona la cultura visuale come focus di ricerca etnografica che implica la necessità di un cambio radicale di paradigmi interpretativi.

Per cultura visuale intendo l'insieme fluido di costituzione di questi nuovi panorami (*mediascape*) che costituiscono i nuovi contesti mobili. Sono cornici scorniciate che praticano i molteplici slittamenti dei codici. Interpretare la personalità dei post-media, la biologia dei *mix-media*, la biografia dei *visual-media*.

La cultura visuale—connessa alla produzione immateriale e al consumo performativo, al *nonorder* metropolitano —dissolve la dicotomia moderna pubblico-privato e il concetto storico di società. Per cui, per interpretare tale nuova cultura si deve indagare sulla personalità dei media, sulla biografia e biologia delle merci-visuali, sulla soggettività incarnata dai nuovi feticismi visuali.

La nuova comunicazione visuale pluralizza e mobilita gli spazi immateriali contro ogni luogo identitario—e li trasforma in zone (*interzone*) visuali.

Anzichè congelarci nelle visioni lamentose e restaurative, il problema della critica antropologica è ben diverso:

- produrre concetti e metodi adeguati alle nuove forme della cultura visuale. Il conflitto è anche sui paradigmi;
- leggere gli stili feticisti sessualmente seduttivi messi in scena dai *videoscape*. Il conflitto è anche nel perturbante;
- sperimentare nuovi moduli narrativi e strategie testuali affinché ogni interpretazione sia anche dissoluzione dei feticci visuali. Il conflitto è anche sulla rappresentazione.

Nuovi tipi di culture visive fortemente pluralizzate e frammentarie scorrono tra i nuovi panorami della comunicazione. I flussi panoramatici sono disgiuntivi. Anche per questo la dialettica perde il suo strumento più classico e potente—la sintesi.

Le classi si frammentano senza più alcuna possibilità per egemonie e mediazioni, così come i conflitti radicalizzano e (som)muovono ogni parzialità. I sincretismi scorrono—*patchwork* pieni di seduzioni e repulsioni—sui corpi-visori di questi nuovi panorami. Una pluralità di culture (stili di vita, identità-a-tempo, vite estetizzate, mode usa-e-getta) frammenta la comunicazione e la dilata senza più confini certi: i confini sono mobili come le identità, confini plurali e polifonici. Confini sconfinati. Il rapporto tra linguaggi e sperimentazione diventa essenziale. La nuova comunicazione non è pensabile nè rappresentabile con la sola forma-saggio. Forme linguistiche polifoniche scorrono e concorrono, si scontrano e si sovrappongono, si isolano e si ibridizzano nel delineare le infinite sfaccettature della comunicazione metropolitana. I panorami sonori (*soundscape*) assurgono a linguaggi decisivi come quelli del corpo (*bodyscape*) o della comunicazione (*videoscape*).

Le molte, disordinate angolazioni prospettiche diluiscono ogni ipotesi generalista, moltiplicano i codici per unità di immagine, disordinano le forme, innovano i linguaggi, decostruiscono i simboli, declassificano le tassonomie, innestano dissonanze, sperimentano discorsi multipli, trame polifoniche, tessuti ibridi.

5. Pixel-zone

Il *nonorder* della metropoli comunicazionale oscilla, convive e intreccia paurosamente quanto seduttivamente *in between* le *interzone*, fatti attraverso una configurazione etnograficamente nuova e alterata di individui e di spazi.

a) *Individuo*: la prima configurazione non è più rappresentabile in termini sociologici—il corpo deride le eredità naturalistiche e pratica la danza-dei-codici. L'*individuo* della metropoli comunicazionale non appartiene più ad una classe, sia nel significato economico-politico che logico; al contrario, è l'individuo a farsi-di-classi, cioè un essere (*entity*) riempito da sezioni interne diversificate, reticolari, multiple che non rientrano dentro la filosofia politica basata sul principio di identità nè sull'ordine dualista e tanto meno simbolico. Un individuo plurale e pluralizzabile, divisibile al suo interno all'infinito. Non più, quindi, individuo come *a-tomon*, il non-divisibile, tormento atomizzato della teologia e della politica. Un individuo atomizzato è, in quanto tale, anomico: è schiacciato dall'anomia, vista da ogni parte ideologica come flaggello anti-sociale, come disperazione solipsistica e irregolare, come emarginazione dalle leggi liberamente accettate.

b) *Spazi*: contro il lamento per la perdita della solidità dei luoghi, i nuovi spazi sono determinati dal consumo performativo (*cyberscape*, discoteche, aree dismesse, spazi vuoti) e dalla comunicazione immateriale (*e-space*). Gli *spazi* hanno dissolto il potere dei luoghi, dove "increspavano" le istituzioni. La filosofia dialettica ha sempre visto nello spazio il disordine incontrollabile, incommensurabile, indefinibile. L'urto tra forze binarie—legate dalle opposizioni dualiste: tesi/antitesi—può avvenire solo dentro i luoghi, secondo le regole del *nomos*. Negli spazi, invece, scorre l'anomia. Quella che era l'orrore irrazionalistico e ingovernabile per le scienze sociali (gli infiniti eredi di Durkheim...), scienze tese a ricondurre il soggetto sociale a una natura classificabile per tipologie, modelli, strutture. I nuovi spazi immateriali (quando non riproducono lo stesso sistema produttivo "materiale") sono come scorrerie fluide che rifiutano ogni tipo di classificazione: non solo, essi individuano proprio nella classificazione una delle fonti della produzione del dominio. Per questo negli spazi scorrono i nuovi concetti liquidi che rifiutano come atto prioritario della post-politica ogni costruzione tipologica. L'aridità del concetto identitario, del potere simbolico, della dialettica sintetica si produce nel risucchiare nell'ordine sistemico dei luoghi tutto ciò che pratica l'anomia spaziale e che scorre negli interstizi anomici.

c) *E-space*: ma ora sia il concetto di luogo che di spazio saranno messi in discussione. Lo spazio è stato visto—filosoficamente—come qualcosa di incontrollabile, di sterminato, di indefinito; mentre, il luogo è configurabile in termini fissi e identitari, circoscritti. Per questo il luogo appartiene al politico nel suo aspetto più istituzionalizzato, mentre lo spazio è il contesto fluido del disordine, dell'irregolare, dell'anomia. L'*e-space* è lo spazio elettronico. Qualcosa che non è più determinabile in termini negativi (nonluogo) o materiali (la città come *polis*), tanto meno che compie delitti perfetti (il detective Baudrillard) o eccessi di velocità (le multe di Virilio). L'*e-space* non è né un a priori né un a posteriori. È un presente dilatato e mobile. Un presente liquido. Nell'*e-space* tutto è simultaneo, come nei desideri dei primi futuristi. Il potere della storia come legge del passato è ininfluente, così come le suggestioni dell'utopia come evoluzione nel futuro. Si parte da un sito e si attraversa tutto quello che si vuole o che si incontra per le autostrade elettroniche. Le cartografie nell'*e-space* hanno sempre meno.

Certamente ci sono rischi di perdite realistiche: ma quello che interessa è se dentro questo fluire sterminato non si immetta nell'*e-space* una liquidazione dell'identità fissa—l'identità ghiacciata e agghiacciante—,dei nazionalismi etnico-religiosi, di enclave politiche autoappagate.

Nell'*e-space* mi posso sentire con chiunque senza conoscerlo e dappertutto senza andarci. La dappertuttità si inserisce nell'*e-space*.

d) *Digital*-collage: ciò che affiora tra le zone immateriali-comunicative della cultura visuale è un flusso di *digital-collage*. Espressioni multivocali.

Spezzare le tipologie classificatorie significa incorporare e scorporare assemblaggi, detriti, concatenazioni, giustapposizioni, sconfinamenti, incomprensioni verso narrazioni multi-sequenziali (*multisequential narratives*). Il *cyberspace* si può precisare sempre meglio come uno spazio multiplo e anomico il cui ambiente (la cui "ecologia") è visuale. È un pixellated environment where the material we recontextualize into new forms of potential meaning is in many ways immaterial.[10]

È un ambiente visuale di tipo nuovo e a nulla valgono i tentativi di ricondurlo dentro le ferree logiche del passato naturalistico e neanche del panorama mediatico tradizionale.

Pixel: piXel ...

L'immagine pixellata è valore (di mercato), è valori (di stile), è valorazione (di percezione).

Pixel è pelle visuale – piXel pelle visore.

As a means of image creation, the pixelated screen is created of both electronic signals and empty space. A pixel, a term derived from the phrase "picture element," composes the electronic image of the television or computer monitor. Pixels are not just points of light but are also memory units.[11]

La differenza disgiuntiva rispetto alle immagini del passato (fotografia, cinema, TV generalista) – che in qualche modo dovevano avere un riferimento a qualche tipo di realtà esterna – sta nel fatto che la "pixelated image reminds us of its necessary artificiality and absence. It is here and not here at once."[12] Così la vita nella *pixel-zone* è di necessità ambivalente, in quanto riesce a creare ciò che Nicholas Mirzoeff chiama *intervisuality*.

La coabitazione tra artificialità e assenza costituisce i panorami immateriali.

L'affioramento immateriale, quindi, diffonde la cultura visuale (*visual media*) come fonte del mutamento e del conflitto. Tale immateriale è di gran lunga più empiricamente concreto del tradizionale concetto – solido, troppo solido – di materiale; quanto rilevabile (non misurabile nè clas-

---

[10] J. Federman, "An Annual Convergence of the Bleak and Absurd," in *Arts 'n Media*, 1998.

[11] N. Mirzoeff, *The Visual Culture Reader* (London and New York: Routledge, 1998), 30.

[12] N. Mirzoeff, *The Visual Culture Reader*, 30.

sificabile o tipologizzabile) con strumenti qualitativi di tipo nuovo.

e) *Mediagenic Reality*: in altri termini, ci stiamo spostando verso quella che mi pare corretto essere definita come una *Mediagenic Reality*. Una realtà—termine di per sé già ambiguo e evanescente, ultimo appiglio degli strenui difensori del passato che pur hanno contribuito a mettere in discussione (Baudrillard)—che è produttrice di media, che genera media e che quindi è anche generata dai media. *Videodrome*. L'importanza politico-comunicativa del termine sta proprio nella contiguità linguistica dei due vecchi termini (genesi e realtà) che ora—nel loro interlacciamento—producono un nuovo senso mediagenico.

La differenza (disgiuntiva) con le generazioni precedenti sia di impostazione politica classica (marxista) che di avanguardia artistica sta nel fatto che

> the artists who create Avant-Pop art are the *Children of Mass Media* (even more than being the children of their parents who have much less influence over them). Most of the early practitioners of Postmodernism, who came into active adult consciousness in the fifties, sixties and early seventies, tried desperately to keep themselves away from the forefront of the newly powerful *Mediagenic Reality* that was rapidly becoming the place where most of our social exchange was taking place.[13]

Così il "gioco" entra dentro la realtà mediagenica, che non potrà rimanere ferma o legata all'"essere."

Il postmodernismo muore sulle soglie *pixelated* di questa realtà mediagenica, dal quale si producono scambi emotivi e comunicazionali, affioramenti immateriali e anomici, conflitti semiotici e visuali. Dalle sue ceneri istituzionalizzate nasce l'*avant pop* che ha imparato a farsi gioco dei media e a trasformare questo gioco in potente conflitto post-politico, conflitto della comunicazione intervisuale:

---

[13] Sukenick, Mosaic Man, Alt-x, <Sukenic@spot.colorado.edu>.

> [it is an] environment from which to engender new contexts of artistic performance and, if possible, create para-media constructs that assault the banal production values inherent in mainstream culture.[14]

Guardare uno schermo, toccare la tastiera, entrare in una *pixel-zone* modifica in primo luogo proprio il sistema percettivo "materiale": vista, udito, tatto, ora anche l'odorato (il senso più arcaico). E il gusto non viene solo mangiando, ma anche guardando chi mangia. Se volessi proprio continuare a utilizzare questa parola disgustosa che, al pari della morte, è usata come una minaccia da ogni forma di inamovibilità del potere, ebbene, allora sì, anche la mia "realtà materiale" è costantemente modificata dal mio *e-space*. E tutto questo modifica ancor di più il mio essere produttivamente "immateriale."

In questa prospettiva, il *videoscape* è la diffusione pervasiva di segni per unità di immagine (*signflation*) emessa dai panorami visuali riproducibili. È l'incarnazione della comunicazione visuale, la comunicazione fatta corpo, è la storia di vita della merce-visuale, il suo farsi feticcio. Personalità. *Videodrome* ...

Lo slittamento non è solo dei confini, ovvero si deve dare al concetto di confine un significato plurale, scorniciato e sconfinato:

- lo slittamento appartiene ai codici, compito politico-comunicativo dei cultural studies;
- lo slittamento appartiene alla ricerca, alla relazione ricercatore-ricercato;
- lo slittamento appartiene al soggetto: l'unità dell'io si frammenta e si fluidifica;
- lo slittamento appartiene ai paradigmi: non è più possibile immaginare il metodo interpretativo che produce concetti universali, inquadrati dentro la cornice de La Storia, La Cultura, La Politica.

---

[14] K. Acker, *Blood and Guts in High School* (New York: Grove Press, 1978).

WORK (AND RESISTANCE) IN PROGRESS
Towards the Many Speeds of the Present

Laura Hengehold

This is an essay about the time it takes to speak and think—not only to draw a breath and pronounce the words, but also the time it takes to identify the events and objects about which one speaks. Without such intervals, which have both political and ontological significance, our perceptions remain private and unformed even to ourselves. The flow of events is measured and broken into manageable segments or objects by the bodily rhythms of breathing, speaking, and thinking, much as we measure the span of a doorway or picture frame with our outstretched hands in the absence of a measuring tape. Moreover, the precision or broadness of our instruments for detecting change affects the kinds of objects and events we are likely to recognize around us; the nightly news gives a different portrait of current events than a yearly poll or a weekly conversation with neighbors at the bar, and age or youth alters the importance we may assign to an individual episode.

But often enough we also find ourselves measured by the doorway we hoped to master, uncertain of its scope because our arms are too short or our stretch unsteady. Anyone who has tried to express him or herself during a public discussion only to find that the topic has shifted by the time he or she finds suitable words recognizes this feeling of frustration with the discontinuous speeds at which events in which we participate take place. The difficulty of recognizing or embodying an unfamiliar timeframe introduces palpable feelings of anger towards the object or person who "disrupts time" by talking or thinking "too fast" or "too slowly." Generations talk past one another, over family meals as well as urban planning sessions, and in both cases we are confronted with genuinely political conflicts over what features of the present are relevant, resonant, or evidently incongruous with a certain shorter or longer past. To mediate the aggressivity and frustration which result from living too many intervals at once, it seems necessary to extend the temporal constraints of one's situation, to show how many smaller segments are implicit in a longer stretch, and to recognize a long span as unified and repeatable in relation to other measures.

In a lecture from the early eighties, Foucault defined the Enlightenment as the search for a difference rather than "a world era to which one belongs, . . . an event whose signs are perceived, [or] the dawning of an accomplishment" (1997, 104-105). Kant's essay "What is Enlightenment?" differs from his other historical writings, Foucault argues, in its attempt to identify the form through which we distinguish *actualité*—the contemporary or the current—from everything that precedes or coexists with it indifferently. Of course, he notes that one can identify "modernity" with a particular epoch in a single direct historical trajectory, by contrast perhaps to the "premodern" or the "postmodern" (115). But he also believes modernity is best characterized as an ethos or desire for self-definition which is both exploratory and inventive, discovering the present state of the self and giving it form. It is a *style* of relating oneself to historical phenomena, not a phenomenon or historical fashion in its own right, a style summed up in the question: "What difference does today introduce with respect to yesterday?" This reading of Kant is influenced by Baudelaire's reflections on the "heroism of the modern age":

> Modernity is often characterized in terms of consciousness of the discontinuity of time: a break with tradition, a feeling of novelty, of vertigo in the face of the passing moment . . . But, for [Baudelaire], being modern does not lie in recognizing and accepting this perpetual movement; on the contrary, it lies in adopting a certain attitude

> with respect to this movement; and this deliberate, difficult attitude consists in recapturing something eternal that is not beyond the present instant, nor behind it, but within it. (114)

More specifically, then, modernity seems to mean relating to history according to a style that detects at the heart of one rhythm or practice the murmur of another undercurrent or transformation. Such a relationship gives rise to a "critical ontology of ourselves" in the sense that the "being" of the modern individual is the result of a critical or resistant intervention in the current of tradition and the rate at which its practices call us to reflect upon ourselves. No theory of the will is needed to understand that a body that feels "out of joint," sympathetic with two ways of carrying out a practice that previously seemed so solid and self-evident as to escape notice, *acts* when it makes this tension or incongruity an object of thought and choice. Self-consciously undertaken, such an act of differentiating is itself a new event, which gathers together various signs from the fringes of perception and finds the span of a doorframe where previously one's hands seemed awkwardly balanced apart. It *is* the opening of a certain freedom for movement.

Leonardo Daddabbo, Bruno Moroncini, and other Italian scholars have recently directed international interest towards the temporal dimension of Foucault's thought, in which the interiorization of modern psychology and the limitations of historical imagination find a common pulse. Technological and economic innovations, by altering the "rate" at which we recognize our present, alter the very forms through which we recognize one another as fellow human beings confronted with common events. *Discipline and Punish,* for example, described some of the techniques through which bureaucrats, prison wardens, educators, military leaders, and industrial engineers trained individuals to break down unruly and idiosyncratic gestures into smaller and smaller parts, and then recombine them in more efficient ways so as to become individuals—but to become individuals in a similar and easily recognizable manner. Foucault characterized his book as contributing to the political "history of the body" begun by historical demographers and pathologists (Foucault 1977a, 25). But his later essays and lectures on the Enlightenment suggest that the historicization of the body is a precondition for any ethical practice of being "historical," that is, taking up historical situatedness as an active project rather than an inescapable fact.

Foucault's suggestion that modernity is a manner of relating oneself to something that inhabits but exceeds the rhythm of our practices, even as they change, implies that the "present" is the crossroads of multiple and simultaneous historical trajectories. In the 1971 essay "Nietzsche, Genealogy, History," for example, Foucault did not discuss the ontological status of the "raw material" of history which is open to multiple interpretations, can be taken up into multiple practices, and thus has many ways of "being" (Foucault 1977b). Nietzsche's historical sense is "the acuity of a glance that distinguishes, separates, and disperses, that is capable of liberating divergence and marginal elements . . . capable of dissociating itself and effacing the unity of man's being through which it was thought that he could extend his sovereignty to the events of his past" (153, translation altered).[1] But Foucault also suggests that historical events and documents should be construed "genealogically" as provocations to an ever-renewed battle over which temporal frameworks and practices should set the terms for identifying and understanding others (Daddabbo 1998, 1999). In retrospect, we can see "genealogy" as consistent with

[1] "Il ne doit être que cette acuité d'un regard qui distingue, répartit, disperse, laisse jouer les écarts et les marges—une sorte de regard dissociant capable de se dissocier lui-même et d'effacer l'unité de cet être humain qui est supposé le porter souverainment vers son passé" (Foucault 1994 (2), 146).

Foucault's ethos of modernity; in "stepping back" to a slower rhythm or "speeding up" to catch previously unremarked details, such writing differentiates time.

However, innovative economic historians from the 20s through the 70s sowed the seeds for this approach to history.[2] Marc Bloch, Lucien Febvre, and Fernand Braudel, among others, suggested that the range of phenomena traditionally studied by historians was too narrow, corresponding to the sorts of political and economic events that could be recognized as significant changes within an individual's life experience, as opposed to long-term changes in highly stable phenomena like staple prices, trade routes, or even land use, on the one hand, and on the other, practices considered too mundane and fleeting to be worth the historian's notice, such as sexuality, crime, death rituals, or urban sanitation. These historians' attempts to identify the *longues durées* of climatic variation or religious ritual which constituted the "backdrop" for other events—phenomena so "self-evident" as to seem outside of history—led to the realization that the history of different phenomena happens at different rates, and that seemingly natural categories such as madness or heresy are "meaningless" and cannot even be said to "exist" before a certain time period when one focuses on the particular legal and medical practices that enabled them to first enter a historical record.[3] Their work, which foregrounded the historiographical problem of what makes an event

---

[2] See Leduc 1999, especially chapter 3, "Découper le temps," for an extensive discussion of historical periodization.

[3] See Farge (1994, 33) for examples of the ways in which the historicality of women's existence has been governed by different focal events and objects than that of men. Farge's approach seems roughly consistent with the nominalist philosophy of history offered by Paul Veyne in the essay "Foucault Revolutionizes History": "For Foucault as for Duns Scotus, the material for madness really exists" at every point in history, "but not as madness"; rather it forms the material for some other object in another regime of practices (1997, 170).

"worthy" of notice or allows us to attribute historical "being" to a phenomenon, was obliquely referenced by Foucault in *The Archeology of Knowledge* as a salutary move away from both "battle-history" and the history of "worldviews," and Foucault participated in this trend to the extent that his histories deal with historical phenomena formerly considered unworthy of historical notice, techniques for ordering bodies and data on which we seldom reflect consciously but which are presupposed by all reflection we recognize as sane and scientific.

> From the political mobility at the surface down to the slow movements of "material civilization," ever more levels of analysis have been established: each has its own peculiar discontinuities and patterns; and as one descends to the deepest levels, the rhythms become broader. Beneath the rapidly changing history of governments, wars, and famines, there emerge other, apparently unmoving histories: the history of sea routes, the history of corn or of gold-mining, the history of drought and of irrigation, the history of crop rotation, the history of the balance achieved by the human species between hunger and abundance (Foucault 1972, 3).

What the coexistence of these diverse histories suggests is that a block of time or an archive can be broken into "events" or "series" in a variety of ways; moreover, at any given moment a society participates in a number of potentially discontinuous histories.[4] The human body at a particular moment in history, Foucault suggests in his essay on Nietzsche, is the crossroads of these simultaneous rhythms and bears the traces of their intersection:

> The body—and everything that touches it: diet, climate, and soil—is the domain of the *Herkunft*. The body manifests the stigmata of past experience and also gives rise to desires, failings, and errors. These elements may join in a body where they achieve a sudden expression, but as often, their encounter is an engagement in which

[4] See also the interview entitled "Sur les façons d'écrire l'histoire," in which Foucault comments on the difficulties of "cutting a certain level of events into history" (Foucault 1994 (1), 586).

> they efface each other, where the body becomes the pretext of their insurmountable conflict. (Foucault 1977b, 148)

This general idea is repeated in *Discipline and Punish,* where Foucault notes that "Historians long ago began to write the history of the body" as economically and biologically needy or in conflict with an environment that changes for historical as well as ecological reasons. "But the body is also directly involved in a political field," he adds; "power relations have an immediate hold upon it; they invest it, mark it, train it, torture it, force it to carry out tasks, to perform ceremonies, to emit signs" (1977a, 25). Above all, the human body is itself a historical artifact, not a metaphysical substrate for such multiple rhythms and temporalities. "Nothing in man—not even his body" Foucault states dramatically in "Nietzsche, Genealogy, History," "is sufficiently stable to serve as the basis for self-recognition or for understanding other men" or to ground a single unifying path of historical development and explanation (153). As Arlette Farge has suggested, specific bodies and forms of embodiment mentioned in the historical record and observed in contemporary life—war-torn, starving, sexually dissatisfied, or racially tagged and exploited—are what must be *explained* rather than an explanatory element in their own right (1997, 22-27). The task of the historian is to "open up the interval" within which such phenomena seem natural or unavoidable and to ask what discontinuities in the field of social and political practice take the form of bodily damage rather than speech.

Kant's essay, written in 1784, attempted to reconcile the state's demand for obedience with the possibility of a scholarly "public space" in which religious and political principles could be debated safely, such that society and eventually the state itself might be "enlightened," that is, grounded in the free exercise of reason rather than blind tradition.[5] Kant characterized this space as a condition for "thinking for oneself" or attaining "maturity," rather than remaining in the tutelage of unquestioned custom. Such a process of intellectual emancipation, Kant believed, was necessary if international relations were to be freed from the customary ravages of economic competition and war. Many political thinkers still regard the ideal of national and international legal norms protecting the individual's right to govern his or her life and to judge and protect his or her interests as the most important legacy of the Enlightenment. They also recognize the importance of some "public space" in which those interests can be researched and debated as essential to the realization of collective and individual self-government. As Habermas has noted, this "public space" includes all the contexts and fora, architectural, political, or mediatic, in which individuals identify and differentiate themselves from one another with respect to the solution of pragmatic issues (1996, 355-370).[6] But today, especially in light of the collapse of the former Soviet countries, it seems difficult to imagine ourselves existing together "publicly" except through legal and economic institutions, which are primarily supposed to protect our "private" interests, moral or economic. At the same time, the proliferation of information technologies calls into question the supposedly natural boundaries of the spaces within which we become public for one another, making it difficult to question the nature of contemporary publicity, and the peace strangely frustrating.

[5] A translation of this essay by Lewis White Beck is available in Foucault (1997).

[6] "Every encounter in which actors do not just observe each other but take a second-person attitude, reciprocally attributing communicative freedom to the other, unfolds in a linguistically constituted public space" (1996, 361). For an extensive discussion of the interaction between formal and informal deliberative spheres in Habermas's conception of democracy, see chapters 7 and 8 more generally; see also Habermas (1989) for a historical treatment.

Foucault differs from liberal inheritors of the Enlightenment project inasmuch as he questions the self-evident existence of "individuals" whose reason founds and is protected by rights—that is, their existence apart from particular historical strategies through which we distinguish ourselves from others or align ourselves with them.[7] The individual whose identity remains constant over time and to whom interests are attributed—including the rational interest in self-government—is one kind of body, one way of gaining a public voice—a historical phenomenon rather than an ontological given. Thus the modern effort to train individuals who would be able to understand their own desires and duties in legal terms went hand in hand with the equally modern effort to establish norms for human functioning which would enable the state to create a situation in which those rights could be exercised. Although the individual was to be respected as a fundamental ontological and moral presence, the state's obligation to protect his or her rights depended largely on the individual's ability to pass as "normal." From this dual rationalization of social and political life arose various phenomena that frequently strike us as irrational and unjust.

As Giovanna Procacci observes, the effects of individuals' liberation from hereditary political roles frequently conflicted with the effects of their liberation from traditional occupational roles (1997, 219). Because they were no longer tied to the land in specific feudal relations, they gained the right to participate in the economy and create capital, but they were also exposed, down to the present day, to new forms of social instability and poverty. The various logics of modernization were protected from catastrophic incoherence by the identification of "abnormal" ontological and moral beings such as the "poor" and the "criminal," whose natures are still hotly debated in contemporary conflicts over the future of the welfare state.

---

[7] For detailed discussions, see Pizzorno (1989) and Ransom (1997).

According to François Ewald, the bureaucratic and medical establishment of "norms" which render individuals equal to one another is one way of addressing the question of justice, but it is also a way of defining the extent to which we "are present" to and with one another—that is, share a public space in our very being (Ewald 1997, 209). Thus Foucault's analyses of normalizing and disciplinary practices, as well as his question as to what "in the present" gives rise to historical reflection, touch on the very practices through which we recognize ourselves as sharing a potentially just public with one another. But they also suggest that identifying modernity with freedom and choice rather than obedience to tradition puts the cart before the horse; in fact, it is the historical techniques for dividing time which render bodies docile to bureaucratic management that enable individuals to replace a seamless traditional pattern with new objects of action.

In *Discipline and Punish,* Foucault's reference to the Panopticon vividly illustrates some of the seemingly insignificant techniques by which individuals' attention to their bodily comportment, and the material rewards for such attention, alter the very physiognomy of the modern individual as well as his or her sense of self. Industrial rhythms, but also those of the modern school, prison, and military corps, give the body an increasingly fine-tuned and infinitely recombinable "beat," breaking down gestures and tasks into the simplest temporal elements so that they can be precisely calculated and their practitioners taught to monitor themselves at exactly the same intervals as their supervisors. Commentators such as Bartky (1990, 71) and Poster (1998, 363-369) have noted that electronic media can provoke styles of self-understanding which require individuals to rely on the very institutions that control them for a sense of agency or freedom. But Alessandro Pizzorno points out that the multiplication of these technologies creates information overloads that threaten the self-evident value of the very right to individual participation which grounds Kant's sense of Enlightenment (1998, 242).

Foucault's interest in the way that bodily gestures function differently and perhaps interchangeably in different technical projects, depending on how these projects are broken down by trainers and engineers, also suggests that the body's form and coherence are also at stake in the various rhythms constituted by the regular publishing of stock prices, the frequency with which the news is broadcast, the length of time allotted to discussion of social or political topics during the office lunch break, even the rate at which the computer screen refreshes a changing Internet page. If information or directions do not come at the proper rate, we are no better able to make use of them than if our limbs move with an ungainly rhythm. In many cases, what an event or project *is* depends on how frequently it is measured, and too-close or fragmentary scrutiny dissolves rather than clarifies many social and historical phenomena. Similarly, our sense of individuality depends upon the frequency with which we are called upon to consider the consistency of our own actions or their difference from the actions of others. To disassemble the many speeds of a seemingly seamless present, therefore, is also to delineate the frontiers along which publicity and conflict exist, and perhaps it is not coincidental that the normalizing imperatives of the modern state gave rise to the same techniques for gathering health and economic data whose results now provoke the most heated uses of "public reason."

But the instruments that allow us to recognize diverse fragments as an "event" also change historically. Such instruments are relevant for the social actor trying to make sense of "current events" as well as for the historian. Where traditionally historical sources were limited to archival texts, and sometimes to personal writings, the scope or timeframe over which historians might draw causal connections was also limited by state restrictions on access to records and the gradual flow of estate papers into private archival collections. But recent technologies such as video recording and satellite transmission, as well as the existence of computers, have made it possible for private individuals and journalists to have access to a wide variety of information in a very short time and to store and recombine it indefinitely; computers, as Krzysztof Pomian points out, have made the statistical treatment of consumer and production patterns far easier to track over both the short and long term. The ability to create "historical sources" at the time of an event's occurrence rather than months or years afterward, as well as the recent willingness of governments to allow access to classified material after a relatively short period of time, has created an interesting situation in which the history of the present can be written and its proper temporal boundaries or salient features contested at the "same time" that it is being written, and often by different generations who lived through these events simultaneously.

> What is the present time, in effect, if not the period lived by generations still living and that which they are in the process of living? Now, the duration of life in the developed countries has increased to such a length that people active more than a half-century ago are always among us, while the delays in term after which archives become accessible have been reduced everywhere by almost thirty years, leaving aside several particularly sensitive files. A confrontation becomes inevitable between, on one side, the work of historians of present times, and on the other, still-painful memories and ideological convictions capable of mobilizing strong passions. (Pomian 379, translation mine)[8]

---

[8] "Qu'est-ce en effet que le temps présent, sinon la période que les générations encore vivantes ont elles-mêmes vécue et qu'elles sont en train de vivre? Or, la durée de vie a gagné dans les pays développés un allongement tel que les personnes déjà actives il y a plus d'un demi-siècle sont toujours parmi nous, tandis que les délais à l'issue desquels les archives deviennent accessibles sont réduits presque partout à trente ans, mis à part certain dossiers particulièrement sensibles. Une confrontation devient donc inévitable entre, d'un côté, les travaux des historiens du temps présent, et, de l'autre, les mémoires encore endolories et

By now we are familiar with critiques of the view, once prevalent in the Western press, that the wars in the former Yugoslavia resulted from reversion to "premodern" ethnic rivalries rather than progress toward enlightened democratic forms of government (Appadurai 1996, 20-21; Schierup 1999, 1-4). One general explanation for recent outbreaks of ethnic and religious fundamentalism has been that both Western and non-Western societies feel the threatened loss of their particular traditions and perspectives as a result of the "success" of universalist political and economic paradigms, i.e., neo-liberalism. Another, related, explanation contends that such fundamentalisms seek the same universality as "fundamentalist" liberalism, and that even the most enlightened universalism promotes some ethnic, religious, and gendered particularity if it is to change the world at all. Yet another approach views renewed attachment to ethnic identities and conflicts, even in the West, as a reaction against "modernity" itself, in the sense of an individualist rather than a traditionalist ethos—or as evidence of a loss of faith in the progressivist hopes which have for two centuries been associated with modernist reflection on historical change. My suggestion is that "modernity" itself, when understood as this ethic of introducing freeing differentiations into time, is neither rejected by nor culpable for such crises; what we face is not Kojève's supposed liberal "end of history" but difficulty in identifying the rhythm or *durée* which subtends our individual and collective embodiment in such a way that we might be able to "exit minority" and become public for one another in a non-liberal manner.[9]

---

les partis pris idéologiques capables de mobiliser des passions fortes" (Pomian 1999, 379).

[9] Moroncini (1998) takes Ewald to task for interpreting our *actualité* as a liberal "end of history" in the sense offered by Kojève. First, he argues that such a reference to Kojève is simplistic because not only is this "end" an end to class struggle and not an end to individual life stories, but Kojève himself discovered

Scholars and survivors seem to agree that the conflict in some of the former Yugoslavian republics had both cultural and economic causes. The cultural conflicts, however, are not the simple "continuations" of ancient rivalries held uneasily at bay by Tito's communist ideology and state-run economy. Rather, the impulse to *return* to ethnic accounts of *l'actualité* (both Eastern and Western European) lay first in the international debt which the former Yugoslavia had incurred under communist rule and whose long-term effects certain economically advanced republics were in a position to avoid suffering if they broke away from the whole in the name of a right to "join" capitalist Western Europe.[10] Faced with this breakaway, which the West encouraged by imposing strict fiscal policies as a condition for refinancing these loans and by readily recognizing the economic and political

---

that the stylized culture of the Japanese contradicted his own Hegelian assumptions about the historical inevitability of such struggles. However, Moroncini's larger argument is that the present "actualizes" when a scene is deliberately repeated, by contrast to Ewald, for whom the present's actuality consists in its as-yet-undiscovered difference from past repetitions.

[10] Yugoslavia, whose communism had been dominated by the "worker self-management" model up until the Soviet collapse, entered the 1990s plagued by serious economic problems caused by regional competition among the republics for federal investment. The "shock therapy" plans proposed by Harvard economist Jeffrey Sachs and by Western lending institutions (aimed at privatizing viable ex-Yugoslavian enterprises, bringing prices and wages into line with international markets, and liquidating those unable to compete) further reduced the central government's ability to prop up regional domestic production through loans or capital infusions. But since Western Europe maintained many of its own trade barriers and had no need of Eastern European imports, lending policies restricting the central government's ability to mediate the effects of immediate conversion to a Western standard of efficiency resulted in staggering unemployment and the destruction of productive capacities that might have been profitable and served industrial as well as consumer needs in a protected, internally or regionally oriented economy. For detailed discussions of the political economy of the Balkans before and after the breakup of Yugoslavia, including its impact on cultural retraditionalization, see Schierup (1999), Gowan (1995), and Chossudovsky (1997, especially Chapter 13). For a brief discussion of Foucault's relevance in former Eastern Bloc countries, see Vladimir Gradev, "La Lecture Brisée" (1997).

autonomy of certain republics on which the others might have depended for a smooth transition to capitalism, politicians in the remaining republics were able to mobilize popular support for a regionally based populism that quickly took a radical nationalist form. But the conflicts were also fed by the radical *disorientation* which citizens of those republics faced at the West's economic and political demands that their governments rapidly convert their political systems and planned economies to multi-party polities and fully privatized economies open to Western investment.

As theorists from many sides of the political spectrum have noted, Communist Yugoslavia (like Russia and other Eastern European nations) lacked the kind of "public space" characterized by multiple parties, a variety of official and unofficial news media and discussion fora, and non-state organizations promoting the interests of social and economic groups and seeking to influence public opinion. It was, to use the terminology of the above paragraphs, a nation in which the "meaning" of publicity and the "manner" of individuals' being-with was officially assumed to be fixed and self-evident; everything important was officially public. In fact, as both Zizek and Pomian note, those same individuals knew that the structures through which their lives intersected and differed were far more complex than the official record would allow them to debate openly, which in some cases led to cynicism with all political activity (Zizek 226-229, Pomian 266-267).[11] Pomian and Schierup suggest that the politics of memory

---

[11] Zizek, it should be noted, is opposed to a theoretical approach to contemporary ethno-nationalist conflict that focuses on the process of individuation out of a more or less chaotic emotional mass, because he believes that such approaches (roughly Deleuzian in inspiration) reinforce the same fear of being "too mixed up with the Other's affects," which persuades individuals to regard the Other as a palpable bodily threat. While agreeing with his overall argument that hatred of the Other arises from panic at the unruly mix of speeds characterizing one's own psychological experience, I still think that an analysis of this temporal confusion might lead to a less "allergic" understanding of conflicted situations.

which are intimately bound up with ethnic "anchoring points" have arisen in large part from nascent discussions between representatives of different communities and generations who suffered these changes in silence and now seek to "catch up" on their own historical identity as individuals and regional or national groups. Given that this "common time," admittedly antagonistic, is nevertheless the precondition for any of the legislative, electoral, or mediatic "public spaces" demanded by the West as proof of democratization, the resulting political strategies that were most readily comprehensible seem to have been those appealing to a memory, even a bio-political mythology, of blood, in order to create stable differences in the flux of the present.

Thus we can see that the rhythm which Western capitalism imposes on other parts of the world refuses to allow them the time to "introduce differences" into their own cultural, economic and political experience (of which the West is necessarily a part). Insistence on the simplicity and self-evidence of this rhythm contributes to the sonic shock crushing the breath out of its own citizens and those of other regions of the world—disrupting ecological, religious, and human physiological cycles of labor and recuperation, throwing the inhabitants into an increasingly undifferentiated confusion from which is unlikely to result the sort of vibrant civil society Westerners expect to accompany capitalist development. All of this brings us back to consider the Enlightenment heritage which is supposedly rejected by ethnic groups outside the West and Western social movements which challenge the idea that their equal power is guaranteed by a form of publicity which coincides with capitalist practices of production and the legal right to assume equal consumer roles. For Foucault, as we noted, the Enlightenment is not this form of publicity per se, but the ethic or desire to introduce a difference between past and present, a differentiating activity which can cut in many ways but which also enables us to identify both when and with whom we exist. To the extent that it denies this differentiating function and seeks to standardize speeds, Western liberalism itself remains pre-"modern" in a certain sense, its occlusion or "forgetfulness" of the historical character of publicity on a par with that imposed by the totalitarian regimes it seeks to replace.

The above remarks have more an exploratory than a definite character, requiring further consideration of temporality in general as well as empirical historical research into particular cases of cultural conflict. Their abstraction and brevity place them in the category of a research program rather than results. Each of those studies would, in turn, have its own temporality and rate of deepening understanding—what I have done is no more than to sketch out a most rudimentary structure for coming to terms with the possible political significance of temporal multiplicity.

WORKS CITED

Appadurai, Arjun. *Modernity at Large: Cultural Dimensions of Globalization*. Minneapolis: Minnesota University Press, 1996.

Bartky, Sandra Lee. "Foucault, Femininity, and the Modernization of Patriarchal Power." *Femininity and Domination: Studies in the Phenomenology of Oppression*. New York: Routledge, 1990.

Chossudovsky, Michel. *The Globalization of Poverty: Impacts of IMF and World Bank Reforms*. London: Zed Books, 1997.

Daddabbo, Leonardo. "Foucault et le temps." *Michel Foucault: trajectoires au coeur du présent*. Ed. Lucio D'Alessandro and Adolfo Marino. Paris: L'Harmattan, 1998. 281-290.

_______. *Tempocorpo: Forme temporali in Michel Foucault*. Naples: La Città del Sole, 1999.

Ewald, François. "Foucault et l'actualité." In *Au risque de Foucault*. Ed. Dominique Franche. Paris: Centre Georges Pompidou, 1997.

Farge, Arlette. *Des lieux pour l'histoire*. Paris: Seuil, 1997.

Foucault, Michel. *The Archeology of Knowledge*. Trans. A. M. Sheridan Smith. New York: Pantheon Books, 1972.

_______. *Discipline and Punish: The Birth of the Prison*. Trans. Alan Sheridan. New York: Pantheon Books, 1977a.

_______. *Dits et écrits, 1954-1988*. 4 vols. Ed. Daniel Defert and François Ewald. Paris: Gallimard, 1994.

_______. "Nietzsche, Genealogy, History." *Language, Counter-memory, Practice: Selected Essays and Interviews*. Ed. Donald F. Bouchard. Trans. Donald F. Bouchard and Sherry Simon. Ithaca: Cornell University Press, 1977b. 139-164.

_______. *The Politics of Truth*. Ed. Sylvère Lotringer and Lysa Hochroth. New York: Semiotext(e), 1997.

Gowan, Peter. "Neo-Liberal Theory and Practice for Eastern Europe." *New Left Review* 213 (1995): 3-60.

Gradev, Vladimir. "La lecture brisée. Notes sur les voyages foucauldiens à l'Est." In *Au risque de Foucault*. Ed. Dominique Franche. Paris: Centre Georges Pompidou, 1997.

Habermas, Jurgen. *Between Facts and Norms: Contributions to a Discourse Theory of Law and Democracy*. Trans. William Rehg. Cambridge: MIT Press, 1996.

_______. *The Structural Transformation of the Public Sphere: An Inquiry into a Category of Bourgeois Society*. Trans. Thomas Burger with the assistance of Frederick Lawrence. Cambridge: MIT Press, 1989.

Kant, Immanuel. *The Conflict of the Faculties*. Trans. Mary J. Gregor. Lincoln: University of Nebraska Press, 1992.

Leduc, Jean. *Les historiens et le temps: Conceptions, problématiques, écritures*. Paris: Seuil, 1999.

Moroncini, Bruno. "La scène du présent. Historicisme et fin de l'histoire chez Michel Foucault." *Michel Foucault: trajectoires au coeur du présent*. Ed. Lucio D'Alessandro and Adolfo Marino. Paris: L'Harmattan, 1998. 93-131.

Pizzorno, Alessandro. "Foucault et la conception libérale de l'individu." *Michel Foucault philosophe: rencontre internationale*. Ed. Georges Canguilhem. Paris: Seuil, 1989. 236-245.

Pomian, Krzysztof. *Sur l'histoire*. Paris: Gallimard, 1999.

Poster, Mark. "Foucault, le présent et l'histoire." *Michel Foucault philosophe: rencontre internationale*. Ed. Georges Canguilhem. Paris: Seuil, 1989. 354-371.

Procacci, Giovanna. "Le grondement de la bataille." In *Au risque de Foucault*. Ed. Dominique Franche. Paris: Centre Georges Pompidou, 1997.

Ransom, John S. *Foucault's Discipline: The Politics of Subjectivity*. Durham: Duke University Press, 1997.

Schierup, Carl-Ulrik, ed. *Scramble for the Balkans: Nationalism, Globalism, and the Political Economy of Reconstruction*. New York: St. Martin's, 1999.

Veyne, Paul. "Foucault Revolutionizes History." *Foucault and his Interlocutors*. Ed. Arnold I. Davidson. Chicago: University of Chicago Press, 1997. 146-82.

Zizek, Slavoj. *Tarrying with the Negative: Kant, Hegel, and the Critique of* Ideology. Durham: Duke University Press, 1993.

THEORY ON BORDERLINES
A Collective Experience and a Free Market

Zeynep Mennan

The theme of the Second Annual Interdisciplinary Conference of Loyola University Chicago announces movement, an active process of change and transformation in places, positions, and postures. The theme also includes the actor of this process, which we all experience today: interdisciplinary studies, a privileged form of knowledge production in the contemporary theoretical arena. I shall focus on interdisciplinarity and depict the contemporary context of what we continue to name as "theory." Theory undergoes a transition in a critical epistemic context marking our present, a transition which remains as yet unresolved. The crisis experienced by theory presents itself under three facets: it is epidemic, that is, it invades all disciplines and research fields; it is epistemic, since theory asks for a redefinition that is not let to stabilize itself in a painful period of paradigm change; and it is representational—theory used to inhabit a metaphorical representation that is currently subject to dislocation. These three features of contemporary theory are intricately bound up with each other.[1]

The rise of interdisciplinary studies marks a new epistemic era in which the very concept of discipline is more problematized than ever, and in which the isolation and self-subsistence of different disciplines melt down in often unimaginable new combinations and forms of inter-, intra, cross-disciplinarity. Writing about the recent effacement of previous categories of discourse, Frederic Jameson notes that

---

[1] Z. Mennan, *An Interpretive Framework for Understanding Architectural Theory's Self-representation* (Ph.D. diss., Middle East Technical University, 1997).

> [A] generation ago, there was still a technical discourse of professional philosophy—the great systems of Sartre or the phenomenologists, the work of Wittgenstein or analytic or common language philosophy—alongside which one could distinguish that quite different discourse of the other academic disciplines—of political science for example, or sociology or literary criticism. *Today increasingly we have a kind of writing simply called "theory" which is all or none of these things at once.* This new kind of discourse, generally associated with France and so-called French theory, is becoming widespread and marks the end of philosophy as such. Is the work of Michel Foucault, for example, to be called philosophy, history, social theory or political science? It's undecidable, as they say nowadays... [italics mine][2]

As Jameson notes, this new theoretical ambience, which indicates the blurring of interdisciplinary frontiers, develops in the wake of post-structuralism and is generally conceived as the product of a growing influence of Foucauldian theory. Post-structuralist analysis brings discourse analysis to the fore, and with the predominance of the latter, associated with the new primacy of language, or what is called the "linguistic turn," a series of sub-disciplines and issues are brought to the center of interest, fields and issues thus far repressed or marginalised.

We have, then, the emergence of sub-disciplines, research programmes or fields such as cultural studies, literary studies, linguistics, social anthropology, feminism, and so forth, which appear on the intellectual scene with renewed interest, together with cross-disciplinary issues shifting to problems of language, text, discursive processes, and interpretation. These changes appear as the cultural products of an essentially interpretivist narrative, gradually debasing, devaluating and disintegrating the previous world picture. Within this overall reorganization, what seems exemplary is that paradigm changes not only

---

[2] F. Jameson, "Post-modernism and Consumer Society," in *The Anti-aesthetic: Essays in Post-modern Culture*, ed. H. Foster (Port Townsend: Bay Press, 1989) 112.

occur within scholarly activities, but also between them. The late '80s and early '90s witnessed an increasing interest in interdisciplinary studies, this manifestation of a new intellectual and discursive spirit, blurring disciplinary frontiers.

This kind of research, in the first place, tends to weaken the traditionally well-defined boundaries between disciplines, and even subdisciplines. It further yields to the emergence of new fields of thought and action, undescribable under conventional disciplinary categories, because emerging thoroughly out of interdisciplinarity, on the intersections of conventional borderlines. Or, traditionally non-authoritative fields and discourses acquire once inconceivable occupations, as has been the case for instance in architectural discourse's recent interest in literary criticism, cinematography, Lacanian psychoanalysis and Deleuzian schizophrenia, and chaos theory, together with the exploitation of new techniques that emerge on interdisciplinary lines, such as collage, pastiche, graffiti, parody, and irony.

It becomes increasingly difficult to draw distinctions between disciplinary fields, to decide about the disciplinary location of a research project. Traditional boundaries becoming undefendable, new insights develop as to their historical artificiality. This undecidability presents itself as the outcome of an epistemological debasement, the most important indication and confirmation of which can be found in interdisciplinarity; indeed, with disciplines coming closer in order to share and compare their production modes of knowledge, interdisciplinarity can be reformulated as a common research and experience on different modes of knowledge, exploded with the fragmentation of a general epistemology. The weakening of disciplinary boundaries is then related to the weakening of epistemological bases.

Interdisciplinarity brings different fields of research closer under common projects, altering their focus in order to meet the changing issues of a changing epistemic posture. Interdisciplinary studies are then set in motion in a critical period of paradigm change; such a period is characterised by troubles in legitimizing accepted research tools and methods. It is no surprise that different fields come closer in their efforts to meet their own disciplinary deficiencies by borrowing theoretical approaches and methodologies from each other.

Opening of disciplinary boundaries denotes an instability in disciplinary formations. Architecture presents one such instance: neither architectural research, nor architectural theory, nor architectural practice can avoid extra-disciplinary references. The sources one consults when designing, theorizing, researching or teaching architecture come from polyvalent contexts. It seems that a syncretism is at work in any of these activities. The discipline of architecture is inherently syncretic and synthetic. The frequent recourse to disciplines outside of itself, which I shall call the onto-epistemological tradition of architecture, points to its disciplinary instability, which necessitates a frame of reference that is more stable and stronger than itself. Architectural history abounds in examples of architecture's extra-disciplinary affiliations—philosophy, natural sciences, social sciences, sociology, psychology, and linguistics—and these affiliations proliferate in ever-expanding directions.

Architecture's recourse to more stable disciplines raises the issue of grounding: grounding a theory, an activity, an inquiry, a method of research. This process foregrounds legitimation, the object of grounding itself. Disciplines proceed in a syncretic fashion in their search for knowledge and validation with the dissolution of a comprehensive epistemological framework capable of gathering and explaining all instances of discourse, itself exploded into a multiplicity of theories with respective, thus differentiated, modes of knowledge. This epistemic situation leaves us with knowledges whose relations to objects cannot be given some unified and guaranteed form, the form of truth; it leaves us with conflicting epistemologies and respective theory-choices. It leaves us with the problem of incommensurability of competing theories. This incommensurability is both the source and the outcome of a co-existence of competing or conflicting stances, liberated with the dissolution of the grounding meta-discourse.

How can theory justify and legitimate its knowledge-claims and truth-claims within such an epistemic context? In order to comprehend alterations in contemporary theory's status and authority, it is necessary to look at its degrees of demarcation from a particular conception and species of theory: the strong concept of theory. The strong concept of theory, which has extensively dominated the field as the only one worth being called theory, originates in and comes affiliated with metaphysical thinking and extends into positivist/objectivist traditions. The powerful self-construction and maintenance of the strong concept of theory can best be understood through recourse to a Cartesian metaphor, the architectural metaphor of the foundation.[3] Theory always represents itself as a kind of

---

[3] Cartesianism in its metonymic form is encapsulated in the metaphor of the foundation, introduced at the opening of Descartes' first *Meditation*: "...I was convinced that I must once for all seriously undertake to rid myself of all the opinions which I had formerly accepted, and commence *to build anew from the foundation,* if I wanted to *establish any firm and permanent structure* in the sciences" (Descartes, cited in R. J. Bernstein, *Beyond Objectivism and Relativism: Science, Hermeneutics and Praxis* [Philadelphia: University of Pennsylvania Press, 1983] 16, italics mine), and the search for an "Archimedean point" for grounding knowledge in the second *Meditation*: "Archimedes, in order that he might draw the terrestrial globe out of its place, and transport it elsewhere, demanded only that *one point should be fixed and immoveable*; in the same way, I shall have the right to conceive high hopes if I am happy enough to discover one thing only which is *certain and indubitable*" (ibid., italics mine). Bernstein notes that Descartes' *Meditations* "has been read as the great rationalist treatise of modern times," indeed representing "the *locus classicus* in modern philosophy," because of the metaphors of the foundation and the Archimedean point; although few philosophers accepted Descartes' claims, these metaphors have inspired many: "There can be little doubt that the problems, metaphors, and questions that he bequeathed to us have been at the very center of philosophy since Descartes..."

building, and as shall be seen, the metaphorical construction of theory's self-representation is a foundationalist structure erected by an architectural theory.

In his "Themes in Post-Metaphysical Thinking," Habermas[4] associates metaphysical thinking and the strong concept of theory. The form of thought which characterizes metaphysical thinking is delineated in Habermas's work as a unitary and totalizing form of thinking which distinguishes itself by the conceptual level at which it relates everything to "the One and the Whole": this feature of metaphysical thinking, that is, its specific construction of the whole, is of particular concern. The One and the Whole is abstracted into something first and infinite, which stands over and against the world of the finite, forming its basis; candidates for this position, notes Habermas, include "a world-transcendent creator-god," "the essential ground of nature," or "lastly, and most abstractly, . . . being," but "in each case, a perspective emerges from which innerworldly things and events, which in their diversity are placed at a distance, can be made univocal as particular entities and at the same time be conceived as parts of a single whole" (30).

This particular relation that metaphysical thinking maintains between the one and the many constitutes the essential feature of this form of thought:

> The one and the many, abstractly conceived as the relationship of identity and difference, is the fundamental relation that metaphysical thinking comprehends both as logical and ontological: *the one is both axiom and essential ground, principle and origin. From it the many is derived – in the sense both of grounding and of originating.* And

(op. cit., 16f). The impact of Cartesianism is indebted to the metaphors that it has produced; these metaphors are construed after problems concerning the foundations of knowledge, the knowledge of the external world – posited as a world standing outside the subjective world – and the ways by which this world can be represented in the mind.

4 J. Habermas, "Themes in Post-Metaphysical Thinking," in *Post-metaphysical Thinking: Philosophical Essays* (Cambridge, MA: MIT Press, 1992) 28-53.

> thanks to this origin, the many is reproduced as an ordered multiplicity. (Habermas, 30; italics mine)

Thus, metaphysical thinking establishes an internal relation between the One and the multiplicity of phenomena, where the One stands as the essence, the unifying order, from which an ordered multiplicity is derived. In Plato, this essence is of a conceptual nature:

> [T]he Platonic Idea is neither pure concept nor pure image but rather the typical, the form-giving, which is extracted from perceptible multiplicity. The Ideas, which are built into what is material, bring with themselves the promise of universal unity because *they taper toward the apex of the hierarchically ordered conceptual pyramid and internally refer to this apex...*(Habermas, 30-31; italics mine)

Within this hierarchical pyramidal organization, the One is extracted and abstracted from the many, and comprises in itself all the multiplicity that it gathers under its organization. The internal relationship of the One to the many is secured through this hierarchical composition in which the many is absorbed within the ideal, universal and supra-temporal One.

In the tradition of metaphysics, the One derives its absolute authority from this established hierarchy, which opposes the One and the many, identity and difference, ideas and matter, the infinite and the finite, the universal and the temporal, the necessary and the contingent, an opposition which gives predominance to the first term of the conceptual pairs (Habermas,30). The symmetrical oppositions between these conceptual pairs, which secure the pyramidal construction, constitute the transcendentalization of the One, which is elevated to the position of the absolute; the One has then precedence over the many, as form has precedence over matter, and identity over difference; the pyramid of metaphysics[5] constructs itself through hierarchical relations of precedence, which culminate in the transcendental apex.[6]

Within the line of metaphysical thinking, this symmetrical opposition points to an equation of theory and philosophy, raised to the transcendental level of the apex. Theory constructs itself as the metaphysical One, allowing then a diverse plurality to be constituted as a totality or as one world, under its totalizing representation. The metaphysical construction of the One opposes theory to experience and secures its precedence over practice. This strong concept of theory, notes Habermas, originates in the notion of theory-as-contemplation:

> Philosophy recommends as its path to salvation the life dedicated to contemplation—the *bios theoretikos*....Theory itself is affected by being embedded in an exemplary form of life. For the few, it offers a privileged access to truth, while for the many the path to theoretical knowledge remains closed. Theory demands a renunciation of the natural attitude toward the world and promises contact with the extra-ordinary. (Habermas, 32)

The strong concept of theory, absolute and self-justifying, is a product of metaphysical thinking, of the ontological

---

[5] See Mennan, *An Interpretive Framework for Understanding Architectural Theory's Self-representation*, for a development of the pyramidal configuration as a representation of strong theory, a visual metaphor haunting the metaphysical and the positivistic traditions of architectural theory.

[6] Habermas notes that the paradox of these oppositions, from which "the history of metaphysics derives its inner dynamic," constitutes the basic deception of idealism about itself, for the One always comprises the many and form always comprises matter; that is, Ideas always contain what they were supposed to exclude as matter and empirical content, from which they are read through comparative abstraction (op. cit., 31). In other words, the pyramidal organization which builds itself through totalizing thinking cannot escape containing what it wanted to exclude through totalization; metaphysical thinking is a simultaneously totalizing and self-referential form of thought. This simultaneous totalization and self-referentiality constitute the basic contradiction within metaphysical thinking; the "logical and ontological" relation of the One and the many is a self-referential relation, to which there can be no escape in the process of totalization: indeed, this tension is what constitutes the inner dynamic of the pyramid.

relation between the One and the many, which allows a diverse plurality to be constituted in the unity of one world, in the participation of the metaphysical One.

The sublimation of theory as the metaphysical One, or the survival of the strong concept of theory, is a resilient form which can also be detected under the positivistic conception of theory. Shifts in the conception of theory correspond to the problematization of metaphysical thought by anti-metaphysical movements, in the face of which metaphysical thinking reconstructs itself, in counter-maneuvers that translate its terms to accommodate these shifts. Renewals in metaphysical thinking are made possible by the translation of the metaphor of the foundation into new terms. But there are also a series of anti-metaphysical movements which gradually devaluate this form of thought. Among these, two paradigm shifts seem significant: notably, the rise of positivism and the shift to the philosophy of language.

The first of these shifts, the rise of positivism, corresponds with the glorification of the methods of the empirical sciences in the seventeenth century: Habermas notes that positivism, as an originally anti-metaphysical movement, renders metaphysical thinking dubious, by the assertion of a new type of procedural rationality through the methods of the empirical sciences, demanding new requirements for justification, and placing confidence solely in the rationality of their own approaches. This is how theory, continuing the empiricist tradition, evolves from a contemplative ideal into a double tentative guiding and informing practice, from a position which is situated outside of experience.

Stanley Fish[7] describes this positivist-foundationalist strategy, mainly appropriated in the natural sciences dur-

---

[7] Stanley Fish, "Anti-foundationalism, Theory-hope and the Teaching of Composition," in *Doing What Comes Naturally: Change, Rhetoric, and the Practice of*

ing the extended hierarchy of the positivist and objectivist traditions, though many branches of the social sciences also fall under this paradigm:

> The foundationalist strategy is first to identify [a] ground and then so to order our activities that they become *anchored* to it and are thereby rendered objective and principled. The ground so identified must have certain (related) characteristics: it must be invariant across contexts and even cultures; it must stand apart from political, partisan, and "subjective" concerns in relation to which it must act as a constraint; and it must provide *a reference point or checkpoint* against which claims to knowledge and success can be measured and adjudicated. (Fish, 342f; italics mine)

Theory then acts as an ahistorical, acontextual and formal description of contingencies, from which a rule of generalized rationality can be derived, acting as the absolute foundation of all action and practice. The foundationalist discourse on theory looks for models and methods which are valid for all and for all time, for ultimate and universal justifications of beliefs and values, with the hope that pretensions to knowledge may be justified by an objective method, instead of the individual beliefs derived from the hazards of education and experience, and that truth may be acquired by correspondence to the fact.

Every foundationalist project assumes the availability of invariance and explicitness, which builds upon the assumption of a ground. The assumption of the availability of a ground is equivalent to the basic conviction of "objectivism," that "there is or must be some permanent, a-historical matrix or framework to which we can ultimately appeal in determining the nature of rationality, knowledge, truth, reality, goodness, or rightness."[8] The gathering of metaphysics and positivism can best be

---

Theory in Literary and Legal Studies (Durham, NC and London: Duke University Press, 1989), 343-355.

[8] R. J. Bernstein, *Beyond Objectivism and Relativism: Science*, 8.

understood under the notion of objectivism, which, as R. J. Bernstein states at the outset of his *Beyond Objectivism and Relativism*, is closely related to foundationalism. Bernstein explains, however, his use of the term "objectivism" "in a way that is far more inclusive than some of its standard uses":

> "Objectivism" has frequently been used to designate metaphysical realism—the claim that there is a world of objective reality that exists independently of us and that has a determinate nature or essence that we can know. In modern times, objectivism has been closely linked with an acceptance of a basic metaphysical or epistemological distinction between the subject and the object. What is "out there" (objective) is presumed to be independent of us (subjects), and knowledge is achieved when a subject correctly mirrors or represents objective reality.[9]

Bernstein's work is significant for understanding the connotations of objectivism, not only in its unquestioned relation to positivism, but also and mainly in its dialectical similarities with transcendentalism. His reading of objectivism stresses the dialectical similarity between "objectivism" and "transcendentalism," to cover both of them under a single term, or under the substantial assumption of the availability of a ground or foundation.

---

[9] Bernstein, 9. Given this standard definition, Bernstein adds that this dominant form of objectivism is only one variety of the species; he gives examples from various philosophers whose works are known to have been carried against objectivism, reading them as bearers of the objectivist bias: His references to Kant's and Husserl's work particularly elucidate this point. Referring to Kant and the tradition of transcendental philosophy "as questioning the very possibility of making sense of the objectivity of knowledge by resorting to metaphysical realism—by appealing to a world of thing-in-itself that is completely independent of the ways in which we condition and constitute experience," Bernstein notes that Kant is no less an objectivist and foundationalist, for he "does not question the need for an a-historical permanent matrix or categorial scheme for grounding knowledge," indeed, insisting upon it "more rigorously than many of his predecessors." Similarly, Husserl, who "thought of himself as pursuing the telos of transcendental philosophy" and who "understood himself as battling against all forms of objectivism in modern philosophy," is an objectivist in Bernstein's reading (ibid., 9f).

It is interesting to note that the rise of positivism, as an anti-metaphysical movement, is not significant enough in displacing the pyramidal representation of theory; indeed, positivism restores this representation it wanted to displace. This is the restoration of the symmetrical opposition between theory and practice. The construction of strong theory, grounded in the architectural metaphor of the foundation, is only one species of the pyramidal configuration, but not the least. It constitutes the fundamental representation, placing theory in a relation of bipolarity with respect to the ground, thus standing at the root of the notion of theory-as-opposed-to-practice. This means that positivism retains somehow the strong concept of theory that was affiliated with metaphysical thinking, and falls back into metaphysics. This restoration distinguishes itself, however, from that of the metaphysical construction.

The pyramid of metaphysics constructed itself through a transcendental foundation. In other words, the construction of the pyramid of metaphysics used to start from the apex, taken as the transcendental foundation, from which the inner relations of the pyramid could be ordered and totalized. Positivism thoroughly reverses this construction to start over from the ground up; the position of foundation is restored to the ground. In a sense, it is with the pyramid of positivism—a product of an anti-metaphysical attempt to reverse the metaphysical construction—that the metaphor of the foundation becomes a genuinely architectural metaphor.

In positivistic thought, the antecedent unity of metaphysical thinking cannot be guaranteed; with the positivistic critique of metaphysics, the anticipation of this unity, governed by the transcendental foundation, is replaced by a confidence in the objectivistic observation of empirical facts, which are independent from theory. Thus, metaphorically speaking, positivism reconstructs a pyramid which, starting from the world of facts and phenomena, tapers towards the apex still throned by theory.

This conception, which opposes theory to practice, retains the notion of theory as "pure," that is, as purged from earthly and empirical origins, and elevated above experience. This symmetrical opposition between theory and practice, which sublimates now the independence of theory, still retains something of the absolutistic understanding of theory: "What remains is the idealistic interpretation placed on distancing the everyday network of experience and interests"(Habermas, 33). The distance created with the ordinary world in the promise of a "contact with the extraordinary" continues to survive and is "inflated into the internally justified precedence of theory over practice" (Habermas, 33), a specter of metaphysical thinking that has not been exorcised from the positivistic notion of theory.

Both the pyramid of metaphysics and the pyramid of positivism taper toward theory, though through different forms of justification and construction. In both of these foundationalist constructions, the apex is retained by theory. The pyramidal representation which builds itself on the metaphor of the foundation is perpetuated either in the form of a universal, ahistorical, foundational philosophical knowledge (the metaphysical tradition), or in the form of a scientism idealising natural science (the positivist tradition), both forms appearing as the major traditions under which a foundationalist theory comes into being. As far as a common ground can be identified, uniting adherents under a common, transcendentalized ideal, the foundationalist representation is left intact. As Habermas, Fish also notes that:

> In the long history of what Derrida has called the logocentric tradition of Western metaphysics, *candidates for the status or position of "ground"* have included God, the material or "brute act" world, rationality in general and logic in particular, a neutral observation language, the set of eternal values and the free and independent self. (Fish, 343; italics mine)

Indeed, foundationalism can accomodate diverse and seemingly contradictory stances that are yet inhabited by this common assumption of the availability of a foundation. This constatation highlights foundationalism as a transdisciplinary position, the first assumption of which can be extended to different areas of inquiry, such as science, philosophy, epistemology, theory, history and hermeneutics.

It is under the foundationalist outlook that a general epistemology could be construed, on the assumption of a common ground uniting all in a common rationality, that is, under the ideal of a metaphysical backdrop, one which is further very specific about its teleology. This backdrop provided for the purity and coherence of the foundationalist world, enabling different discourses to maintain isomorphic relationships. The legitimacy of this paradigmatic world was acquired from the ruling episteme, i.e., a correspondence theory of truth, which used to justify theory's epistemological stand and its form of power uphold. This epistemology built itself on the conviction that there exists an objective world, one which is the object of inquiry and from which facts are derived and studied by objective methods. The acquisition and the validation of truth and knowledge rest on the assumption of a subject-object dichotomy, a dialectical opposition between the outside objective world standing out there to be discovered and the scientist or researcher who tries to uncover its hidden rules and patterns through objective methods. The scientific method provides here the link between the inner and outer worlds, between the subject and the object, and appears as the primordial guarantee of objectivist inquiry standing firm against all forms of subjectivism and relativism.

The world as depicted by foundationalism is characterized by the purity of its outlook, sustaining the epistemological, philosophical and historical narratives in cohesion. This cohesion and purity is contaminated by an anti-foundationalist critique which recurs around and problematizes foundationalist themes such as "metaphysics," "transcendentalism," "grand narratives," "logocentrism," "anthropocentrism," "universal reason," "universal history," the "founding subject," the "centering of the subject," and "subject-object humanism," to cite just a few, all themes which acquired validity under the foundationalist outlook, and which are vigorously brought into question mainly in the post-Nietzschean, post-Heideggerian or post-positivistic trends of thought. Anti-foundationalism originates in philosophy—that is, from the top of the pyramid—and spreads to other disciplines and fields, in which it is excessively appropriated. As Robert Mugerauer notes, "Dismantling comforting forms and meanings currently is the 'hottest' alternative."[10] Theory is no exception; it undergoes significant dislocations within this critical context.

Anti-foundationalism manifests itself as an active denial of the possibility of absolute foundations and a continuous erosion of all notions of ground. It is the embodiment of the conception of the world as a conflict of interpretations, with a growing unwillingness to endow any of them with grounding authority, the embodiment of uncertainty and undecidability, of in-betweenness. The idea of in-betweenness comes as a manifestation of the threat and challenge which interpretation poses to the certainty of method.

With the rise of interpretation, or the linguistic turn, world-views and narratives multiply, under which different epistemic versions of the world can now accommodate themselves. Intellectual constructions or interpretations, which multiply the "single objective world" estimated to provide for the object of all inquiry, multiply the objects of

---

[10] R. Mugerauer, *Interpretations on Behalf of Place: Environmental Displacements and Alternative Responses* (Albany: State University of New York Press, 1994) 12.

inquiry, and put into doubt the credibility of the previous unified world picture, and above all its certainty. By denouncing the possibility of recovering the foundations of knowledge, anti-foundationalism also denounces the cumulative or accretionary view of knowledge on which natural sciences ground themselves. Interpretation thus poses a powerful threat to the grounds on which natural sciences establish themselves, and more specifically, to the positivistic modes of inquiry. It is important to note that the linguistic turn is a turn towards the social sciences, with the new valuation of language and interpretation. A series of dissolutions are then set forth: the dissolution of the distinction between subject and object; the dissolution of the disciplinary boundaries; and the dissolution of the dichotomy between the natural and the social sciences. Anti-foundationalism perpetually contaminates the unity and purity of the foundationalist outlook, casts doubt on the certainty of its picture, and stresses our embeddedness in a world which is no more stable than the historical and conventional forms of thought that bring it into being. It thoroughly destabilizes the foundationalist picture and the isomorphic relations held by different discourses.

This destabilization, however, does not settle into a self-establishment of anti-foundationalism. Indeed, anti-foundationalism is a movement which, by its very nature, resists instaurating itself as a new paradigm or a new epistemology. Anti-foundationalism is a form of critique which maintains tension by continuously launching oppositions between its own position and the ground of its critique, and by maintaining these oppositions in a continuous critical co-habitation. The present context should be understood through this critical co-habitation of conflicting stances that give way to and maintain a state of crisis. In other words, an anti-foundationalist context denotes a critical context.

This pluralistic and fragmented epistemic context is co-habited by competing theories having no privileged epistemic status over each other. Statements uttered from a theoretical position cannot claim the legitimacy of the knowledge they produce. Anti-foundationalism redistributes legitimating power between different modes of knowledge and suspends the universality of validity claims. Theoretical statements, confined to the specific language-games they have been uttered from, cannot transcend their context. The incredulity towards the grand narrative—or the incredulity towards universal truth-claims—articulates the irreducibly local character of all argumentation and discourse.

Within this cultural context, diversity, plurality and undecidability appear as the companions of an epistemological debasement. Anti-foundationalism questions prevalent epistemological frameworks, exploded into different forms of knowledge, the modes of production of which constitute the experimental theme of interdisciplinary research, bringing different fields together in new, unconventional encounters. Interdisciplinarity, then, is the name of a collective experience characterized by the coexistence of competing theoretical statements, the plurality and diversity of which are being promoted by an epistemological debasement. This promotion further accelerates the debasement, to the point that the critique of epistemology may also lead to its own ruin, placing the age under the frustrating sign of undecidability.

The blurring of traditional boundaries and the accompanying epistemological discomfort indicate still another aspect of the recent context, namely, the loosening and gradual effacement of power relationships between traditional disciplinary categories. The rise of interdisciplinarity indicates also a non-hierarchical reorganization of disciplines and sub-disciplines.

Theory in an anti-foundationalist world is a special product of a paradigm that is searching for an ever-increasing articulation of difference and heterogeneity, and altering its self-definition. Theory transforms itself into a new critical instrument pursuing knowledge along interdisciplinary lines. It is then released from disciplinary possession and becomes collective. The dispossession and collectivisation of contemporary theory—or critical theory, or collective theory—appear as significant indications of the degree of its destabilization with respect to foundationalist theory and as the most important manifestation of the contemporary theoretical context.

Anti-foundationalist theory significantly displaces its status from the strong concept of theory: it does not hold the relation of precedence to practice (sustained by positivist theory) and comes as a product of anti-foundationalist detranscendentalization. This process of detranscendentalization is consequential to the rise of interpretation. With interpretation occupying the center of the present intellectual climate, the alleged unity of the foundationalist world picture is brought into question and attacked on many fronts, and through different anti-foundationalist perspectives. Anti-foundationalism's denial of transcendence is expressed in its critique of totalizing thinking, which attempts to sustain the unity of the foundationalist world-picture and to gather the Whole under a single global interpretation. This global interpretation is now considered to be suspect, and its criticism explodes into a multiplicity of interpretations, threatening the epistemic orthodoxy of foundationalism. Interpretation dissolves the unity of the foundationalist world.

It seems clear that anti-foundationalist theory, as depicted so far, can no more be represented under the pyramidal figure previously developed. In terms of metaphorical imagery, the transcendentalist construction, the concept it represented, and the relations of hierarchy it sustained, all dissolve together. The transcendentalist organization collapses through philosophy's self-interrogation, initiating a series of radical and irreversible transformations in terms of the disciplines, discursive forms, and narratives that it had been containing, released with the collapse of the metaphor of the foundation. Robert Mugerauer uses a similar metaphor to depict the present context: "As with the Berlin wall, it is hard to understand the sudden collapse of the established disciplinary boundaries, the radical subversion of what institutions had enforced for hundreds of years" (Mugerauer, 3).

In the anti-foundationalist world, theory appears in an incongruous form; its configuration cannot be traced. The "architecture" of the recent critical context conceals itself through a continuous presentation of ambiguity, heterogeneity and incongruity. Boundary construction (and destruction), a traditionally architectural act, displaces itself to become the cultural product of an epistemological debasement. Erection and trespassing of boundaries are being secularized by their constant immaterialization and permeability, creating a fragile in-between condition, a rather uncomfortable and unstable architecture, an intangible space called interdisciplinarity in which all disciplines are forced to dwell.

Dispossessed from traditional disciplinary and epistemological anchors, theory's self-construction and self-representation remain, however, increasingly local and historicist. European or Continental thinking, an essentially interpretivist and critical culture, distinguishes itself in the contemporary discourse of/on theory, defined by a growing discomfort in the face of ever new uncertainties of a post-foundationalist age. This age seems to be an "age of Europe" when the significance and magnitude of the "linguistic turn" is remembered: The hegemony of Europe is related with the worldwide hegemony of interpretivist schools (in philosophy, in the arts, in architecture, in humanities, and so forth), as interpretation constitutes the most distinct practice of European tradition(s).

The valuation of language and textual interpretation intensifies the controversies between Continental and Anglo-Saxon schools of thought. The rather late discovery of hermeneutics in Anglo-Saxon philosophy can be related with its positivistic, natural sciences-oriented aspirations, as differentiated from and devaluated by the culturalist and interpretivist schools of Continental thinking. The distance the Anglo-Saxon world has kept with textual interpretation is not only spatial, but is rapidly recovering through an intense importation of the so-called "critical theory" into the North American theory market.

I would like to end by introducing a new metaphor for the apprehension of contemporary theory in its interdisciplinary form: the military metaphor of the Trojan Horse. The city hosting this conference inspires and legitimates the development of this metaphor, when we remember that the foundation myth of Rome, according to Virgil, is traced back to Aeneas, son of the goddess Venus and the mortal Anchises, who fled from Troy when it was captured, and landed at the mouth of the Tiber. Virgil's association of the myth of Aeneas with that of Romulus and Remus (in order to strengthen the national myth of the founding of the city)[11] and extending it to Troy becomes further significant, as it recalls and indicates the Roman admiration and importation of Greek theoretical material, a situation that seems to echo itself in the theoretical exchanges occurring between the two sides of the Atlantic.

Contemporary theory replaces and multiplies the Trojan Horse, this first historical instance of trespassing a boundary. As the Trojan Horse, it displaces itself without

---

[11] See P. Zanker, "The Mythical Foundations of the New Rome," in *The Power of Images in the Age of Augustus* (Ann Arbor: University of Michigan Press, 1990). Zanker explains that the mythological aspect of the Augustan program consisted of the combination of two myth cycles, the legend of Troy and the story of Romulus "[I]n the version employed by Virgil, Mars has seduced Rhea Silvia, daughter of the king of Alba Longa, and has thus become father to the twins Romulus and Remus and ancestor of the Romans. But Rhea Silvia belonged to the Trojan family of Aeneas and could therefore be incorporated into the family tree of Augustus....Venus and Mars were then both ancestors of the Romans, though by different partners" (195).

opposition: it is welcome in foreign land. Theory immaterializes the Trojan Horse, renders it intangible. It thus travels and invests in foreign territories. It also releases new material and accounts for the epidemic and imperialistic propensity of interpretivist narratives, or of the antifoundationalist argument.

Transiti di scrittura

Isabella Vincentini

C'è una geografia nuova, tutta da ricostruire in questo inizio di millennio dove siamo appena entrati. Gli anni Novanta, che ancora stentiamo a considerare conclusi, ci hanno lasciato in eredità, come dice il titolo del nostro convegno: uno *slittamento dei confini e una negoziazione dei luoghi* che ci chiede di ridefinire lo spazio in cui ci troviamo ad agire. Uno spazio in cui siamo stati proiettati dagli eventi che hanno chiuso il Novecento, un secolo di espansione, di cambiamenti vertiginosi, rapidissimi, tanto da giustapporsi gli uni agli altri, fino a creare la nostra epoca della simultaneità, della globalizzazione e dell'omologazione.

Proprio mentre lo spirito epocale spinge verso l'identità dei valori, azzerando differenze e radici culturali, esplodono a macchia d'olio conflitti di razza e di religione, guerre etniche e genocidi. I luoghi delle mediazioni (dalle istituzioni civili al progetto sociale, fino alla politica culturale dell'integrazione), non riescono a contenere ma solo ad offuscare, problemi essenziali pronti a riaccendersi all' improvviso.

Non credere alle mediazioni non vuol dire estetizzare romanticamente il dissenso, come rifiutare l'unificazione non vuol dire illudersi di coltivare le differenze. Tra il luogo dell'inclusione e quello dell'esclusione, si può cercare un altro luogo: quello dell'Individuazione e sarà uno spazio protetto dal suo *genius loci*.

In arte, i capolavori non sono mai stati il frutto di un negoziato ma dell'inquietudine, delle disperazioni e del disordine, del conflitto e della solitudine, della violenza dell'energia centrifuga. Da sempre i pensatori più incisivi hanno sfidato la morale comune, il *political correctness* degli intellettuali convenzionali ed hanno denunciato i crimini dell'attualità, la barbarie della civiltà. Sono i dissidenti, i pensatori "contro." Già all'inizio del Novecento, la critica al concetto di Civilizzazione (*Zivilisation*) contrapposta al concetto di Cultura (*Kultur*) con autori come Spengler o il Thomas Mann delle *Considerazioni di un impolitico*, aveva delineato l'aspetto artificioso, rigido, prossimo alla decadenza della Civilizzazione. Il richiamo ai valori più autentici dell'individuo, alle sue pulsioni naturali ed istintive, alle sue forze interiori corrotte dall'automatismo della civilizzazione, è un discorso che attraversa l'intero Novecento.

Demonizzare oggi la tecnica o abbandonarsi all'enfasi apocalittica, è sicuramente una strada inutile che conduce ad una sterile lamentazione e al pathos del catastrofismo. All'opposto è ugualmente vano inseguire euforicamente gli *input* dell'attualità credendo di cavalcarne l'onda per non rimanere indietro. Probabilmente è molto più utile prestare ascolto ai sintomi del disagio: che si presentano con la stessa faccia della malattia, in quanto spesso non viene da aspetti contrapposti (come sano o malato) una possibilità di guarigione, ma dal virus stesso iniettato come anticorpo.

Se la civiltà rappresenta l'ambito del dentro, gli artisti si sono sempre spostati verso l'esterno, il confine, il limite.

La Modernità con il Novecento ha inaugurato uno spostamento dello spazio dal finito verso l'Infinito: con Baudelaire, Leopardi, Rimbaud, Eliot e Mallarmé, dal deserto di un mondo che già prefigurava una società metropolitana commercializzata e tecnicizzata, si apriva verso l'ontologia negativa del Mistero e dell'Ignoto.

Lo *slittamento dei confini* si orientava verso il Lontano, verso i Paradisi artificiali, l'oltrepassamento dei limiti. La geografia dell'inizio del moderno fa *slittare i confini* verso il Nulla, il Mistero, verso una Natura selvaggia e lontana, in contrapposizione con la vita moderna prefigurata. È un moto di evasione che porterà nell'Abisso, inseguendo la speranza di vedere il Nuovo.

La geografia successiva vede i poeti cimentarsi con l'attraversamento del Vuoto, del Deserto, del Nulla, cercando un'escatologia della storia come impegno etico o civile. La poesia e l'arte sono ancora strettamente legate all'elaborazione creativa del destino di un'epoca, segnano la coscienza dell'epoca. L'arte è vicina all'ontologia, anche se ad un'ontologia nichilista, si interroga sul destino dell'esistenza, sul "male di vivere." Nello spazio aperto del mondo, il poeta pur avendo p0erso la sacralità del proprio luogo protetto e difeso all'interno della comunità, ha ancora un eremo, come gli stiliti, da cui continua a parlare.

La fine del Novecento presenta uno scenario del tutto cambiato. Ogni luogo è stato desacralizzato, i non-luoghi delle utopie cancellati, è stata rimossa l'antinomia ontologica tra il dentro e il fuori, l'interno e l'esterno, tra il vicino e il lontano.

Ma cosa è avvenuto negli ultimi trent'anni del Novecento per creare una frattura così forte con la produzione artistica precedente?, per creare quella spaccatura che separa il nostro tempo anche dai tempi più recenti?

In campo letterario le ultime avanguardie artistiche si sono manifestate negli anni Sessanta. È pur vero che, all' interno della poesia italiana contemporanea, a trent'anni di distanza, si è tentato di riprendere il discorso delle avanguardie e di fondare un movimento, il Gruppo 93, che riprendesse, innovandole, le istanze dell'omonimo Gruppo 63 di cui si dichiarava erede diretto.

In realtà da tale movimento non è nata nessuna letteratura, né alcuna innovazione, ma solo elaborazioni teoriche di una metaletteratura ormai giunta alla fine.

Segnali veri e proficui di vitalità sono venuti invece, negli anni Settanta, da poeti cresciuti sulle letture dei maestri francesi: da Roland Barthes a Foucault, da Blanchot a Deleuze e Guattari, da Lacan a Derrida.

Sicuramente i *maitrés a penseér* francesi, prima del loro viaggio in transatlantico per fecondare le scuole postmoderne e del decostruttivimo americano da Paul de Man a Hans Blumenberg, Harold Bloom fino al distruzionismo di Spanos e Bové, hanno creato un luogo di sconfinamento ed estensione, di decodifica e di relazioni ricche di nuovi elementi, di inquietudine e di circolazione di forze tale da penetrare in tutti gli spazi confinanti: dalla letteratura alla critica letteraria, dalla saggistica alla poesia, dall'ambito delle teorie a quello della riflessione filosofica.

A partire dagli anni Settanta si è sviluppata una tendenza letteraria nella filosofia: gli scritti di pensatori come Blanchot, Barthes, Deleuze, Lyotard, Lévinas ed altri, sconfinavano con il loro linguaggio fortemente metaforico, nel campo letterario. D'altro lato poeti come Edmond Jabes, René Char o Yves Bonnefoy si facevano interpreti delle inquietudini del pensiero contemporaneo.

Anche in Italia la filosofia si spostava sul terreno letterario e la letteratura si avvicinava alla speculazione con autori come Umberto Eco, che da esperto semiologo diventava uno scrittore di best-sellers, o con filosofi come Cacciari, Agamben, Gargani o Magris che non solo per i temi indagati spesso di ambito letterario, ma per la loro stessa densità di scrittura, si situavano oltre i confini delle discipline. O, ancora, le *Lezioni americane* di Italo Calvino, così acute di riflessioni sui cambiamenti epocali, oppure la forte consapevolezza teorica degli studi linguistici di un poeta come Andrea Zanzotto.

La critica letteraria, accademica o scientifica, cominciava ad essere attraversata da spinte centrifughe che sconfinavano nel campo delle teorie e da queste alla prosa saggistica. Alla figura del filologo e dello studioso, sempre più si andava sostituendo la figura del critico-scrittore che si nasconde dietro i libri di cui parla, per rivelare attraverso di essi, la propria identità.

Il passaggio dagli anni Sessanta agli anni Settanta ha rimodellato lo spazio della scrittura prima confinato in un sistema preciso di discipline, trasformando lo strutturalismo praghese e il formalismo russo in un campo semiotico allargato all'antropologia come alla psicanalisi, alla nuova storiografia e alla sociologia. Erede oltre che dell'ortodossia strutturalistica anche della grande tradizione russa degli studi sul folclore e sulla cultura popolare, dagli studi di Propp sulla fiaba all'antropologia strutturale di Levi Strauss, il post-strutturalismo francese è stato probabilmente una delle espressioni più forti e feconde degli ultimi anni. È proprio a partire da questo sovraccarico di spinte e tensioni si è sviluppato il dibattito contemporaneo.

Mentre la filosofia post-nietzscheana francese assumeva caratteri letterari come era nello stile del maestro, il linguaggio letterario sempre di più abbandonava le forme tradizionali dando vita ad una commistione di versi e prosa, forma lirica e forma narrativa, dialogica e riflessiva, filosofica e frammentaria.

È stato proprio il post-strutturalismo francese ad inaugurare il panorama della contemporaneità. È da lì che è partita la più significativa rivoluzione del pensiero attuale. Le nuove nozioni di Deterritorializzazione, Disseminazione, Forclusione, Smarrimento, Perdita, Assenza, Mancanza, Manque, Differenza, Simulacro, Ripetizione, Deriva, Linee di fuga, Rizoma, Traccia, Frammento, Debolezza, Molteplicità, Desiderio, Follia, Altro, Eros, Scarto, Impossibile, Gioco, Paranoia e Schizofrenia, hanno fatto *slittare i confini* delle teorie e della scrittura abolendo *i luoghi* delle precedenti rappresentazioni.

Con lo sbriciolamento dell'egemonia del pensiero post-strutturalista francese nella visione del decostruttivismo postmoderno e dell'ermeneutica, ci si è trovati non solo alla fine delle grandi narrazioni, ma anche delle teorie e della possibilità di proseguire.

Gli anni Ottanta sono stati caratterizzati dallo sviluppo e dalla storicizzazione delle teorie, mentre, negli anni Novanta, abbiamo assistito ad un rimaneggiamento eclettico del *nouveau mélange* venutosi a formare alla fine di queste innumerevoli tensioni.

Svuotato dall'interno, lo spazio della scrittura si è trovato dislocato nel campo dell'Irrealtà. Situata nella Casella Vuota del Simbolico e dell'Immaginario, la scrittura non sembrava più appartenere alla geografia del mondo reale.

Chiusa dello spazio del Simbolico, la scrittura non trovava più la rete di relazioni che le permettevano di spostarsi dalle cime agli Abissi, dalla prefigurazione della metropoli moderna ai paradisi selvaggi ed artificiali, dal mondo noto all'Ignoto. Collocata nello spazio dell'Irrealtà simbolica, alla scrittura è stata negata la connessione con lo spazio pubblico e sociale.

Per riportare la scrittura, esiliata da anni dentro questo spazio chiuso, all'interno di una geografia compatibile con la comunicazione, è sembrato necessario dislocarla da quella Casella Vuota del Simbolico dove l'aveva situata lo strutturalismo prima e la decostruzione dopo, all'interno di uno spazio Culturale che avesse in sé tutti gli elementi dell'utile e delle pratiche sociali.

È stato necessario ripensare la scrittura come Cultura per uscire dalle pastoie di una riflessione che aveva saturato lo spazio della produzione teorica.

Ma, mentre lo spazio Culturale e lo spazio Sociale sono dislocati sullo stesso piano, dentro la sfera della storia, dei sistemi di vita e del progetto comune, lo spazio dell'arte è un percorso solitario.

"Uno scrittore che si rispetti vive accanto alla sua società," ha affermato Ernst Junger. "È come se ne sfiorasse i caratteri per capirne meglio l'essenza. Il suo compito, diversamente da quello del politico o dell'economista, non è di natura sociale". "L'uomo romantico in qualche modo fugge dalla realtà e si costruisce con la fantasia poetica o con il sogno un proprio tempo e un proprio spazio. L'Anarca invece conosce e valuta bene il mondo in cui si trova, ed è capace di ritrarsi da esso quando gli pare. In ciascuno di noi c'è un fondo anarchico, un impulso originario all'anarchia. Ma non appena si nasce esso viene limitato dal padre e dalla madre, dalla società e dallo stato. Sono salassi inevitabili che l'energia originaria dell'individuo subisce a cui nessuno sfugge. Ma l'elemento anarchico rimane latente, e può erompere come lava: può liberare l'individuo ma anche distruggerlo."[1]

---

[1] A. Gnoli and F. Volpi, *I prossimi titani: Conversazioni con Ernst Junger* (Milano: Adelphi, 1977), 56-57.

La fine del millennio che stiamo attraversando si presenta sotto il segno di un cambiamento in atto ma, come sempre, da vicino siamo affetti da presbiopia per cui possiamo solo limitarci ad azzardare ipotesi.

Come da un lato unificare le differenze equivale a soggiacere all'ideologia dominante, allo stesso modo la rivendicazione della diversità è semplicemente la sua maschera rovesciata, che crede di opporsi al sistema, in realtà criticandolo non lo destabilizza, ne agevola la dialettica interna del mantenimento.

Anche l'arte provocatoria e d'avanguardia si è perfettamente istituzionalizzata ed è entrata – senza alcuna difficoltà – in tutti i musei, come i recenti movimenti di contestazione sono diventati le nuove direttive del cambiamento.

Alla fine di questo percorso di *slittamento dei confini e negoziazione dei luoghi,* siamo giunti ad un luogo di *transito,* che non può *con*-cludere ma solo cercare di *in*-cludere tutto ciò che è rimasto *ex*-cluso dentro una nuova territorializzazione.

E cos'è che è rimasto *ex*-cluso in questi anni?

L'elemento perturbante dell'arte che è ben diverso dall'iter provocatorio dell'arte contemporanea, la quale ha cercato in questo modo di sfuggire all'isolamento e all'impotenza in cui si è venuta a trovare nel mondo di oggi. È venuto a mancare il guizzo perturbante di un'identità psichica che come un anticorpo grida la sua non acquiescenza all'insignificanza, alla frustrazione e all'indifferenza. È venuto a mancare l'elemento anarchico latente che la società limita e sottopone a continui salassi. L'empietà di Socrate che per questo fu condannato a morte. L'inattualità di Nietzsche e di tutti i solitari, gli Anarchi o i dissidenti da Kafka a Céline, da Camus a Borges.

Abbiamo imparato ad attraversare la letteratura come una morfologia di motivi, categorie e astrazioni. Abbiamo imparato che tra la categoria dell'agricoltura e quella della guerra esiste una mediazione: il termine intermedio di CACCIA.

Abbiamo imparato che l'*usanza di seppellire i morti* è coincisa con il *passaggio alla sedentarietà* nella storia umana. Ed abbiamo dimenticato la potenza delle tombe a cupola degli Atridi, il fascino della porta dei Leoni di Micene, la grandezza delle fortificazioni delle mura ciclopiche.

Abbiamo dimenticato le costanti emozionali dell'uomo e della vita, come ad esempio il dolore che (come scrive Junger) non è valutato con lo stesso metro in ogni epoca:

> Esistono alcuni grandi e immutabili parametri in base ai quali il valore dell'uomo dà la misura di sé. Uno di questi è il dolore; esso è la prova più dura in quella catena di prove che è, some si suol dire, la vita.
>
> [...] Il dolore come unità di misura è immutabile, ciò che muta, invece, è il modo in cui l'uomo si pone di fronte a tale unità di misura.
>
> [...] Il dolore è una di quelle chiavi che servono ad aprire non solo i segreti dell'animo ma il mondo stesso. Quando ci si avvicina a quei punti in cui l'uomo si mostra all'altezza del dolore, o superiore ad esso, si accede alle sorgenti della sua forza e al mistero che si nasconde dietro il suo potere.

Se l'omologazione della Cultura si è trasformata in una dimensione artificiale, falsamente pubblica e stereotipata, è proprio in quella sensazione di malessere e spaesamento che il modello produttivo cerca di inquadrare e sopire, che dovremmo ricercare il nostro luogo di *transito.*

Non cercare dunque un luogo dove stare, ma lasciarsi portare in tutti i luoghi dove la natura, i nostri demoni come dice Hillman, le nostre radici biologiche come dice adesso la psicanalisi delle neuroscienze ci chiamano.

Sarà un percorso ardito, ad alta percentuale di rischio, perché mentre la collettività seleziona il più adatto, la natura seleziona il più forte. I poeti e gli artisti, a loro spese, lo hanno sempre fatto. Ed allora lasciamo, per concludere, a loro la parola:

Lo spirito ha lasciato il mondo. Temo i corpi morti che si dispongono attorno a me, i cadaveri dell'umanità, contaminati e coperti di cenci. Temo gli zombie dirigenti, gli zombie negozianti, gli zombie ecclesiastici, gli zombie letterati, tutti che si esprimono per luoghi comuni, temo la lingua dei morti, che scambiano gli hobby per le passioni, temo la follia dei morti.

Quando tutti parlano la stessa lingua il poeta non ha più parole. Il linguaggio si arricchisce se viene nutrito dalla differenza. Dove non c'è differenza non c'è ricchezza. Non c'è distinzione dai morti.

Mangiate le stesse mele, spunta il giorno scende la notte. Leggete gli stessi giornali, spunta il giorno, scende la notte. Accendete la televisione, spunta il giorno, scende la notte. Affermate la vostra individualità con una sola voce. Spunta il giorno, scende la notte.[2]

[2] J. Winterson, *Arte e menzogna* (Milano: Mondadori, 1996), 79.

Part II -Constructing National & International Identities

Un approccio di Antropologia del Diritto al problema dell'armonizzazione europea
l'esempio nordamericano

Barbara Faedda

L'Antropologia del diritto ha, tra i propri terreni di ricerca, le situazioni giuridiche di convivenza fra elementi di civiltà moderne, postmoderne e tradizionali. Essa intende approfondire le interazioni dinamiche tra diritto, cultura e organizzazione sociale e focalizzare l'attenzione sulle relazioni tra il diritto e l'uomo. La tradizione giuridica classica normalmente studia ciò che i giudici, i legislatori e gli avvocati fanno e dicono. L'antropologia del diritto invece intende scoprire, dall'interno, come i membri di una società considerano le proprie relazioni giuridiche e come esse influenzino la loro vita.[1]

Importanti ricerche sono state condotte, in tempi recenti, proprio nel cosiddetto *Quarto Mondo* e precisamente nelle *Rich Countries,* ambito prescelto anche per via della caratteristica compresenza d'alta industrializzazione e forte tradizione. Le Rich Countries, come afferma Riccardo Motta, sono *zone di frontiera culturale,* ricche di risorse naturali, che vedono coesistere nello stesso territorio gruppi urbani di tipo occidentale con redditi procapite tra i più alti del mondo e gruppi autoctoni ad economia tradizionale con redditi molto bassi.[2] Queste aree sono state in passato facile bersaglio di ghettizzazioni degli etnodiritti, ma oggi, finalmente, sono diventate lo scenario di aperture etnogiuridiche rilevanti. Le ricerche svolte in quest'ambito sono fondamentalmente incentrate sul problema dell'armonizzazione del diritto nazionale, statale, federale, comunque un diritto positivo, con il diritto tradizionale di gruppi di nativi, immigrati o rifugiati, vale a dire molto

[1] N. Rouland, *Antropologia giuridica* (Milano: Giuffré, 1992).
[2] R. Motta, *L'addomesticamento degli etnodiritti* (Milano: Unicopli, 1994).

spesso un etnodiritto *homegrown*. Mi riferisco soprattutto agli studi di Norbert Rouland, del già citato Riccardo Motta, di Laura Nader e Rene Gadacz,[3] così come alle linee di ricerca di *anthropology of law* o di *legal anthropology* seguite in alcune università nordamericane quali, per esempio, quelle canadesi di Calgari e di Saskatchewan, quest'ultima con il suo *Native Law Centre*,[4] o quella di Bloomington nell' Indiana. Il maggior numero di ricerche di tal genere si deve proprio al nordamerica, che ne ha fatto una prestigiosa tradizione accademica.

Ora che l'Europa continua il suo lungo cammino verso una completa unificazione economica, politica ed anche giuridica, non si può non considerare preziosa tutta la lezione nordamericana, ovviamente tenendo ben presenti le evidenti diversità storico-culturali; soprattutto, si deve valutare con attenzione ciò che sta accadendo in questi ultimi anni proprio nel Canada e negli Stati Uniti. Per noi europei la vera ricchezza consiste nel considerare le tappe, le metodologie ed anche gli inevitabili errori che gli operatori del diritto nordamericano hanno compiuto nel loro tentativo che fu, inizialmente, d'assimilazione ed oggi, soprattutto con riferimento al Canada, d'armonizzazione. Si dovrebbero oramai evitare sbagli, dimostratisi a volte irreparabili, quali l'imposizione del diritto positivo, la violazione della pluralità dei sistemi giuridici autoctoni, l'introduzione di regole estranee, la coercizione.

Si deve tenere conto di tutto ciò allorquando l'Unione Europea, oltre a riunire sotto un unico organismo amministrativo numerosi Stati, si trova a dover gestire il problema politico delle minoranze[5] e quindi, di seguito, anche delle particolarità giuridiche di gruppi e comunità distanti culturalmente e giuridicamente dalle realtà nazionali all'interno delle quali vivono.

---

[3] R. Gadacz, *Towards an Anthropology of Law in Complex Society: An Analysis of Critical Concepts* (Alberta: Western Publishers, 1982).

[4] Native Law Centre <http://www.usask.ca/nativelaw/index.html>.

[5] W. Kymlicka, *La cittadinanza multiculturale* (Bologna: Il Mulino, 1999).

Oltreoceano gli Inuit,[6] che abitano territori ricchi di giacimenti, sono stati vittime, per molti anni, di atteggiamenti aggressivi e prevaricatori da parte di speculatori bianchi dell'Alaska, e di modalità paternalistiche da parte del Canada. Ma ciò che in questo contesto vorrei sottolineare è che il loro sistema di giustizia tradizionale era, fino a pochi anni fa, praticamente scomparso, e così anche tipiche istituzioni quali il *song-duel*, metodo di risoluzione pacifica dei conflitti mediante sfide canore a contenuto ironico-satirico. La cultura giuridica di questi popoli è stata nel tempo indebolita e le loro istituzioni tradizionali ignorate ed isolate. Di questi popoli si sono interessati molti studiosi d'antropologia del diritto: tra questi Hoebel e Pospisil. Riguardo ai duelli canori[7] Hoebel descrive il loro svolgimento sottolineando che in gioco è l'abilità nel canto e nella parola, non la forza fisica. Nella risoluzione del conflitto si valuta cioè la capacità di elaborazione artistica attorno ad un nucleo di concetti base che sono i punti deboli dell'avversario. Il pubblico, con i suoi applausi, decide a chi assegnare la vittoria, ma colui che risulta sconfitto deve mostrare sempre e comunque di non adirarsi o incollerirsi per l'esito della tenzone. Qualsiasi sia stato il risultato, è costume che le parti in causa si riconcilino scambiandosi doni: l'importante è che sia restaurato l'ordine e ristabilita l'armonia all'interno della comunità. Anche Pospisil,[8] nei suoi studi, ci offre un esempio del cosiddetto *ordine negoziato*. Egli, parlando dei Nunamiut, descrive la figura dell'*umealik*: questi detiene l'autorità di risolvere i conflitti usando come strumenti giuridici i rimproveri pubblici e l'assegnazione di un soprannome di cui il colpevole sentirà il peso sociale per molto tempo. Anche in questo caso la sanzione corporea è stata ampiamente evitata.

---

[6] Nunatsiaq News, Nuvavik Edition, Canada <http://www.nunatsiaq.com/cgi-bin/mainpage>.

[7] F. Remotti, *Temi di antropologia giuridica* (Torino: Giappichelli, 1982).

[8] L. Pospisil, *Anthropology of Law: A Comparative Theory* (New Haven, CT: HRAF Press, 1974).

Il Canada rappresenta senza dubbio un vero e proprio laboratorio di ricerca per l'antropologo del diritto. In passato il governo di questo Paese è stato accusato di aver manipolato o addirittura negato il sistema giuridico autoctono e, non a caso, la vita di questi popoli fu interamente regolata da legislazioni federali fino al 1951, anno in cui i Nativi furono consultati dal governo per la prima volta. Oggi invece, in conseguenza di un'apertura giuridica multiculturale, questi stessi gruppi riescono ad amministrare e gestire circa l'80% del budget governativo destinato loro. L'accordo ratificato dagli Inuit nel 1992, firmato dal Primo Ministro canadese nel 1993 e passato al Parlamento nello stesso anno, è la maggior risoluzione circa le rivendicazioni territoriali nella storia del Canada; tale accordo ha stabilito chiare regole di proprietà e controllo su un'area che rappresenta circa un quinto del territorio canadese, e sulle relative risorse.

La terra, del resto, è sempre stata il principale problema legato all'innesto di diritti occidentali sulle consuetudini autoctone: nelle società tradizionali la proprietà è intesa fondamentalmente come comunitaria e inalienabile, a differenza delle nostre legislazioni che a tal riguardo parlano di proprietà individuale e trasferibile.[9] Allo stesso modo lo sfruttamento delle risorse legate alla terra nel periodo di conquista fu regolato da norme commerciali tipicamente occidentali, sconvolgendo e sbilanciando così il sistema e gli equilibri autoctoni. Oggigiorno le cose sono cambiate, soprattutto per opera dell'*Office of Native Claims*, creato dal governo federale canadese nel 1974, che è riuscito a condurre transazioni economiche e finanziarie di grande importanza giuridica. In una causa[10] di un nativo contro la corona inglese sul diritto di pesca in un particolare territorio, la discussione giuridica si è incentrata sul problema del conflitto tra più norme applicabili. Ci si è trovati di fronte alla presenza simultanea di diritto cana-

---

[9] M. G. Losano, *I grandi sistemi giuridici* (Torino: Einaudi, 1988).

[10] Native Law Centre, *Canadian Native Law Cases*, University of Saskatchewan, <http://www.usask.ca/nativelaw/cnls.html>.

dese, diritto coloniale e diritto autoctono, e indicative sono state le parole di commento alla sentenza: "Invero il diritto di proprietà aborigeno è stato riconosciuto come una specie distinta di common law federale piuttosto che un semplice sottoinsieme di common law o civil law o diritto di proprietà operante all'interno della provincia."[11] Dopo tanti anni e tante battaglie s'inizia solo oggi a riconoscere al diritto autoctono carattere di autonomia.

Nell'anno 1996, il Dipartimento federale per la Giustizia approva *l'Aboriginal Justice Learning Network,*[12] un programma inserito nella cosiddetta *Strategia per la Giustizia degli Aborigeni.*[13] Tale strategia guida le comunità locali a costituire sistemi alternativi di giustizia ed indica come tali sistemi possano essere inseriti all'interno di un più largo contesto d'autogoverno. Il Network, a sua volta, studia la flessibilità di cambiamento all'interno del sistema di giustizia vigente e ricerca la modalità più adatta per rimanere, allo stesso tempo, saldamente in linea con i valori e le tradizioni autoctoni.

Nella città di Winnipeg un nuovo progetto, creato nel 1998 e denominato *Servizi Legali Aborigeni di Winnipeg*, offre opzioni alternative all'attuale sistema giuridico. Esso riguarda una particolare istituzione giuridica autoctona: il *Sentencing Circle,*[14] il Consiglio di comunità. Esso è composto di uomini, donne, giovani e un anziano, tutti aborigeni, che siedono con l'imputato e la vittima per condurre un processo per così dire "di aggiustamento." Il Consiglio, infatti, non determina il colpevole o l'innocente, ma raggiunge una decisione basata sul consenso. In questo processo, in cui il colpevole ammette la sua colpa e si assume la responsabilità delle sue azioni, il ruolo dell'anziano *Peacemaker* è importante: diventa un componente interattivo, una figura di equilibrio, che lavora con l'accusato e la vit-

---

[11] *Regina v. Batisse* (1978) (Ont. D.C.), Canadian Native Law Cases, Hunting and Fishing Rights, <http://library.usask.ca/native/cnlch.html>.

[12] <http://www.usask.ca/nativelaw/jah_AJLN.html>.

[13] Aboriginal Justice Strategy (AJS), Canada.

[14] <http://www.usask.ca/nativelaw/jah_scircle.html>.

tima per raggiungere insieme un accordo sul da farsi. Adottando l'istituzione autoctona del *sentencing circle* si è registrato un abbassamento del numero di crimini e la riduzione degli individui imprigionati. Con questo sistema alternativo la comunità è impegnata in modo diretto a far slittare l'attenzione dal concetto di castigo a quello di restituzione, reintegrazione, riparazione e riabilitazione. Specifici criteri, inoltre, sono stati sviluppati al fine di assicurare consistenza applicativa: l'accusato deve essere pienamente d'accordo ad essere giudicato dal *sentencing circle* e deve avere profonde radici nella comunità nella quale il *circle* è tenuto e all'interno della quale sono scelti i partecipanti. I *circles* sono tenuti in sedute informali dove ad ognuno è data la possibilità di parlare.

L'impegno della comunità in questa vicenda conferma il profondo radicamento dei valori aborigeni, e rappresenta un passo importante nella realizzazione dell'autodeterminazione e dell'autonomia. Il *sentencing circle* sostituisce il sistema tradizionale punitivo anglo-europeo con uno in cui l'obiettivo è quello di restaurare l'armonia nella comunità. Gli autoctoni non ritengono che esista un modello universale per la giustizia restitutiva: ogni comunità deve trovare il suo modo e sviluppare un modello che rifletta i propri valori, ma il controllo sul processo *deve* rimanere all'interno della comunità. A Saskatchewan l'uso di *sentencing circle* si è allargato anche ai centri urbani.

I nativi asseriscono che la cultura giuridica angloamericana tenta di controllare le azioni che potenzialmente considera dannose per la società attraverso l'interdizione e la punizione di comportamenti nocivi: l'enfasi quindi è posta sulla punizione del deviante come mezzo per rendere la persona conforme e per proteggere gli altri membri della società. Nelle società aborigene, la proposta di un sistema di giustizia alternativo consiste nella restaurazione della pace e dell'equilibrio all'interno della comunità e nella riconciliazione tra l'accusato e l'individuo che ha danneggiato, oltre che con la sua coscienza. Considerando fondamentali la riconciliazione tra accusato e vittima e il mantenimento dell'armonia e dell'ordine della comunità si è di fronte significativamente ad una sfida al presente sistema giuridico. I nativi ritengono, inoltre, che una ridistribuzione di funzioni all'interno della comunità aiuti a modificare e riformare la struttura gerarchica e paternalistica del sistema giuridico nazionale ed occidentale.

È interessante notare che inizialmente le critiche degli autoctoni al sistema convenzionale furono interpretate come rivendicazioni dettate semplicemente da diffidenza, rifiuto e rabbia. Probabilmente, anche in questo caso, risaliva a galla l'atavica chiusura etnocentrica tipica della cultura occidentale. Solo in un secondo momento si è notato che tali critiche riflettevano, invece, una differenza fondamentale nell'intendere la giustizia e il processo. Si comprese quindi che tale divario era generato da una *differenza giuridico-culturale*. Si capì, cioè, che il concetto di assimilazione era un totale fallimento, sia dal punto di vista culturale che specificamente giuridico.

Il giudice Robert Yazzie, Presidente della Corte di Giustizia della Nazione Navajo, in un suo intervento sulla rivista specialistica *Justice as Healing*,[15] tenta di spiegare il concetto di giustizia degli aborigeni. "Quando parli di diritto tradizionale o di common law indiano la gente non sa di cosa tu stia parlando. La comune definizione di diritto cita tre elementi: le norme, le istituzioni e la forza. Molte definizioni insistono sul fatto che senza forza, senza la possibilità di punire, senza tribunali e prigioni non ci possa essere diritto, ma questo tipo di diritto può solo danneggiare; non può guarire. Quando io sentii questa definizione per la prima volta ero confuso. Chiesi se le emozioni umane rientrassero nella definizione, se facessero parte del processo. Non dovrebbe essere così? Per comprendere come i tribunali navajo definiscano il diritto si

[15] *Justice as Healing* è una newsletter del Native Law Centre, nata per dibattere circa i concetti aborigeni di giustizia, soprattutto in considerazione delle esperienze legate al colonialismo, al razzismo, alla dominazione e all'oppressione, per un reale recupero della tradizione autoctona. <http://www.usask.ca/nativelaw/jah.html>.

deve considerare prima il termine *norma*. Le norme per noi sono valori e sentimenti condivisi circa il modo di fare le cose. Il navajo dice: fa le cose in un modo giusto. Come indiani noi sappiamo cosa significhi fare le cose in un modo giusto. È per questo che i sentimenti condivisi dalla gente si riversano in quel vasto termine che è la parola diritto: per dargli significato. Troppo spesso la gente rigetta la parola *moralità* a causa di reconditi significati religiosi, ma essa significa qualcosa di più - è l'insieme dei sentimenti condivisi circa la giusta modalità di comportamento. Per completare la nostra definizione di diritto, devono essere incluse le istituzioni indiane tradizionali: la famiglia, il clan, le autorità cerimoniali e le società; ed anche la gente nelle sue relazioni quotidiane. Gli esploratori europei nel passato dissero che gli indiani non avevano un diritto perché non vedevano polizia, uniformi e prigioni; ma essi non vedevano neanche i clan, che sono così importanti per le nostre istituzioni giuridiche. Noi ci relazioniamo l'un l'altro in modo di evitare gli scontri e l'uso della forza. La coercizione e la pena non sono necessarie per avere il diritto. Diverso è anche il modo di guardare alle figure dei giudici. Per gli angloamericani un giudice è una persona con profonda conoscenza della legge che prende decisioni per altri. Si suppone che egli/ella sia così saggio da decidere per il meglio e, in un tribunale americano, un giudice non parla mai (né si consiglia) con le parti. Per noi un giudice è una persona che ha un problema, ma è la gente coinvolta nella disputa che prende una decisione circa tale problema. Il giudice è una persona considerata saggia, che proprio per questo non prende decisioni per altri, bensì incoraggia le parti a parlare dei loro problemi e le aiuta a proporre soluzioni attraverso la sua mediazione. La nostra è giustizia restitutiva."[16]

---

[16] Robert Yazzie, Chief Justice of the Navajo Nation, *The Navajo Response to Crime: Indians, Ant Hills and Stereotypes* in *Justice as Healing* Vol. 3, n. 2, (Summer 1998), <http://www.usask.ca/nativelaw/jah_yazzie2.html>.

Eppure l'ordine negoziato e la tendenza alla conciliazione non sono aspetti tipici solo delle società tradizionali: a ben vedere, si riscontra abbondantemente anche nelle società moderne (sebbene permanga una certa tradizione storico-culturale che valorizza in ogni caso l'ordine imposto). Lo stesso Rouland afferma, dopo numerosi studi da lui condotti in Francia, che l'ordine negoziato è assai più presente di quanto si possa supporre dai manuali di diritto e dai codici. La differenza sta nell'interpretazione di questo principio: per le società tradizionali l'ordine negoziato "è l'espressione di una visione del mondo e della vita sociale fondata sulla nozione di comunità; le società moderne lo reinventano in una cultura individualista, e spesso per rimediare alle insufficienze dello Stato."[17] Procedure alternative quali la mediazione, la conciliazione e l'arbitrato sono sempre più presenti nelle culture giuridiche moderne. Sono definite modelli a somma positiva, poiché conducono ad un risultato nuovo tra le parti, che non comprende un vincitore ed un perdente. Anzi, con queste soluzioni si giunge alla pianificazione delle relazioni future e al ristabilimento di rapporti non conflittuali.

Questi stessi scopi si prefigge la risoluzione pacifica delle dispute anche nella cultura giuridica giapponese. Molti immigrati nipponici si sono scontrati con la giustizia nordamericana. Nella loro cultura le relazioni sociali e il parentado sono più importanti dei singoli individui e, poiché le dispute mostrano disarmonia, devono essere evitate a tutti i costi. Nella risoluzione di una disputa ci si deve sempre impegnare per preservare i rapporti di parentela e il bene sommo delle relazioni familiari.

Numerosi law cases riguardanti americani d'origine giapponese mostrano il dilemma della cultura contro il diritto. Nel caso Yamanaka, una coppia chiese ai vicini di casa di fare da baby-sitter al figlio di tre anni. I vicini presero il bambino con loro e lo portarono al mare, dove purtroppo annegò. I coniugi Yamanaka citarono in giudizio i

[17] N. Rouland, *Antropologia giuridica* (Milano: Giuffré, 1992).

loro vicini per negligenza e furono risarciti con 24.000 dollari. Dopo la sua vittoria in tribunale, la coppia ricevette centinaia di telefonate di denuncia per il suo comportamento. Gli stessi individui della loro comunità erano, non solo sconcertati del fatto che avessero ricevuto denaro dai vicini, ma anche perché avevano citato i vicini in giudizio. La famiglia non sopportò a lungo la pressione sociale e, dopo meno di un mese, tornò in tribunale per restituire la somma e ritirare le accuse.[18]

Il caso Kimura è forse uno dei più strazianti e complessi. La signora Kimura, abitante a Los Angeles, ricevette un giorno una telefonata da una donna che le confessò di intrattenere un rapporto di lunga data con il marito. Alla notizia la signora Kimura decise di annegare se stessa e i suoi due figli. Durante questo tentativo di omicidio-suicidio intervennero due ragazzi ma essi riuscirono a salvare solo la donna: i bambini morirono entrambi. Dopo l'arresto la signora Kimura raccontò della telefonata e dell'infedeltà del marito; spiegò che la vergogna era ricaduta su tutta la famiglia ma soprattutto su di lei, poiché per la sua cultura ella aveva fallito come moglie. Nella cultura giapponese un modo onorevole di sollevare la famiglia da tale vergogna consiste nel compiere una forma di suicido genitore-figli chiamato *oyako-shinjo*. Poiché la cultura giapponese vede i figli come estensione della loro madre, anche i bambini dovevano morire. Rimanere vivi avrebbe rappresentato per loro una terribile situazione: sarebbero stati vittime di ostracismo, disprezzo e ridicolo per tutta la vita.[19]

In casi come questo armonizzare due culture giuridiche sembra davvero impossibile. Gli stessi problemi ovviamente si presentano, nel nordamerica come in qualsiasi altro Paese di accoglienza, per i rifugiati. Il noto concetto statunitense di *melting pot* volle essere in passato la risposta all'ideale che guidava molti gruppi d'immigranti nel

[18] Macella Monk Flake, *The Impact of Culture*, Yale - New Haven Teacher Institute, <http:// www.yale.edu/ynhti/curriculum/units/1996/1/96.01.08.x.html>.
[19] Vedi nota 18.

loro desiderio di diventare individui interamente integrati, ma questa stessa idea fu anche strumento di coercizione e traumi. Oggi questo criterio di assimilazione è comunemente considerato superato, ma il problema della convivenza nella diversità, collegato alla consistenza numerica di immigrati e rifugiati, è ancora molto attuale.

Le più recenti stime dell'ONU dichiarano che, nel mondo, più di 11 milioni di individui fuggono dalla loro terra d'origine a causa di guerre e politiche persecutorie. In quest'ultimo decennio, alla Germania è spettato il primato mondiale delle richieste d'asilo; il Canada dal 1995 ad oggi ha accolto 50mila rifugiati, soprattutto d'origine somala, iraniana e singalese, ma ogni anno deve far fronte a circa 25mila nuove richieste. Gli Stati Uniti detengono il primato mondiale di accoglienza permanente di rifugiati: dal 1990 ad oggi hanno offerto accoglienza a più di un milione di persone e per l'anno prossimo è stato progettato un programma d'insediamento che riguarderà oltre 90mila individui.[20]

Avviene così che, oltre ai nativi, altre categorie facenti parte delle fatidiche *minoranze,* vivano dure esperienze legali come diretto risultato delle loro differenti pratiche culturali.[21] Sorgono quindi molti problemi circa la mancata armonizzazione del diritto nazionale con le peculiarità di diritti tradizionali, per così dire, *d'importazione*. Ma, come ho affermato all'inizio del mio intervento, fortunatamente si registrano oggigiorno notevoli passi avanti in tal senso: gli Istituti di Correzione del Canada, per esempio, riconoscono e rispettano le diversità etnoculturali attraverso programmi e pratiche operative ispirate da principi d'*armonizzazione etnogiuridica*. Esiste un Consiglio Multiculturale per il penitenziario di Saskatchewan[22] che include gli operatori

[20] *National Geographic Magazine Italia,* "Un mondo in fuga" (Roma: National Geographic Society, febbraio 2000).

[21] Per questo tipo di considerazioni giuridico-culturali si rimanda anche all'*International Journal of Canadian Studies* (*I.J.C.S.*), Canada.

[22] Native Law Centre, *Canadian Native Law Reporter* (*C.N.L.R.*), University of Saskatchewan, <http://www.usask.ca/nativelaw/cnlr.html>.

del carcere e gli stessi detenuti: il Consiglio organizza sessioni informative sulla diversità culturale, poichè la varietà etnoculturale nelle prigioni aumenta. Esistono specifiche iniziative regionali in tutto il Paese: ad esempio, la Facoltà di Educazione Permanente dell'Università di Montreal propone un modulo formativo d'intervento interculturale nella regione del Quebec e corsi in comunicazione interculturale per le comunità etniche dell'Ontario e delle regioni Atlantiche.

Il Dipartimento di Giustizia del Canada[23] è un'istituzione tra le più attive e moltissime sono le sue iniziative: i vari uffici regionali consultano regolarmente le comunità sulle questioni giuridiche che esse considerano più importanti. Una consultazione pilota è stata già utilizzata per sviluppare il primo programma intensivo d'educazione dei contesti sociali. Il Dipartimento gestisce, inoltre, attività educative legali online che forniscono ai gruppi di donne immigrate accesso ad internet e agli strumenti d'aggiornamento etnogiuridico, così che possano dialogare anche per via telematica. Il Dipartimento finanzia, poi, l'Associazione Canadese di Black Lawyers per la produzione di un rapporto sul modo, per gli avvocati, di contribuire alle comunità presso le quali prestano le loro competenze. Un altro organismo, il *Centro canadese per le Questioni delle Minoranze* di Toronto, riceve ugualmente finanziamenti dallo stesso Dipartimento per sviluppare una maggiore cooperazione tra le organizzazioni principali per la prevenzione del crimine e le comunità nere e caraibiche della città. Attraverso il *Settore per le Operazioni Legali*, il Dipartimento conduce poi un programma di consapevolezza etno-culturale per i procuratori e gli avvocati e programmi d'educazione permanente per i giudici. Si progettano anche programmi per facilitare l'accesso alla giustizia agli individui che non leggono la lingua inglese o francese: emblematica la sua pubblicazione intitolata "L'abuso è

[23] Department of Justice of Canada, <http://canada.justice.gc.ca>.

sbagliato in ogni lingua," ora tradotta anche in spagnolo, cinese, punjabi e nella lingua degli Inuit.

Il problema, quindi, sembra consistere nel far fronte al senso di smarrimento che colpisce i membri della comunità locale nel loro incontro/scontro con il sistema giuridico convenzionale e nel ricordare che armonizzazione è il mezzo per il raggiungimento dei comuni obiettivi. Oggi, per alcune nazioni come il Canada, si può riconoscere che spesso, fortunatamente, gli obiettivi della giustizia statale coincidono con quelli della giustizia autoctona. Invece, per quanto riguarda l'Europa, se cerchiamo di approfondire il termine *armonizzazione giuridica* attraverso testi di diritto comunitario, scopriamo che tale concetto è riferito essenzialmente alla normativa fiscale, al diritto delle società, al diritto dei servizi finanziari e al diritto industriale.[24] Il campo d'azione, in altre parole, permane quello politico-economico e per gli aspetti culturali si nota un veloce quanto insufficiente accenno. Eppure l'Europa è scenario di rivendicazioni particolaristiche che danno origine a situazioni di conflittualità permanente.

In Europa, ancora oggi, si sente il bisogno di riaffermare che il diritto non è solo quello scritto, codificato e che anche le minoranze e i popoli altri hanno elaborato e prodotto una loro cultura giuridica. Il *pluralismo giuridico* è principio, come abbiamo visto, quasi banale per il Canada o gli Stati Uniti, ma non per l'Europa. Oggi, più che mai, si dovrebbe parlare di *multiculturalismo giuridico* e incominciare a sensibilizzare il legislatore comunitario (che è ancora il Consiglio dei Ministri, e non il Parlamento) su grandi questioni quali, per esempio, la presenza dei musulmani o dei due milioni di Rom, Sinti e Jitanos che vivono e si muovono all'interno dell'Unione Europea. Deve essere affrontata la questione delle prigioni sempre più multietniche ed anche il problema di una mediazione giuridico-culturale nei procedimenti legali, che vada al di

[24] L. Ferrari Bravo and E. Moavero Milanesi, *Lezioni di diritto comunitario* (Napoli: Editoriale Scientifica, 1995).

là del semplice servizio di traduzione linguistica. Tra i grandi progetti di carattere giuridico riguardanti l'Unione Europea, vi è quello ambizioso di unificazione normativa del Codice Civile. Nelle varie sessioni di lavoro, nei convegni internazionali e nelle due risoluzioni in cui il Parlamento europeo ha promosso la redazione di un codice unico, gli elenchi dei partecipanti hanno visto professionisti ed esperti nel campo giuridico, ma non in quello della mediazione interculturale. Fino ad oggi si è parlato di rispetto per il pluralismo giuridico-culturale e per le tradizioni storiche, ma non si è pensato ancora di considerare quest'aspetto come quello fondamentale.

TRANSIDIOMA/TRANSIDIOMATIC PRACTICES

Marco Jacquemet

Drita è Albanese, ha lasciato Tirana agli inizi degli anni 90, prima per la Germania e poi per New York, dove abita ad Astoria, nel Queens in un quartiere di greci cristiano-ortodossi. Questa residenza è stata scelta dal marito, Gencit, dopo essersi convertito alla fede ortodossa in Grecia, durante una permanenza durata 5 anni. Drita parla correttamente albanese, tedesco ed inglese, parlicchia e capisce l'italiano. Gencit parla correttamente albanese, greco, inglese ed italiano.

Drita ha un fratello ed una sorella. Il fratello vive nello stesso abitato, due piani più in alto. La moglie del fratello, Susan, è di nazionalità tedesca, frutto di un matrimonio multietnico, il padre un immigrato turco, la madre una del posto. Susan ha vissuto 6 mesi a Tirana nella casa di famiglia ed ora parla albanese, tedesco e inglese. L'estate scorsa se ne è andata in vacanza nel villaggio d'origine del padre, in una zona della Turchia centrale dove si erano installati molti gruppi d'albanesi. In quel periodo ha fatto amicizia con delle vicine di origine albanese, in grado ancora di esprimersi in un albanese vecchio di 200 anni. Ha scoperto che usando l'albanese imparato a Tirana poteva comunicare agevolmente.

La sorella di Drita, Ilirijana, vive anche lei a New York, nel Bronx. È sposata con un cittadino americano, George, nipote d'immigrati italo-albanesi venuti negli Stati Uniti all'inizio del secolo. La famiglia di George parla in privato *arberesh*, l'albanese delle comunità residenti in Italia, ed in pubblico inglese. La famiglia di George comunica con Ilirijana usando un albanese cinquecentesco, fissatosi all'epoca della migrazione di cattolici albanesi in Italia.

Questo esempio di gruppo multilinguistico non è certamente un nuovo fenomeno, da sempre gruppi sociali limitrofi, e non, si sono appropriati delle rispettive lingue per scambi di ogni genere, tendenza solo acceleratasi nei secoli, soprattutto a causa del ruolo svolto dalle varie politiche mercantili e coloniali occidentali nella creazione di varie lingue franche, *pidgins*, e linguaggi creoli. Quel che più impressiona di questo fenomeno multilinguistico tardomoderno, che chiamerò il transidioma, sono innanzitutto due fattori: 1) l'impressionante rapidità e velocità d'espansione di un multilinguismo planetario con creazioni linguistiche innestate sulla struttura linguistica dell'inglese (rapidità dovuta in gran parte alla mobilità dei media e delle migrazioni, su cui tornerò più sotto); e 2) la sua presenza soprattutto nelle aree occidentali, in quei territori cioè dove per gli ultimi due secoli, governi nazionali, intellettuali, e gruppi di potere si sono agitati per la progressiva standardizzazione della lingua, riducendo bilinguismi, sanzionando creolizzazioni e multilinguismi, distruggendo varietà dialettali, tutto per la creazione della lingua nazionale—ritenuta condizione necessaria per lo sviluppo di un'identità nazionale, e quindi per la creazione di uno stato-nazione solidale.

Questo fenomeno transidiomatico è uno dei prodotti del passaggio dal mondo delle nazioni all'universo della globalizzazione transnazionale. Dopo due secoli di sovranità delle nazioni, ora la supremazia politica, sociale e culturale passa nelle mani degli organismi internazionali (FMI in testa, e poi ONU, NATO, CEE, ANSEA,...), delle corporazioni multinazionali, delle holdings di aiuti umanitari, delle varie forze di intervento militare. In questo contesto cambia il regime di appartenenza, non più—o non solo—legato ad una terra, una lingua, un popolo, bensì ad un area cosmopolita (fatta di aeroporti, hotels e ristoranti, luoghi di transito), ad un linguaggio globale, ad una comunità diasporica, *corporation* o organismo internazionale (governativo o non).

In quest'ottica, il transidioma è la pratica comunicativa dei dipendenti delle organizzazioni internazionali, dei nuovi nomadi del lavoro globale, dei cibernauti, di una nuova classe sociale che da più parti stanno cominciando a chiamare il cognitariato. Il transidioma a disposizione di questo cognitariato è il risultato dell'intrecciarsi delle due forze sociali di diterritorialità che stanno definendo la configurazione comunicativa di questa tarda modernità: la mobilità delle persone e la comunicazione elettronica.

E per affrontare il discorso della deterritorializzazione delle popolazioni, effettuerò il mio primo *shifting* transidiomatico, passando alla seconda lingua di questo convegno, l'inglese, per evocare appunto l'universo globalizzante e deterritorializzato rappresentato da questo linguaggio.[1]

One of the legacies that linguistic studies has inherited from the philosophy of the French Enlightenment (especially from Condillac) and German Romanticism (especially from Herder) is the identification of a language with a people and, consequently, the recognition of peoplehood according to the criterion of language. Since the nineteenth century, social scientists have seen the linkage between territory, cultural tradition, and language as a continuous field. Anthropological interest in local populations and face-to-face encounters led the discipline to think of human populations as bounded entities, culturally and linguistically uniform. A people came to be viewed as a social formation held together by shared behavioral norms, beliefs and values mediated by a common language.[2]

With the globalization of migration, nomadism and all forms of human mobility (where the growth of the "international community" joins the older process of labor migration and colonial movements) the crisis of a territorially based notion of culture comes to the foreground: it is now impossible to talk of culture as a fenced garden, an objecti-

---

[1] D. Crystal, *English as a Global Language* (Cambridge: Cambridge University Press, 1997).

[2] S. Gal, "Commentary," in B. Schieffelin, K. Woolard, P. Kroskrity, ed., *Language Ideologies: Practice and Theory* (Oxford: Oxford University Press, 1998); see also B. Anderson, *Imagined Communities: Reflections on the Origin and Spread of Nationalism* (London: Verso, 1983).

fied reality. It was always a conceptual gambit; it is now exposed as an empirical chimera.

This problematization of the territory is highlighted by new social practices that no longer require physical proximity for interaction. This is the case of the deterritorialized sites, made possible by the technological mediations operated through electronic media. The media have produced an intense acceleration in the dynamics of social interaction, an acceleration that does not progress along straight lines, but follows the centrifugal, rhyzomatic, and chaotic interweaving of multiple channels, voice, and audiences.

As Appadurai points out,[3] the most important new phenomenon facing an anthropology of late modernity is the encounter between media and migration, between mobile texts and mobile people. He considers this interaction an ideal entry point for investigations of the social and cultural mutations of the last decades and of contemporary social formations.

The contemporary pervasiveness of electronic media transfigures all mediated communications, including established forms of social communication such as print and political meetings. Electronic media have the capacity to comprehend all other forms of communication, from talk to print to visual. Electronic media constitute a wider field of communicative mediation than that of any single established form. As Appadurai discusses, phenomena in the field of electronic media such as the synergy of information and entertainment, the tension between the public spaces of cinema and the more private spaces of video watching, the immediacy of the penetration of media messages within public discourses, the role of computer-mediated communication in the constitutions of new subjectivities, and the media's aura of cosmopolitanism and of being on the cutting edge, transform and appropriate all

---

[3] A. Appadurai, *Modernity at Large: Cultural Dimensions of Globalization* (Minneapolis: University of Minnesota Press, 1996).

other communicative forms.

The media offer new rules and resources for the construction of social identity and cultural belonging. As Appadurai states,

> when the rapid, mediated flow of images, scenarios, or emotions merges with the flow of the many social formations of deterritorialized audiences, the result is a recombination in the production of modern subjectivity.[4]

When Moroccan families tape their weddings to be sent to relatives who migrated to Italy, when Italians in New York follow soccer broadcasts in Italian via satellite, or when Pakistani taxi drivers in Chicago listen to sermons recorded in mosques in Kabul or Teheran, we witness the encounter of mobile media practices and transnational people. In this encounter, a new, deterritorialized social identity takes shape, light-years away from the corporative logic of the nation-state, which coagulated around a sentiment of belonging that can no longer be identified with a purely territorial dimension or with a single language.

A final switch to conclude and reclaim the language of our hosts.

Mediazioni elettroniche e migrazioni sociali subiscono un'intensa accelerazione dovuta all'acquisita velocità e multidirezionalità delle comunicazioni, per cui ora il mondo può essere attraversato non solo in 24 ore ma in più direzioni e modi. È questo sviluppo rizomatico e centrifugo che caratterizza la modernità diffusa. I centri metropolitani perdono o vedono diminuita la loro capacità attrattiva perchè possono essere facilmente superati per raggiungere direttamente il villaggio dove vive il cugino o la parte più distante di un continente (permettendo ad esempio ad un europeo di by-passare New York per dirigersi direttamente in California). In questa deterritorializ-

---

[4] A. Appadurai, *Modernity at Large*, 21.

zazione parliamo tutti la stessa lingua, l'inglese, solo per poi accorgerci che nella pratica comunicativa dobbiamo considerare le numerose varietà locali se vogliamo essere capiti. Come il consumo può essere solo locale, così la ricezione dei messaggi comporta questa capacità d'articolare flussi culturali globali nelle specificità del proprio essere nel mondo. Mediazioni e migrazioni fanno oggi la differenza perché sono diventate massicciamente globalizzate, attive cioè su larghi ed irregolari territori transnazionalizzati, e sono in grado di esprimersi nell'intersezione tra globale e locale.

Vista in quest'ottica, la modernità sembra aver sempre meno a che fare con quella linea retta che va dall'Illuminismo ai progetti per lo sviluppo del terzo mondo elaborati nel dopoguerra, e sempre di più con il groviglio di micronarrazioni cinematografiche, programmi televisivi, spot pubblicitari in tre lingue, accenti di *Indian English* nei corrispondenti di CNN, musica *banghra* mixata da un DJ algerino in un club di New York, ed tutte le possibili forme comunicative utilizzate da pubblici diasporici per la costituzione del proprio (effimero) territorio.

Tutto ciò ci permette di riscrivere il concetto di modernità diffusa non nei macrolinguaggi delle politiche nazionali o internazionali, ma nei molteplici transidiomi dei flussi culturali planetari.[5] Tutto ciò, infine, ci permette d'incominciare a capire turbolenze migratorie e pratiche comunicative di gruppi sociali in grado d'immaginarsi, interagire e mutare tra il paradossale desiderio di spostarsi per stabilirsi ed il turbinio mobile, elettronico e digitale che li avvolge come una spessa coltre di nuvole.

---

[5] S. Gruzinski, *La Pensée Métisse* (Paris: Fayard, 1999).

SUBSIDIARIZED PLACES, REIMAGINED COMMUNITIES
Stateless Regions in a United Europe

Kyriaki Papageorgiou

On February 20, 1999, Bretons from all around the world could, in just a few seconds, transport themselves to a traditional Breton village by simply logging onto the Internet. This virtual village was constructed to host the first Breton cyber-festival, which featured Breton traditional music and dance.[1] Brittany is one of the many regions in Europe with a distinct sense of identity that has been discriminated against in the making of a homogeneous state. Throughout the process of French nation-state construction, Breton language and identity were labeled as separatist movements and thus forcefully subordinated. During the Third Republic the inscription "No spitting and no Breton" featured prominently on public buildings.[2] By manipulating the means of information and through a forceful bureaucratic administration, the French central authorities, like many others in Europe, were thought to have successfully replaced distinct regional identities with a homogeneous state identity.

In the late 1960s, however, the image of well-integrated and indivisible Western European states was shattered. Indigenous regional minorities arose from centuries of suppression and asserted their rights with new vigor, confidence, and sometimes violence exhibited in demonstra-

---

[1] Michael Crabb, "France to Host International Cyber Festival of Breton Culture," *CBC Infoculture* (10 Feb 1999): 1; 2 Feb 2000 <http://www.infoculture.cbc.ca/archives/newmedia_02101999_breton.html>. The site where the festivities were held can be accessed through <http://www.antourtan.org>.

[2] Suzanne Berger, "Bretons and Jacobins: Reflections on French Regional Ethnicity," *Ethnic Conflict in the Western World*, ed. Milton J. Esman (Ithaca, NY: Cornell University Press, 1977), 166-167.

tions that spread over Western Europe.[3] It seemed as if "all those people 'without history' that Engels had ridiculed—the Basques, the Bretons, the Slovenians, the Welsh, etc.—had come back to haunt him"[4] and all those who foretold the disappearance of non-state cultures. These communities that were silenced when the nation-states were formed have become salient in the making of a united Europe by constructing themselves around the slogans of "Independence in Europe" and "Europe of Regions." Local languages and dialects have been brought back to life and local traditional cultural activities are becoming increasingly visible through art and music.

This phenomenon has often been explained as an indicator of a cultural renaissance generated to combat the loss of community and "authenticity" caused by the forces of globalization and capitalism, or in the European case, by a united European identity. From a different angle, "cultural renaissance" can be interpreted as local communities' response to larger power structures. By reinventing their identity on the basis of an aestheticized culture that is distinct from the nation-state identity, local communities can justify their claims for greater political participation and economic position at the European and global levels while bypassing the nation-states. At the forefront of this reassertion is the Committee of the Regions, which through elaborating on the principle of subsidiarity and the importance of local cultures has provided a new arena in which substate communities in Western Europe can assert themselves and enhance their status.

---

[3] Milton J. Esman, ed., *Ethnic Conflict in the Western World* (Ithaca, NY: Cornell University Press, 1977); David H. Fortier, ed., *Nations Without a State* (New York: Praeger, 1980).

[4] Joseph R. Llobera, "The Future of Ethnonations in a United Europe," *Rethinking Nationalism and Ethnicity: The Struggle for Meaning and Order in Europe*, ed. Hans-Rudolf Wicker (New York: Berg, 1997), 51.

REGIONALISM IN WESTERN EUROPE

Regions, like nations, are "imagined communities."[5] Regions "are not a given fact of life, or a historic relic,"[6] but are constructed within particular historical processes, and are constantly being recreated, reshaped and reimagined.[7] Regions today have set out to provide a powerful principle for collective identity by adopting a similar strategy that nation-state builders did after the French Revolution: that of inventing traditions. Many substate groups are revisiting and reinterpreting the past in which they discover, and then reclaim, an old culture—the nucleus of a new identity.

Different regions have contrived different avenues by which they reimagine their identities. Aspects of Gaelic culture, such as tartan, bagpipes and whiskey, were pertinent to Scotland's representation of the Highlands and articulation of contemporary Scottish identity.[8] Catalonia's claims to be a pre-Iberian nation were largely based on archaeological discoveries.[9] Brittany's Celtic identity has been popularized through music and dance, and is exhibited and reinforced every year at the Interceltic Festival, a very popular event that brings together many Celtic communities.[10] Padania, a recently invented region, brainchild of Italy's Lega Nord leaders, has revised Italian history by claiming a North Italian Celtic ancestry.[11] Incidentally,

---

[5] Benedict Anderson, *Imagined Communities: Reflections on the Origin and Spread of Nationalism* (New York: Verso, 1991 [1983]), 5-7.

[6] Michael Keating, *The New Regionalism in Western Europe: Territorial Restructuring and Political Change* (Northampton: Edward Elgar, 1998), 109.

[7] Also see Sharon MacDonald, *Reimagining Culture: Histories, Identities and the Gaelic Renaissance* (New York: Berg, 1997), xvi.

[8] MacDonald, 3-8.

[9] Margarita Diaz-Andrev, "Archeology and Nationalism in Spain," *Nationalism, Politics, and the Practice of Arcaheology*, ed. Philip L. Kohl and Clare Fawcett (Cambridge: Cambridge University Press, 1995), 39-56.

[10] Bretagne.com. "The 28th Interceltic Festival Lorient," 13 Feb. 1999 <http://www.bretagne.com/english/Doc/culture/FESTIVAL. htm>.

[11] Lega Nord, "The Foundations of a Nation," 3 Apr. 1998. Accessed from <http://www.leganordsen.it/eng/index.htm>.

during the 1998 Breton Festival the Padanias paraded for the first time with their new flag.[12] This making and remaking of regions has intensified as the European Union placed on its agenda the issue of regional economic development and political decentralization, and consequently created the Committee of the Regions.

THE COMMITTEE OF THE REGIONS

The creation of the Committee of the Regions (COR) in 1994 marks an important stage in the restructuring of the European Union. Until the COR was established, substate levels of government were excluded from official representation at suprastate institutions. The Committee was a product of the EU authorities' realization that constraints existed for formulating and administering their projects via the national governments. Consequently, substate authorities were given more attention as potential means through which national bureaucracies could be bypassed, while assisting the process of European integration.[13] Today regional and local authorities are considered to be an indispensable part of the process of European unification and a response to the "democratic deficit" of the Union. Since 1994, the role bestowed on the regions has been further elaborated and reinforced.

The Committee of the Regions is an advisory assembly of the European Union composed of 222 representatives of local and regional authorities. According to official documents, this assembly was established to ensure that the European Union consults authorities closest to the citizens, such as mayors, city and county councilors, and regional presidents, in matters that directly relate to them.[14] Re-

[12] Europadania.com, "Padania in Europa a Lorient," 15 Feb. 1999 <http://www.europadania.org./Lorient/festival.htm>.

[13] Cesare Onestini, "National and Regional Attitudes to the Committee of the Regions: A Synopsis," *Regions in Europe*, ed. Joachim Jens Hesse (Baden-Baden: Nomos Verlagsgesellschaft, 1995), 210-211.

[14] Committee of the Regions, "Introducing the Committee of the Regions," 8 Feb. 2000 <http://www.cor.eu.int/overview/Intro/intro_eng.html>.

gional membership of the committee, as well as regional structure, power, and resources, varies widely, depending on the nation-state.[15] In Germany, for example, each one of the sixteen Länder has one seat in the Committee, with an additional seat to the four Länder with the largest population. Also, three seats are given to the representatives from unions of local authorities. Spain has seventeen seats allocated to its autonomous communities and four to local authorities. Both in Spain and Germany the members are democratically elected. In France, representatives are selected by the Prime Minister on the basis of geographic and political criteria, as well as the recommendations of the Minister of Interior, who is in contact with the different local associations.[16]

Despite its limited status and functions when it was first conceived, the COR has altered the institutional architecture of the EU, offering unlimited potential to the regions' political and economic enhancement.[17] The Amsterdam Treaty, which was put into force in May 1999, empowered the COR by expanding its responsibilities. In addition to its already established areas of influence, such as structural and cohesion funding, trans-European infrastructure networks, public health, education, and youth and culture, the Committee of the Regions can issue opinions on issues concerning the environment, employment, vocational training, transport and other social

[15] See Onestini, 219-222; Udo Bullmann, "The Politics of the Third Level," *The Regional Dimension of the European Union: Towards a Third Level in Europe?*, ed. Charlie Jeffery (Portland: Frank Cass, 1997), 4; and Committee of the Regions, "The Contributions of the Committee of the Regions to the Construction of Europe" (Brussels, November 1999), 17.

[16] Committee of the Regions, "The Selection of Representatives to the Committee of the Regions: The Process in Different Member States" (March 1997). Accessed from <http://www.cor.eu.int>. Also see Onestini, 219-222, and Udo Bullmann, 4.

[17] John Loughlin, "Representing Regions in Europe: The Committee of Regions." *The Regional Dimension of the European Union: Towards a Third Level in Europe?*, ed. Charlie Jeffery (Portland: Frank Cass, 1997), 156-158.

matters.[18] By having a say in these issues the COR hopes to bring the European Union closer to its citizens and to assure that supranational authorities take into account the interests and demands of substate authorities. The COR is firmly committed to the basic principles of democracy at all levels of government and in all sectors of society and is "above all, the guardian of the principles of subsidiarity and proximity."[19]

Regional Cultures and the Principle of Subsidiarity

The principle of subsidiarity is a concept with politically charged connotations. The substance of this principle is that decisions should be taken at the scale most appropriate to the problem. According to Article 3B of the Maastricht Treaty, "in areas which do not fall within its exclusive competence, the region shall take action in accordance with the principle of subsidiarity, only if and so far as the objectives of the proposed action cannot be sufficiently achieved by the member states and can therefore, by reason of scale effects of the proposed action, be better achieved by the community."[20] The COR argues that application of this principle will ultimately create a strong sense of European citizenship because it brings European-wide action to the local level, making the European Union's actions and possibilities visible to its citizens. Furthermore, the principle of subsidiarity safeguards and enhances the status of regional cultures, which in turn can reinforce a new European identity. The means through which this idea of strengthening diversity would be achieved was discussed in a special forum entitled "A Europe of Cultures in a Europe of Regions."[21]

---

[18] Committee of the Regions, "The Contributions," 17.

[19] Ibid., 13.

[20] Maastricht Treaty, Article 3A, quoted from Richard A. Griggs, "Geopolitics and the Fourth World in Europe," *Fourth World Bulletin* 3 (July 1994): 4.

[21] Committee of the Regions, "Roundtable: A Europe of Cultures in a Europe of Regions," *Forum: A Europe of Cultures in a Europe of Regions*, 14 Feb. 2000 <http://www.cor.eu.int/Archive/arkiv/menuhin/round1.html>.

This forum took place concurrently with the Committee's plenary session held in February 1999, and it brought together representatives of various cultural communities and organizations for a "debate on the plight and rights of Europe's minorities."[22] The presentations addressed the following two topics: "Using Subsidiarity to Protect Europe's Different Cultural Identities" and "Cultural and Minority Groups within the Multicultural Reality of Europe." During the forum there was an "exhibition of cultures," which featured indigenous, as well as immigrant, groups from Western and Eastern Europe, such as the Moldavian Csago in Romania, Roma/Gypsies, Pomaks in Bulgaria, Sami from Finland, and Africans in Portugal.[23]

The representatives of the various regional groups stressed that their specific experiences could be very useful in the process of European unification, and that they were optimistic that the European Union's new cultural programs would enhance minority cultures. Their statements demonstrate that the Committee of Regions has become a new arena in which minority groups may contest and question the states' practices, while at the same time asserting their rights and identity. Opening the plenary discussion, the President of the Committee reminded the audience that modern European history features attempts to erase and forget its cultural minorities. The aim of these communities today, the President recommended, should be "to build a Europe of subsidiarity and diversity, where regional and local authorities welcome cultural communities and minority groups as fellow citizens."[24] The repre-

[22] Committee of the Regions, "Overview of the Forum," *Forum: A Europe of Cultures in a Europe of Regions,* 14 Feb. 2000 <http://www.cor.eu.int/Archive/arkiv/menuhin/overview.html>.

[23] Committee of the Regions, "An Exhibition of Cultures in a Forum of Cultures," *Forum: A Europe of Cultures in a Europe of Regions,* 14 Feb. 2000 <http://www.cor.eu.int/Archive/arkiv/menuhin/exhibit.html>.

[24] Manfred Dammeyer, qtd. in Committee of the Regions, "Minority Cultures in Europe: The Beginning of a New Dialogue," 14 Feb. 1999 <http://www.cor.eu.int/Archive/arkiv/MoreEurope/MoreEurope.html>.

sentative of the Spanish Gypsy community said that the gypsies' experience could enlighten the European Union about how to open borders and could assist European citizens in reconfiguring their identity by interlacing their membership to the state with their membership to the European community.[25] The Commissioner of the President of the Basque Government for External Relations argued that the principle of subsidiarity is an important instrument that would allow minority communities to "live in their own culture—politically, financially and administratively."[26] Professor Jacquard stressed the need to encourage the documentation of "disenfranchised social groups" because the lack of "documents, or images of themselves" oftentimes leaves them at "the mercy of faceless administrators." These groups are "the culturally disabled," and as such, they suffer the most in today's societies.[27] For these groups, one of the speakers for the COR asserted, "special efforts may be needed to bring culture to them...[because]...everyone has the right to culture."[28]

The term "culture" holds a central role in the rhetoric of the Committee of the Regions and the European Union.[29] Official EU documents present culture and cultural heritage as a medium that nourishes the feeling of a common European identity, while at the same time respecting diversity and triggering economic growth. According to one document, cultural heritage "creates jobs, directly (administrative offices and field work) and indirectly (jobs created thanks to growth due to the effects

---

[25] Juan de Dios Ramirez, qtd. in "Minority Cultures," 3.

[26] José María Munoa Ganuza, qtd. in "Minority Cultures," 5.

[27] Albert Jacquard, qtd. in "Minority Cultures," 4.

[28] Christina Tallberg, qtd. in "Minority Cultures," 3.

[29] Marcelino Oreja, "Culture and European Integration: Foundations of the European Community's Cultural Activities" (Vienna, 6 March 1997), 5 March 1998 <http://europa.eu.int/comm/dg/oreja/0603en.html>.

of cultural tourism)."[30] Culture here connotes a commodity that has the ability to unite people and to give them a sense of shared belonging "in a world where economic competition may cause hardship and division, where familiar reference points and values may be swept away by the tide of globalization."[31] Culture is presented as a necessary asset small communities must possess in order to cope with the new challenges of globalization, capitalism and the crisis of identity and the state.

Eroded Borders and Reconfigured Territories

The nation-state is today considered to be "too big to run everyday life, and too small to manage international affairs."[32] Its legitimacy and powers are being challenged, on the one hand, by suprastate forces, such as globalization and capitalism and entities like the European Union, and on the other hand, by substate actors that demand greater political participation and economic benefits.[33] The nation-state today has lost its most powerful sources of legitimacy—"the intensity of its meaningful presence in a continuous body of bounded territory."[34] It can no longer safeguard its borders and the movement of its citizens, or manage and manipulate people's "imaginaries." Today, the nation-state has to compete against those of "unsettled communities and of global electronic media."[35]

Although globalization has blurred nation-state borders, it has not eroded the sense of place—rather, it has

---

[30] The European Commission, "Action by the European Commission Regarding Preservation of Cultural Heritage," 5 Feb. 1998 <http://www.europa.eu.int/en/comm/dg10/culture/en/heritage/raphael.html>.

[31] Oreja, 7.

[32] John Newhouse, "Europe's Rising Regionalism," *Foreign Affairs* 76 (January-February 1997): 67.

[33] Bullmann, 4-5.

[34] Arjun Appadurai, *Modernity at Large: Cultural Dimensions of Globalization* (Minneapolis: University of Minnesota Press, 1996), 189.

[35] Ibid., 198. Also see p. 31.

augmented its significance. Globalization has forced a "*re*territorialization of space,"[36] providing new structures within which identities are reconfigured and powers renegotiated. As Gupta and Ferguson observe, "as actual places and localities have become even more blurred and intermediate, *ideas* of culturally and ethnically distinct places and identities become perhaps even more salient."[37] Because of this renewed importance of distinction, regional groups are becoming aware of the enhanced instrumental and negotiating value[38] a traditional aestheticized culture and identity has in improving their positions in the current power configuration. Regions are conscious that international capital is increasingly less concerned with state boundaries,[39] and that investment decisions are based on the attributes of places where there is a "local traditional culture" such as Wallonia or Flanders instead of Belgium, Baden-Wuttermberg instead of Germany, and Catalonia instead of Spain.[40]

Brittany offers an illuminating example of how identity and culture are used in the deliberate activities of Bretons

---

[36] Akhil Gupta and James Ferguson, "Beyond Culture: Space, Identity and the Politics of Difference," *Culture, Power, Place: Explorations in Critical Anthropology*, ed. Akhil Gupta and James Ferguson (Durham, NC: Duke University Press, 1997), 37.

[37] Gupta and Ferguson, 39.

[38] See Navidad Gutierrez's discussion of ethnicity, "Ethnic Revivals Within Nation-States? The Theories of E. Gelner and A.D. Smith Revisited," *Rethinking Nationalism and Ethnicity: The Struggle for Meaning and Order in Europe*, ed. Hans-Rudolf Wicker (New York: Berg, 1997), 171-172.

[39] According to Newhouse, 69-72: "many and probably most of the wealthiest provinces of Western Europe are interacting with one another (and in some cases with parts of Central Europe) and together creating super-regions—large economic zones that transcend national boundaries... In 1988 the regions surrounding Stuttgart, Barcelona, Lyon and Milan—Baden-Wurttemberg, Catalonia, the Rhone-Alpes, and Lombardy—formed the Four Motors Association. The idea was that the four would together become the engine of European growth.... Some say that the association's real function is to coordinate regional policy with Brussels and work around disputes between EU members over integration issues."

[40] Richard A. Griggs, "Geopolitics and the Fourth World in Europe," *Fourth World Bulletin* 3 (June 1994): 6.

to attract economic advantages.[41] Le Coadic's study[42] illustrates that Breton entrepreneurs, farmers and fishermen are becoming increasingly self-conscious about the economic value of their Celtic identity. Many Breton companies invite large foreign investors to Brittany, in hope that their sales will increase because their clients would associate the products with the beauty of Brittany's countryside. These entrepreneurs are organizing themselves under the label "Produit en Bretagne." Le Coadic's study also reveals another significant phenomenon—the revival of Breton language in the cities, and its decline in rural areas. Children belonging to the executive or middle classes take advantage of bilingual education, or take private Breton lessons, sometimes for their own pleasure, while many rural Bretons, who have been using the Breton language for centuries, now have difficulty understanding the new urban Breton language.

This lore invites an array of questions and concerns. Is "cultural renaissance" an elite class phenomenon? What is at stake in creating a Europe where cultural diversity is portrayed as "a cosmorama" or "a peep-show?"[43] Difference in the form of aestheticized, exoticized, and romanticized cultures is desired and encouraged by the processes of European integration and the forces of global capitalism. In the midst of European integration, global capitalism, and eroded state borders, small groups strategically position themselves as distinct cultural communities by adopting tactics similar to those of the architects of the nations. The Committee of the Regions further facilitates regional resurgence by elaborating and advocating the principle of subsidiarity and by providing an arena at the

---

[41] See Appadurai's discussion of culturalist movements, 15.

[42] Ronan Le Coadic, *Breton Identity*, 1 Mar. 2001 <http://www.breizh.net/identity/index.htm>. This web site offers a summary of Le Coadic's book *L'Identité Bretonne* (Rennes: Presses Universitaires de Rennes, 1998).

[43] Lisa Malkki, "Citizens of Humanity: Internationalism and the Imagined Community of Nations," *Diaspora* 3 (Fall 1994): 50-51.

European Union level in which regions can assert and reimagine themselves. At the outset of the twenty-first century, Europe's burgeoning multilayered geopolitical structure demands new economic arrangements, political administration, and ways of imagining community.[44]

[44] This paper is an outgrowth of my honors thesis, "Reimagining Identity in an Integrated Europe," completed at Macalester College, Saint Paul, MN, in May 1999. I am grateful to Victoria Berlhant, Jim von Geldern, Arjun Guneratne, Anne Sutherland, and Jack Weatherford for the advice and support they provided me at Macalester. I want to thank my professors and classmates at the University of California, Irvine, who listened to a presentation of an earlier version of this paper and gave me valuable comments. I owe special thanks to Lisa Malkki and Bill Maurer for their guidance and support. Finally, I want to express my gratitude to the graduate students of Loyola University Chicago and the University of Rome "La Sapienza" for adeptly organizing the conference "Shifting Borders, Negotiating Places."

SEXUAL HARASSMENT IN THE CONTEXT OF A GENDER-EGALITARIAN CULTURE
The Example of the Philippines

Patrocinio P. Schweickart

Let me begin by posing a question: Does a high incidence of sexual harassment imply a culture that devalues women? In this paper, I will argue that the example of the Philippines suggests that the answer to this question is, "Not necessarily."

In June 1999, under the sponsorship of the Center for Women's Studies, I gave talks on sexual harassment at several campuses of the University of the Philippines (UP). The talks were part of an educational effort to encourage awareness of the problem and discussion of the newly adopted University policy against sexual harassment. My audience consisted of University officials and administrators, faculty, students, and often members of the larger community. The audiences were generally large, and in one campus, well covered by the local media. The discussions were lively as well as tense. Some members of the audience (generally male) manifested defensiveness; many (mostly women) manifested considerable anger. I came primarily with information about sexual harassment and sexual harassment policy in the US context. Although I grew up in the Philippines, I have lived in the US for over thirty years, and had returned only for brief visits. I was knowledgeable about the US context, but not about the situation in the Philippines. However, as the sponsors of the lecture tour had expected, my talk prompted discussion about the Philippine situation.

Clearly, all issues regarding gender and sexuality are highly dependent on cultural variables—this is the case with sexual harassment. In this paper, I report some completely predictable facts about sexual harassment in the Philippines. To put it bluntly, it happens with depressing frequency. However, my main concern is really to articulate my reflections about what I learned and observed this summer. The views I express will be controversial—they contradict standard American feminist perspectives on gender and on sexual harassment. I also expect that Filipino feminists (the women I had discussions with last summer) will not readily agree with them. I offer my reflections hypothetically, as ideas for further research.

The Philippines has come relatively late to addressing the problem of sexual harassment. The Philippine Congress passed the "Anti-Sexual Har-assment Act" in July of 1995.[1] In July 1998, the University of the Philippines adopted a sexual harassment policy following the provisions of the law.[2] The law and the UP policy are the culmination of approximately six years of research and political advocacy. The immediate inspiration, I was told, were the US Senate hearings on the charges brought by Anita Hill against Clarence Thomas, then a nominee for a seat in the US Supreme Court.

According to the Philippine law, unwanted sexual advances, solicitation of sexual favors, and other visual, verbal or physical advances of a sexual nature constitute sexual harassment when:

> a) compliance is obtained as a result of explicit or implicit promises of employment or academic benefits, or of threats of the withholding of benefits or other punitive consequences in the event of noncompliance; or when
> b) the behavior described above results in an intimidating or hostile environment for the employee or the student.

In this definition we clearly see the two forms of sexual harassment identified in US law and in American feminist

---

[1] Republic Act No. 7278 was passed by the Philippine House of Representatives and the Senate on February 8, 1995.

2 The University of the Philippines Board of Regents ratified the policy for "Implementing Rules and Regulations of the Anti-Sexual Harassment Act of 1995" on July 30, 1998.

theory—the so-called *quid pro quo* and *hostile environment* forms. However, there are interesting differences between the US and the Philippine law:

a) In Philippine law, sexual harassment is a crime punishable by imprisonment (one to six months) and a fine ($250-$500). In the US, it is not a crime, but an actionable civil offense. Victims may sue for reinstatement and damages. Incidentally, rape is a death penalty crime in the Philippines.
b) In the US, the law against harassment is based on the principle of equal opportunity in employment and academic pursuits. Sexual harassment is illegal because it is discriminatory. In the Philippines, the law against sexual harassment is based on the state interest in protecting the dignity of all citizens. It is illegal because it is a violation of human rights.

The second difference is very significant. In conversations with the faculty members and administrators at the UP who were instrumental in framing the University policy, the theme of human rights came up frequently. I observed that it is not clear from the policy who has responsibility for handling complaints; I said that in the US, sexual harassment is generally related to the issue of equity and the policy is often administered by the affirmative action officer. To my surprise, I was told that the affirmative action framework would not work. There is no need for affirmative action because gender parity has been achieved at all levels of the University. In fact, women predominate in all areas. They form the majority of undergraduate and graduate students (60%), and faculty (53%). They are slightly underrepresented among deans and associate deans (47%), but they constitute 50% of the highest university officials (chancellors and vice chancellors of regional campuses, and university system vice-presidents), except the president, who, so far, has always been male.[3] It is

---

[3] *Women and Men in the University of the Philippines*, University of the Philippines Center for Women's Studies (Diliman: Quezon City, 1995-96).

interesting that the one "affirmative action" program at the University is affirmative action for males. The College of Medicine has a gender-balance policy, which in practice sets significantly higher admission standards for women (roughly an A- GPA) than for men (roughly a B/B-). It is reasoned that if applicants were allowed to compete according to identical standards, women would predominate in the college.

Let me now advance some controversial, and in some ways speculative, theses.

Thesis 1. There is a high degree of gender egalitarianism in the Philippines; Philippine culture accords women a higher status than Western culture.

The Philippines was a colony of Spain for over 300 years (1521-1898), and then a colony of the US for 48 years (1898-1946). Today it is a very westernized, strongly Americanized culture. (Catholicism is the majority religion; English is a principal, even dominant, language of the public sphere, including education, the media, and politics.) The gender egalitarianism stems from the indigenous culture and has persisted in spite of the male-dominant values of the colonizing western cultures. Philippine culture does not fit the stereotype of a Third World (Asian) culture that is oppressive to women. Let me present some evidence supporting the claim of gender egalitarianism.

1. There is gender parity in the distribution of highly valued goods, including education. Literacy rates are comparable. According to the 1990 census, the basic literacy rate (based on the ability to read and write simple messages) is 93.2% for women and 94% for men. The functional literacy rate (based on the ability to read and write simple sentences and perform basic computational tasks) is 85.9% for women, 81.7% for men (1994, Functional Literacy Education and Mass Media Survey). There are more females than males who have never gone to school, and more boys than girls in elementary school. However,

more females than males are enrolled in secondary schools and college; the rate of degree completion is also higher for females.[4]

2. There are no "missing women." In general, "normal" birth and death rates result in populations with slightly more women than men. Economist Amartya Sen's studies of world populations found that in certain areas of the world (such as India and China), the number of women in the population is significantly less than normal. These less-than-normal ratios of females to males correlate with the inferior status of women—with preference for male offspring, practices such as selective abortion on infanticide of female children, poorer nutrition, and neglect of girls and women. The Philippine population has the normal distribution of men and women.

3. There are no indigenous practices that are indicative of the devaluation of women, such as dowry, suttee, foot binding, sequestration of women, female infanticide, genital mutilation, or mistreatment of brides by groom's family.[5] In the Philippines, traditionally, the groom's family shoulders the cost of the wedding, and provides a certain portion of assets for the new couple (symbolized in the wedding ceremony by a bag of antique coins given to the bride). Married women remain close to their kin; there is parity in the status and authority of the man's kin and the woman's kin.

4. There are no ritual practices and myths that associate pollution with female sexuality and biological processes.

5. There are no misogynistic myths; the most well-known myths (e.g., the myth of Maria Makiling) feature

[4] See *Women and Men in the University of the Philippines*, 2.

[5] The situation in the Philippines is in stark contrast to the traditional "lethal discrimination" reported by Ellen Goodman in her column "'Honor Killers' of Women Get Away with Murder," *International Herald Tribune*, March 28, 2000 (originally published in the *Boston Globe*): "In 1997, more than 300 women were victims of honor killings in just one Pakistan province. In 1998, some 200 women were victims of acid attacks in Bangladesh. Every year 5,000 women in India are killed over 'dowry' arguments."

powerful female deities. There are no misogynistic terms in the native languages, which would be indicative of devaluation of women as women. Women's body parts are not used as curse words. The misogynistic curse words in current use are invariably derived from Spanish or English.

6. Filipino languages, unlike European languages, are not sexist. Filipino languages have no grammatical category of gender, and therefore no generic masculine pronouns. Generic terms—for example, *tao*, meaning "person"—do not carry androcentric connotations. Sexism in language is a feminist concern, but in the Philippines, this concern is entirely associated with sexism in the English language. The UPCWS primer on "Gender-Fair Language" argues that attention to sexist usages in English is important because this language, "handed to us by colonizers," is a major language of education and public life, and therefore instrumental in the formation of ideas, attitudes, and cultural values.[6]

7. There is a high degree of economic initiative and influence among women. Among peasants, women have a high degree of participation in agricultural work: men plow the field, women sow and participate in other processes. Women and men also tend vegetable and fruit gardens, and raise chickens, ducks, pigs, and goats. Women set up small businesses and cottage industries. Traditionally, women are the treasurers of the household—a woman manages her income as well as that of her husband. It is my contention that the traditional sexual division of labor is egalitarian. Women and men have different roles, but the labor and authority are equitably distributed.

8. There has been a remarkably rapid rate of the integration of women in the professions and in public life. The traditional gender division of labor is breaking down un-

---

[6] *Gender-Fair Language: A Primer*, University of the Philippines Center for Women's Studies (Diliman: Quezon City, 1998).

der pressure of contemporary conditions and has been in the process of renegotiation this last thirty years. Before the twentieth century, women did not enter the professions, except for a few traditionally feminine ones, such as teaching and nursing. But they have been entering virtually all professions at an accelerated rate since 1960. At the University of the Philippines (1992-93), women are well integrated in all departments, ranging from the traditionally feminine disciplines of Home Economics (80%) and Nursing (82%); to less traditionally feminine disciplines, such as Dentistry (85%) and Arts and Letters (78%); to traditionally masculine disciplines, including Economics (65%), Business (62%), Science (55%), Law (50%), Medicine (50%), and Engineering (36%).[7]

Women are still a minority in most professions, and they are underrepresented at the highest levels. This condition can be regarded as a legacy of the traditional division of labor; but the rapid rate of integration of women into the professions and public life now that the traditional division of labor has begun to break down is indicative of the basic gender egalitarianism of the culture—the absence of the gender-discriminatory barriers in employment and education that women in the West have faced.

Thesis 2. Coexisting with gender egalitarianism are three conditions that are generally thought to be indicative of the oppression of women.

1. Philippine society is characterized by gender polarity (e.g., the masculine ideal of strength and courage vs. the feminine ideal of beauty and modesty) and a sexual division of labor whose modern, urban form parallels the division between public and private spheres, between the formal economy of employment in wage-earning work outside the home and the informal domestic economy, which includes unpaid reproductive work as well as income-generating cottage industries and small businesses.

---

[7] *Women and Men in the University of the Philippines.*

2. There is a double standard of sexual morality: men are promiscuous and sexually assertive in courtship; women are supposed to be chaste and modest. Sexual transgressions are tolerated in men, disapproved of and punished in women. Women find sexual harassment offensive, but men often are unable to distinguish it from "normal" courtship behavior.

3. Relations between the sexes are not necessarily harmonious. There is tension and conflict—a battle of the sexes—and a high incidence of sexual harassment.

In standard American feminist theory, these three conditions would generally be taken as evidence against gender egalitarianism. Gender polarity and the sexual division of labor are thought to be root causes of the oppression of women; the sexual double standard is regarded as a key indicator of male dominance. My claim is that the Philippines presents a rare counter-example to this view.[8]

In spite of gender egalitarianism, however, Filipino women have to endure sexual harassment. One survey of students and faculty at the University of the Philippines indicated that about 20% of the respondents had personally experienced sexual harassment, and 25% knew of someone who had experienced sexual harassment.[9] It is not clear what is the exact nature of these incidents. However, the literature and my own conversations with people identify familiar kinds of incidents, such as: requests or demands for sexual favors (such as a date) by a boss or a professor with intimations of bribery or threats; being grabbed, kissed, or fondled, by a professor, a superior, a co-worker, another student, or by a fellow pas-

---

[8] Another counter-example is the Minangkabau of West Sumatra, a large (over a million people), modern ethnic group that combines gender egalitarianism (it is matrilineal, and senior women have decisive influence in clan matters) and gender polarity and a sexual division of labor. See Evelyn Blackwood, *Webs of Power: Women, Kin and Community in a Sumatran Village* (Oxford: Rowman & Littlefield, 2000).

[9] Elena Samonte, "Sexual Harassment: Perceptions of UP Students and Faculty," *Review of Women's Studies* 3.2 (1993): 107-143.

senger in a public vehicle; men exposing themselves on buses and in secluded public places; lewd comments at work, in school, or on the street; dirty jokes in the classroom; and general unwelcome, offensive sexual attention from men.[10] My own personal experience and knowledge of the experience of friends and family members makes me believe that virtually every Filipino woman has experienced at least one physical form of sexual harassment in her lifetime. Filipino women show a high level of umbrage towards these disrespectful behaviors. (At one large public meeting, a woman got up and seriously offered the Lorena Bobbitt method as a strategy for dealing with sexual harassers; the women in the audience laughed, but they appreciated the poetic justice in this method). Men, not surprisingly, are more "understanding" even when they do not condone the behavior. They generally place the responsibility for preventing and stopping the behavior on individual women.

If there is gender egalitarianism in the Philippines, and if women are highly valued, then why do men sexually harass them? If the cultural norm dictates respect for women, why do men disrespect them? Of course, it must be said that only a small minority of men are harassers. Because harassers tend to be serial harassers, each one can account for a high number of incidents. Still, why do some men harass, and why are the majority of men generally "understanding" of harassers?

Thesis 3. American sexual harassment theory does not fit the pattern of the phenomenon in the Philippines. In the Philippines, sexual harassment is a form of sexual opportunism that may suggest certain socially problematical aspects of masculine sexuality, but is not necessarily indicative of gender stratification.

In American feminist theory, rape and sexual harass-

---

10 See *What is Sexual Harassment?*, University of the Philippines Center for Women's Studies (Diliman: Quezon City).

ment are said to be about power rather than sexual pleasure. Men rape and harass women, viewing them as sex objects, because they want to dominate them. Images of women as sex objects for men pervade the culture, from the highest level of art and literature to the most vulgar pornography. Thus, it is argued, the desire to dominate is encoded in male sexuality. This explains both why a significant number of men rape and harass, and why those who don't "understand" those who do.

The strong influence of American feminist theory in the Philippines is evident in the literature on sexual harassment, which characterizes Philippine society as patriarchal, and rape and sexual harassment as evidence of male power and women's oppression. (American texts predominate in the bibliographies of the Philippine sexual harassment literature.) Filipino feminists will point out that especially in the urban centers, there is a thriving sex trade that objectifies and commodifies women's bodies—in prostitution and pornography as well as in mainstream advertising and popular culture. Everywhere in Manila, one can see images catering to predatory male sexuality. The women I talked to repeated the American view that sexual harassment is about power, not about sexual pleasure, and I expect that they will not readily agree with the view I am attempting to articulate. Still, certain features of the situation in the Philippines do not fit the American model.

1. In the US, hostility and disrespect for women are implicit and often explicit in a lot of sexual harassment—the most obvious case, where pornography or obscenity is used by men in the workplace to make women uncomfortable, is a form of backlash against affirmative action. This is also true with harassment in schools and colleges. The behavior is intended to bully its targets, and is analogous to racist or homophobic harassment in schools and workplaces.

In the Philippines, men will often say they do not intend to harass or disrespect when they proposition women, whistle at them in the street, rub up against them, repeatedly make sexual advances even when they are unwelcome, and so forth. While these disclaimers are not necessarily to be believed, I think the sort of hostile, resentful misogynistic component of sexual harassment is relatively rare in the Philippines. (This would be a good topic for further research.)

2. When I asked women to characterize the offense in sexual harassment, they invariably said that it is an abuse of power. Indeed, this is its legal definition—the inappropriate abuse of the power of a superior over an employee, or a professor or university official over a student. Yet, when asked to give everyday examples, the women turned quickly to inappropriate behavior by male peers, by strangers (usually in public transportation), or by social inferiors. When I asked my Filipino colleagues to give me vernacular terms for sexual harassment (the English term is the one generally used), they struggled for a while, and eventually came up with the term "chancing," a widely used vernacular derivation from the English word "chance." "Chancing" is the term used to characterize the behavior of a suitor who "steals" a kiss or some other sexual favor, and in this sense it is a part of the normal mating game. This widely used term suggests that sexual harassment is viewed as a form of sexual opportunism rather than of hostility or dominance. Women feel harassed, exploited, preyed upon, disrespected by the sexual opportunism of men—men who do not intend to disrespect or harass, but only to take advantage of opportunities to grab sexual pleasure. Of course, some men in positions of power will take advantage of the opportunities offered by that position. The Philippine law and the University of the Philippines do not take any position on the intentions of the perpetrator, but they recognize the detrimental consequences of male sexual opportunism (it subjects women to indignities; it is a breach of decorum; and it is detrimental to the good of the service or the institution). It is significant that the

Philippine law upholds the *dignity* of women as human beings, not just their right to equal employment or academic opportunities, and identifies sexual harassment as a form of sexual misconduct, rather than of gender bias.

Thus, although the Filipinos I spoke with echoed the American view that sexual harassment is about power rather than sexuality, and is indicative of the social and cultural inferior status of women, a careful study of the concrete situation would indicate that in the Philippines, sexual harassment is a form of sexual opportunism, and does not necessarily imply that the culture devalues women.

I offer the following tentative conclusions from my experience in the Philippines as hypotheses for further research.

1. Patriarchy and male dominance are not universal. The assumption of the universality of patriarchy and male dominance—and specifically, the higher degree of oppression of women in "underdeveloped" countries—is an artifact of Western theory, and obscures rare but illuminating examples of gender-egalitarian cultures.

2. Gender egalitarianism can coexist with gender polarity and a sexual division of labor, as well as with disharmony and discontent in heterosexual relations.

3. A high incidence of sexual harassment can coexist with gender equality, and with high regard for women and femininity. My hypothesis is that in the Philippines, sexual harassment is not driven by power motives, but by sexual opportunism. The significant frequency of sexual harassment and the tolerant attitude men take towards it is not indicative of the social inferiority of women or of men's derogatory attitude toward them, but rather, more directly, with socially problematic features of male sexuality. It follows that to understand sexual harassment in the Philippines, one requires not a theory of power, but a theory of sexuality that addresses the problematic relationship of men to their sexuality, and of individual sexual desire to the norms of social conduct.

4. The Philippine example also shows that even in a gender-egalitarian culture, women are vulnerable to the sexual aggressiveness of men. This, it seems to me, is explainable in terms of differential capacity for physical force, without resorting to any assumptions regarding superior cultural or social power. However, clearly, cultural and social male dominance can make women more vulnerable and less able to defend themselves, and men more sexually predatory. Under conditions of male dominance, masculine sexuality is inevitably implicated in misogynistic attitudes, and becomes an instrument of the exercise of male power over women.

5. The Philippine example indicates that the US feminist theory that attributes rape and sexual harassment to power motives may be too simplistic. In the Western context (as in the Philippine context), issues that have to do with sexuality—problematic features of masculine sexual desire, a mismatch between male and female sexuality, and the social necessity to regulate sexual conduct—are masked by the emphasis on the issue of power.

"La Massa è Donna": *La Giornata della "fede"* and Re-membering Fascist Italy

Anne Wingenter

The crowd loves a strong man. The crowd is a woman.
—Benito Mussolini[1]

On the morning of December 18th, 1935, two months into the Italo-Ethiopian war, a crowd of people converged on the Piazza Venezia in central Rome to take part in the *Giornata della "fede"* (Day of wedding rings).[2] The carefully orchestrated event was the culmination of a metal drive aimed at helping Italy withstand economic sanctions imposed by the League of Nations. By the end of the day a reported 250,000 Romans, the vast majority of whom were women, had donated their wedding rings to the nation's coffers. In cities, towns and villages all over Italy and in foreign countries with large Italian émigré populations, other crowds gathered by the thousands to offer their wedding bands.[3]

That the *Giornata della "fede"* was a powerful symbol and effective piece of propaganda seems indisputable. Even allowing for fascist exaggeration and figure inflation, the numbers are staggering. Moreover, the "plebiscite of gold," as the fascists dubbed it, survives intact in postwar accounts of the fascist period as unproblematic proof of the years of consensus for the regime.[4] Close examination re-

[1] Emil Ludwig, *Colloqui con Mussolini*, trans. Tomaso Gnoli (Verona: Arnaldo Mondadori, 1965 [1932]), 52. All translations are my own unless otherwise noted.
[2] "*Giornata della 'fede'*" is translatable as both "day of wedding rings" and "day of faith." It seems clear that both meanings were intended; the word "*fede*" appears in quotes throughout the primary documents.
[3] *Corriere della sera* (Dec. 19-22, 1935). It is possible, even likely, that the press exaggerated the numbers; nonetheless, participation was high and the event was quite clearly a success.
[4] The use of the notion of consent stems largely from the work of Renzo De Felice, whose multi-volume biography of Mussolini determines that the Fascists

veals that this "proof" hinged upon the careful presentation and mobilization of women—the feminization of the masses. Fascist ideologues and producers of mass culture attempted simultaneously to reinforce and to transform long-term cultural assumptions, mapping modernizing projects onto the seemingly "natural," and therefore immutable, category of gender. By appealing to the supposedly unassailable "truth" represented by gender stereotypes, the fascists sought to elide distinctions between public and private, rendering the regime and its acts articles of unexamined faith.

It is not my intention to argue in this brief paper the ultimate success or failure of a fascist identity project, but rather to examine closely a specific event in order to demonstrate how the regime articulated such a project. I have chosen to analyze the *Giornata della "fede"* because it marked what both contemporaries and historians have suggested was the high point of consent for, and thus individual identification with, fascism.[5]

Italian forces invaded Ethiopia on October 3rd, 1935. Fascist propaganda presented the war to the Italian people as the cause of "civilization" against "barbarism"; accounts of atrocities against Italian missionaries, raids against Italian property and slave trading abounded.[6] Drawing on

---

enjoyed a period of general support between the signing of the Lateran Agreements in 1929 and 1936. See Renzo De Felice, *Mussolini il duce: I. Gli anni del consenso 1929-1936* (Torino: Einaudi, 1974).

[5] M. Macciocchi, *La donna 'nera': 'Consenso' femminile e fascismo* (Milan: Feltrinelli, 1976); Ruggero Zangrandi, *Il lungo viaggio attraverso il fascismo* (Milan: Feltrinelli, 1976), 56; Frank Hardie, *The Abyssinian Crisis* (Hamden, NJ: Archon Books, 1974); and Denis Mack Smith, *Mussolini's Roman Empire* (New York: Penguin, 1977). For a discussion of the inherent distortions of a "consent" model of interpretation which nonetheless asserts the dominance of such a model over scholarship prior to the late 1980s, see Robin Pickering-Iazzi, "Unseduced Mothers: Configurations of a Different Female Subject Transgressing Fascistized Femininity," *Feminine Feminists: Cultural Practices in Italy*, ed. Giovanna Miceli Jeffries (Minneapolis: UP of Minnesota, 1994), 16-20.

[6] *Corriere*, almost any issue from Aug. 1935 to May 1936. For an example from Catholic women's literature, see the account of a "martyred" missionary in Antonietta Fallacara, "Giustino De Jacobis," *Il solco: Rivista di cultura e di attività femminile* (Nov. 1935): 580-86. Such accounts were not entirely new; episodes of

imperialist sentiment that had remained an insistent, though usually marginal, presence in Italian political discourse since the *Risorgimento*, Mussolini assured his nation that the conquest of Ethiopia would affirm Italy's status as a Great Power, provide an internationally recognized symbol of the new Roman empire, satisfy the "virile," growing nation's need for space, and be a general economic boon. Using Mazzinian rhetoric, the party propaganda machine presented the conquest of Ethiopia as the acme of modernity, and the true test of Italy's mission to lead other nations in the modern era.[7] In addition, the struggle would avenge the humiliating defeat (the humiliation was de-emphasized, of course, and substituted with references to treachery and Liberal-era inefficiency) of Italian troops in the Italo-Abyssinian war of 1896.[8] Newspapers carried daily dispatches from the war describing glorious Italian victories and the loyalty and gratitude of the natives who were being "civilized" and "rescued."[9]

These accounts of the fighting can be viewed as the culmination of an extensive propaganda campaign preparing Italians for a colonial role. The misadventures of the late nineteenth century had left the majority of the population disinclined to get involved in expensive overseas ventures, and the argument that Italy needed colonies to accommodate her overflowing population failed to convince those for whom extant emigration patterns had become an accepted way of life. The regime made a vast ef-

---

"barbarism" featured heavily in the African adventure stories found in *Gioventù fascista* throughout the early 1930s. For secondary accounts of such justifications, see De Felice, 765-775, and Hardie, 30.

[7] For an account of colonial rhetoric throughout the post-*Risorgimento*, see John A. Thayer, *Italy and the Great War: Politics and Culture, 1870-1915* (Madison and Milwaukee: UP of Wisconsin, 1964). For Mussolini's presentation of the war, see Smith, 70.

[8] For a fascist account of Italy's colonial history and "destiny," see Alessandro Lessona, *Il fascismo per le colonie: Le colonie italiane nel quadro europeo* (Istituto Coloniale Fascista, 1932).

[9] *Corriere, Il Popolo d'Italia, Il Resto del Carlino*, etc. (Oct. 1935-May 1936).

fort to overcome such dispositions and to persuade the people of the value of colonies and the heroic nature of the undertaking. Adventure stories and accounts of Italian explorers in Africa had been standard fare in periodical literature for youth; tales of missionaries combating "heathen" and Muslim beliefs filled secular and Catholic magazines, many of the latter directed at women. Films, both documentary and fiction, took Italy's "destiny" in Africa as their subject.[10]

The imposition of economic sanctions by the League of Nations against Italy was something of a turning point for popular opinion about the war. Not only, went the rhetoric, was Italy fighting for European civilization against the barbaric Africans; she was being persecuted by the very countries whose way of life she sought to defend. According to this line of reasoning, the sanctions constituted

> ignoble blackmail, in which the League of Nations made a joke of our moral influence: the reasons of Italy were not considered; the documentary reminders of Italy—about Abyssinian violations, about Ethiopian atrocities, about slavery and raids—were not taken into any account.[11]

At issue then, was not only the right to empire but also the very status of Italy as a European power and thus "civilized" and "civilizing" nation. Furthermore, the sanctions, no matter that they were half-heartedly applied, allowed for an image of Italy as alone and in danger, a country requiring loyal citizens to rally to her defense.[12]

As the household accountants and shoppers, women were held to play a key role in the successful resistance against the sanctions. By buying local and by keeping up

---

[10] See, for example, the years 1931-1935 of any of the following: *Famiglia fascista*, *Gioventù fascista*, *Lidel*, *Lumen*, and *Il solco: Rivista di cultura e di attività femminile*.
[11] Introduction to Mussolini's December 2nd speech to the women of Italy, *Scritti e discorsi dell'Impero (Novembre 1935-XIV—4 Novembre 1936-XV E.F.)* (Milan: Ulrico Hoepli, 1936), 11.
[12] Hardie, 31.

family morale in spite of sacrifice, women were taking up a place on "the front lines" against sanctions just as soldiers were fighting on the front lines in Ethiopia.[13] In order to teach and encourage Italian women how to be equal to the task, the government appointed the National Association of Mothers and Widows of the Fallen of the Great War, "who represent in spirit...all the women of Italy,"[14] to visit homes giving advice and encouragement. The involvement of the "Mothers and Widows" reinforced both the notions of battle and of moral sacrifice. They could, "with a moral authority that no other women [held]...ask Italian women not to ignorantly sabotage the sacrifice of the living and even more the sacrifice made by the dead for a greater and more worthy Italy."[15]

In addition to doing without foreign goods, Italians were expected to undertake the positive action of donating gold, silver and copper to the nation's coffers. Leading citizens made public donations. Newspapers published ongoing lists of donors and their donations and kept a running tally of the total addition to the treasury. Stories of priests giving the chalices from their first masses, war heroes giving up their medals and peasants turning over copper cooking pots appeared daily.[16]

Then, on December 1st, a delegation of the "Mothers and Widows" presented Mussolini with a declaration announcing their intention to "consecrate December 18th as a day of 'faith' (*fede*) for offering to the Nation (*Patria*) their wedding rings, an offering which will occur simultaneously in every Italian community, at monuments to fallen soldiers or in war cemeteries."[17] The declaration was presented to the public as originating with the "Mothers and

---

[13] F. Prosperini, "Pregare, Obbedire, Combattare," *Il solco: Rivista di cultura e di attività femminile* (Nov. 1935): 577-579.

[14] *Corriere* (Dec. 1, 1935): 3.

[15] Giovanna Canuti, "Cronache Sociali," *Il solco: Rivista di cultura e di attività femminile* (Nov. 1935): 620.

[16] *Corriere, Il Popolo d'Italia, Il Resto del Carlino* (Nov. 20-Dec. 18, 1935).

[17] *L'Italia ha conquistato L'Impero*, Vol. 6 (Rome: Pinciana, 1936), 101.

Widows," though there is evidence this event that was to take place in less than three weeks time in "every Italian community" was centrally planned. In any case, Mussolini's response was to thank the women for their "spontaneity" and praise them as the "*avant garde* of this feminine Italian exercise to which the Regime has entrusted the task of reacting methodically, with energy and with inflexibility against the shameful economic siege that grips Italy."[18]

A complex, gendered discourse surrounded the *Giornata* and by extension, the metal drive and the Ethiopian war itself. While the battles in Ethiopia continued to be represented to the public with traditional masculine rhetoric of conflict, violence and active combat, on the home front the struggle against the League of Nations' "siege" became feminine and reactive. Mussolini himself insisted that so-called feminine qualities were required to prevail: "The Party, the Regime counts on you, on your sensibility, on your patience, on your tenacity, and it counts above all on that spirit of ardent patriotism that beats in the hearts of all the women of Italy."[19] Because a war on foreign soil was involved, the "home" country, masculine at the abstract level, was feminized in reference to its geographic locus, population and quotidian reality.[20] Soldiers fought for the Nation (*Patria*) but returned home to "Mother Italy" (*Madre Italia*). The glory of the *Patria* was at stake in the struggle for empire, but "Mother Italy" was threatened by the League of Nations' siege. This gendering neatly answered the propagandic need to claim victim status for

---

[18] *Scritti e discorsi*, 12.

[19] Ibid.

[20] It has been suggested that soldiers after WWI had trouble readjusting to life at home because of the chasm that separated their experiences on the front lines from those of the home front. Their disaffection often manifested itself in hostility and violence towards women. It seems to me that this suggests a certain identification of the home front as female the way that the home, in the modern era, became so identified. See Renate Bridenthal, Claudia Koonz and Susan Stuard, ed., *Becoming Visible: Women in European History* (Boston: Houghton Mifflin, 1987), 374-497, and the introduction to Renate Bridenthal, Atina Grossman and Marion Kaplan, ed., *When Biology Became Destiny: Women in Weimar and Nazi Germany* (New York: Monthly Review, 1984), 1-29.

Italy—a position more reconcilable in fascist ideology with women—while at the same time lauding the masculine "soldier-hero."

The rhetoric and images surrounding the *Giornata della "fede"* specifically, can be read as an attempt to bring the country into line with national goals and ideology, a symbolic union of "Mother Italy," embodied by Italian women, with the *Patria*, represented by the fascists and the army. By targeting Italian women, and particularly those women who were acceptable in the fascist cosmology, generic wives and mothers, the regime could lay claim to the support of "the people" as a whole. The *Giornata* was, as we shall see, designed as a wedding ceremony, not between individual women and the state, but between the "masculine" state and its "feminized" subjects. In it, the metal drive, by early December already officially referred to as the "plebiscite of gold," gained its most central and enduring metaphor.

Accordingly, the stage had been carefully set. In Rome the *Vittoriano* monument, popularly known as "The Altar of the Nation (*Patria*)," was draped with tricolor pennants. On the platform at the top of the stairs leading up to the monument were three large incense burners situated behind bronze urns; representatives of the Mothers and Widows of the Fallen stood on either side of them along with various representatives of the Grand Council. Further down, at the tomb of the unknown soldier, uniformed fascist Youth stood guard over the eternal flame and numerous chests of steel rings. Two lines of people were formed to come forward and place their gold wedding rings, or *"fedi,"* in the urns and to receive steel wedding rings, or *"vere,"* in their stead. Queen Elena of Savoy began the event, donating her wedding ring and that of the King and receiving her *"vere"* from the war widow of an Italian general. The ladies of the court followed suit and then the women of Rome in a procession that reportedly lasted the entire day.[21]

In other locations around Italy, the event was similarly structured, taking place at local monuments to the unknown soldier, in chapels dedicated to the "fallen in war," or on platforms constructed in war cemeteries. Local noblewomen opened the donations and fascist officials and representatives of the National Association of Mothers and Widows of the Fallen presided over the day.[22]

These women were central to the overall metaphor of consent; they were *Madre Italia* incarnate. They had sacrificed their men, and thus their individual identities, for the ideals of the *Patria*. They were defined by their bereavement, symbols collectively of the country's sacrifice. Their position was identified from the initial pronouncement of the *Giornata* as synonymous with besieged Italy, who sent her sons to fight for the causes of the *Patria* and of civilization in general. Over and over again in accounts of the "iniquitous sanctions" Italians were reminded that their sons had died defending the very countries that now ranged themselves against them.

By gathering these women at the tomb of the unknown soldier, or in war cemeteries around Italy, the regime underlined their identification with *Madre Italia* and evident dedication to the *Patria*. Such a message was not a new one, as the Mothers had been cast in this role annually at the commemorations of the "March on Rome," and in various other ceremonies where the presence of the "fallen" was evoked.[23] It is significant that it was primarily they who handed out the "*vere*" to the women of Italy.

---

[21] *Corriere* (Dec. 19, 1935): 1.

[22] Ibid., 1-4; also Dec. 18 and 20. See the front-page stories on the same dates in *Il Resto del Carlino, Gazzetta di Venezia* and *Il Popolo d'Italia*.

[23] For an overview of commemoration ceremonies during fascism, see Patrizia Dogliani, "Constructing Memory and Anti-Memory: The Monumental Representation of Fascism and Its Denial in Republican Italy," *Italian Fascism: History, Memory and Representation*, ed. R. J. B. Bosworth and Patrizia Dogliani (New York: St. Martin's Press, 1999).

One need not overly tax the imagination to arrive at the conclusion that the ceremony resembled, indeed was planned to resemble, the mass fascist weddings that were frequently held and reported on in the media.[24] The procession up the steps of the "Altar" or, outside Rome, the tomb of the unknown soldier, the exchange of rings with a war widow, witnessed by a fascist official, the air "blue with incense," all contributed to the nuptial-like scene. Just in case there was any doubt, the *Corriere della sera* provided an official interpretation of the event: "Wife and mother, Elena of Savoy opened the innumerable procession of wives and mothers who in an unparalleled act, in a donation that was not a renunciation but the reaffirmation and consecration of a pact of love with the *Patria*, fulfilled a rite of faith."[25]

The fact that it was necessary to stress that the contribution of one's wedding ring "was not a renunciation" suggests that there was concern that the *Giornata* might be interpreted as impinging upon wives' subservience to their husbands[26] and that the wedding-like nature of the event did not escape its architects. However, they were careful to stress that marriage was not one which involved individual women but rather "a rite of faith" which joined "innumerable" women to the goals of the *Patria*, the body of the state to the will of the state, the Motherland to the Fatherland.

The "feminine" nature of the offering conveyed, at least in the opinion of its organizers, a special "purity" upon it. The exchange did not involve "vile" gold, "streaked with blood from the wild competition of its seekers," but

[24] Government-sponsored "splendidly showy" group weddings were one of the many ways the dictatorship attempted to raise the birth rate in Italy. Victoria De Grazia, *How Fascism Ruled Women: Italy, 1992-1945* (Berkeley: UP of Calfornia, 1992), 137.

[25] *Corriere* (Dec. 19, 1935): 1.

[26] De Grazia, 77-78. De Grazia, in fact, suggests that the Giornata was interpreted thus by many Italian women.

> honest, clean gold...in which came to be known the sweetest and most sacred moments of life. Gold that was bathed in blood, yes, but in the blood of heroes [...] [It] flowed from the hand of the humble and the rich alike, from that of the Church dignitary and from the hand of the mother of the hero, generous and munificent, to the Nation in need.[27]

Such gold might be transformed for the "base" purpose of foreign exchange and end in the coffers of Italy's enemies, but "what will remain the firm and enduring richness of the Italians is the marvelous force that put this gold and transformed it and fused it and made it an offering worthy of Italy the great mother"[28]—pure gold, from the Motherland, to be used as the Fatherland required.

The metal drive as marital exchange, as harmonious cooperation between the people and the state, is further suggested by a linguistic complication that is not immediately translatable into English. The Italian word "*fede*" can be rendered in English as "faith" and the word "*vera*" as "true" or "genuine." Both words are colloquially used to refer to wedding rings, or "*anelli nuziali*." Thus, women were giving and receiving wedding rings as well as exchanging their individual "faith" for the nation's collective "truth." Likewise, as the fatherland received the masses' love, the masses in turn were promised protection and strength.

In Ada Negri's poem "The Ring of Steel," published in the *Corriere della sera* on December 18th, this exchange is stressed. The poem is an ode to Mother Italy (*Madre Italia*), "never more dear than today...when you wear on your ring-finger an indestructible circle of steel...ring of superb nuptials." The gold of the donated wedding rings, the "*fedi*," is made of all Italian women's "spirit and flesh,

[27] G. Canuti, "Cronache Sociali: Oro," *Il solco: Rivista di cultura e di attività femminile* (Dec. 1935): 671.
[28] Ibid., 672.

willing blood, breast milk, long-suffering tears, loved love, flame and sacred ashes from the hearth." The "*vera*" is a "talisman and a weapon...sharper than a spade, or more burning than fire, or more secure than any defense."[29] While the "*fedi*" are pledges from the hands of individual women of a malleable, precious metal associated with tradition and personal wealth, the "*vere*," of modern, "national," and immutable steel,[30] mark and protect *Madre Italia*. In their exchange, the very symbol that, in fascist terms, gave a woman identity as someone's wife and a potential mother [31] was sacrificed in order to subsume her into the collective *Madre Italia* and unite her with the goals and "ideals" of the *Patria*. In this way the private act of marriage itself became synonymous with public loyalty and patriotism. The *Corriere della sera* enthused, "With the offer of the golden circles, the 'yes' that united two lives becomes a more grandiose shout of love, a pious, austere, ardent vow."[32]

If we consider that the *Giornata della "fede"* was designed as a metaphor for the union of the "feminized" masses of Italy, the "besieged" home country or *Madre Italia*, with the fascist government and military, the warrior state or *Patria*, the question remains: Why was it necessary to separate it from the rest of the metal drive, already quite successful? Why was this carefully constructed, obviously feminine metaphor required as a sign of national solidarity?

Flowery, official explanations can be found in contemporary publications. The *Corriere della sera*, for example, explained:

---

[29] Ada Negri, "L'anello d'acciaio," *Corriere* (Dec. 18, 1935): 3.

[30] In fact, the "*vere*" were made of cheap tin, though they were claimed to be steel.

[31] Attempts in fascist Italy to desti gmatize illegitimacy and separate childbearing from marriage were unsuccessful and all but abandoned under pressure from the Catholic Church. De Grazia, 61-64.

[32] *Corriere* (Dec. 16, 1935): 2.

> [The ceremony] shows not only a national spirit tempered to every trial, but an absolute, total, spontaneous solidarity, because women from every social background, from the Queen to the most humble peasant, offer to the *Patria* the dearest pledge of their love, the most precious reminder of their married life. But every woman is the center of a family, every one of them is wife and mother: one could not conceive of such a unanimous offering if there did not exist unanimity in the breast of every Italian family.[33]

Having established that a show of support from women is equal to the support of all Italy, the article goes on to suggest the political implications of the symbolic act: "It is political because the Italian family in the fascist regime is not an organism unto itself, but part of a collective society, a cell of the Italian social tissue."[34]

The war heroes who gave up their medals, priests who donated gold chalices and plates, noblemen who gave up their heirlooms, even the peasants who turned over copper pots and pans—all of them could be cited as examples of the support of particular segments of society for the nation, but no one of them could be extrapolated to constitute the approval of the masses. Only women, conveniently styled as a monolithic, ultimately homogenous group of soldier-bearers, could fill that role, and fill it well enough to disappear into a declaration of general popular consent. Thus a contemporary account of the Ethiopian war could end its brief account of the *Giornata* with the assertion, "Proletarian and fascist Italy stood up [to the League of Nations] and won!"[35]

Despite the difficulty of assessing the contemporary reception of the *Giornata*, it is likely that audiences did not accept fascist interpretations unproblematically. Women's behaviors during the regime as a whole shows that they understood themselves in ways that did not necessarily

---

[33] *Corriere* (Dec. 18, 1935): 1.
[34] Ibid.
[35] *L'Italia ha conquistato,* Vol. 6, 107.

conform to fascist prescriptions. Historian Victoria De Grazia, among others, has suggested that the very mobilization of women under fascism, the fact that they were brought into the public sphere in such a visible and organized fashion, challenged in the minds of many the gender assumptions that the regime hoped to reinforce.[36] Likewise, attitudes toward colonialism, and even those towards the First World War and its exacted sacrifices, were not unanimous. As the overall metaphor of the *Giornata* was based upon these inherently unstable symbols, there was clearly room for alternative readings of the event.

It is likewise important to recognize that this so-called "plebiscite of gold" did not necessarily stem from a spontaneous outpouring of patriotic sentiment. Archival evidence demonstrates elements of coercion. Various associations kept detailed reports about who had or had not donated their wedding bands and applied direct pressure to insure full cooperation. Also, the fact that the *Giornata* involved an exchange, meant that one could not simply remove her ring and store it until the situation changed. The steel ring was a necessary talisman against accusations of sabotage.

In his memoir *Christ Stopped at Eboli*, Carlo Levi recalls such pragmatic motivations:

> [W]hen the government asked for the donation of wedding rings and all other objects in gold to supply funds for the prosecution of the war with Abyssinia, they responded in full measure....When the government's gold collection took place they were given to believe that contributions were obligatory, that severe punishment awaited evaders, and that the Pope himself had ordained the sacrifice of all the gold in the churches.[37]

[36] De Grazia, 77-83.

[37] Carlo Levi, *Christ Stopped at Eboli: The Story of a Year*, trans. Frances Frenaye (New York: Farrar, Straus, 1963), 243-44.

Nonetheless, the orchestration of the *Giornata* shows that the regime engaged in an attempt to control and utilize gender in its quest to manufacture consent. Every aspect of the event was not only carefully choreographed, but also meticulously and repeatedly explained in the press. Women were brought out of their private context, made public as the embodiment of Italy. Their public presence was then interpreted as universal consent for the regime.

Part III - Language & Text

LINGUAGGIO MUTAZIONE NET-PIDGIN

Franco Berardi

1. DIASPORE

L'infosfera è l'ambiente nel quale gli organismi si formano come cellule interconnesse. Il linguaggio costruisce questo sistema di innervazioni e si finge una comunità, una appartenenza; è nel linguaggio che viene costruita la finzione dell'origine, che è un'illusione di riferimento fondante, utile a fondare identità fittizie ma non perciò inefficaci.

In questo senso le grammatiche sono finzioni, perché nella realtà la comunicazione è un processo dispersivo: ogni lingua è dispersione. Pierre Calvet[1] propone il modello delle nuvole per descrivere il comporsi e decomporsi dei fenomeni linguistici.

Non vi è propriamente contaminazione e sovrapposizione tra sistemi linguistici rigidamente strutturati, ma continuo flusso e ricomposizione.

Possiamo parlare, certo, di una lingua come fenomeno strutturato, come esecuzione di un programma grammaticale—ma si tratta di un'astrazione. La realtà parlata, vissuta di una lingua è di tutt'altro genere, è un processo fluido, un equilibrio instabile nel divenire delle diaspore.

Ancor più che da una radice, il linguaggio procede da una diaspora.

Cosa è una diaspora? Il procedere da un luogo (illusorio, puramente mentale, proiezione nostalgica, allucinazione della memoria e finzione di identità) verso tutti gli altri luoghi.

Diaspora è allora la dispersione di una verità e di una coerenza originaria, che non è però che un'astrazione no-

[1] P. Calvet, *L'ecologie des langues* (Paris: Fayard, 1999).

stalgica. Dispersione di una finzione condivisa. Entropia di un'illusione proiettata verso il passato.

> Non c'è universalità della lingua, non c'è universalità degli atti linguistici. Ad ogni sequenza di espressione linguistica è associata una rete di catene semiotiche di ogni natura (percettive, mimiche, gestuali, pensieri per immagini ecc...). Ogni enunciato significante cristallizza una danza muta di intensità che si gioca al tempo stesso sul corpo sociale e sul corpo individuale. Dalla lingua alla glossolalia, tutte le transizioni sono possibili.[2]

Ogni lingua parlata è il punto di incontro transitorio e sfuggente di differenti diaspore, di vari allontanamenti da passati luoghi virtuali puramente nostalgici.

La tarda modernità è l'epoca in cui l'intera umanità è sottoposta ad uno sradicamento: una diaspora fatta di emigrazioni e di colonizzazioni culturali incrociate, ma anche di una costante emulsione informativa che filtra attraverso ogni poro della vita quotidiana.

Le tecnologie di comunicazione mettono in moto un processo di deterritorializzazione generalizzato e costante, che si manifesta come sradicamento ed ubiquità, e come aleatorietà del rapporto tra segno e referente. In realtà questa deterritorializzazione tardomoderna non fa che lacerare i veli illusori della referenzialità e dell'identità che il pensiero moderno portava dentro di sé come eredità dell'illusione identitaria e come culto romantico dell'appartenenza.

Il vigore totalitario della modernità, l'integralismo, l'economicismo, il fascismo, il socialismo autoritario sono tutte manifestazioni di una ossessione dell'origine che si oppone disperatamente alla deterritorializzazione, ma è al tempo stesso permeata.

---

[2] F. Guattari, *L'inconscient machinique: Essais de schizo-analyse* (Paris: La Recherche, Fontanay sur Bois, 1979), 31 (traduzione nostra).

Arjun Appadurai[3] descrive il fenomeno della globalizzazione in termini di sovrapposizione e intreccio di mediascape e di etnoscape deterritorializzati.

I taxisti pakistani che a Londra ascoltano le orazioni islamiche di muezzin che parlano da Lahore e gli esuli che trasportano frammenti di cultura nazionalista nei campi per rifugiati in cui incontrano i livelli più avanzati della tecnologia di comunicazione planetaria sono esempi di questo intreccio, che pervade profondamente, e irreversibilmente, l'immaginario delle nuove generazioni.

L'inconscio sociale reagisce alla deterritorializzazione con una sorta di paura panica. Gli investimenti sociali del desiderio dipendono dal bisogno di un ancoraggio identitario. Esposto all'immaginario globale, questo ancoraggio si rivela fantasmatico, fragile, e reagisce all'invasione immaginaria con gli strumenti dell'integralismo, del localismo aggressivo, della xenofobia.

La deriva è divenuta condizione del consistere, il vuoto destino del conoscere.

I centri da cui promana il flusso di informazione si moltiplicano e si rendono invisibili fino a produrre un effetto di inflazione incontrollabile.

Inflazione significa: sempre più danaro compra sempre meno merce.

L'inflazione semiotica si manifesta come un regime in cui sempre più segni comprano sempre meno senso.

> Coloro che dovrebbero essere guida per la popolazione vedono troppi aspetti di ogni questione ascoltano tante cose e scoprono che si possono dire tante di quelle cose a proposito di ogni cosa, che non provano più sicurezza a proposito di nulla. Un senso opprimente non solo della relatività delle idee, ma di una enorme quantità ed incoerenza dell'informazione, una cultura di incroci e di

[3] A. Appadurai, *Modernity at Large* (Minneapolis: University of Minnesota Press, 1996).

energie inestricabili—questa è la sensazione primaria del nostro tempo.[4]

La sovrastimolazione coincide con una sorta di anestesia dell'apparato cognitivo e particolarmente dell'attenzione. I segni proliferano oltre la capacità di ricezione attenta, ed oltre la capacità di decodificazione cosciente.

I segni non sono più soggetti ad interpretazione. Divengono piuttosto un oceano nel quale si naviga attraverso catene di associazione.

2. Net pidgin

Nelle lingue possiamo riconoscere un funzionamento strutturato, che si può identificare per astrazione dal flusso reale della comunicazione, ed un movimento dispersivo costante: ogni lingua è lingua di frontiera, punto di incontro fuggevole e subito ridefinito.

Nella fase dell'insediamento la comunità tende a sopravvalutare ed enfatizzare la struttura, la costanza, la comprensibilità. Ma poi ecco che le popolazioni di parlanti si mescolano, si spostano: ed allora si rendono necessarie delle lingue di comprensione intermedia, fluttuanti e semplificate. Quando gli schiavi vennero importati dall'Africa e depositati nelle isole caraibiche per essere poi inviati nelle piantagioni americane, quelli che provenivano dalle stesse aree vennero separati intenzionalmente per evitare che potessero comunicare tra di loro e complottare. Gli africani appartenenti a diversi gruppi linguistici, per potersi comprendere tra di loro, cominciarono allora a prendere in prestito l'unico linguaggio comune, che era quello degli europei schiavisti. In questo modo presero inizio le contaminazioni linguistiche che sfociarono in varie forme di pidgins, e poi, attraverso un'evoluzione ed una stabilizzazione posteriore, si trasformarono nelle lingue creole che si sono consolidate nell'epoca più recente nell'area carai-

[4] C. Newman, *The Post-modern Aura* (Evanston, IL: Northwestern University Press, 1985), 9.

bica (un'area che per secoli è stata deposito di forza lavoro schiavistica di provenienza africana).

Ma ai nostri giorni i pidgin si moltiplicano informalmente, ogni qual volta si creano flussi di migrazione o circuiti di comunicazione transitoria. Il pidgin è la lingua instabile e flessibile che viene creata fra due parlanti che non conoscono la stessa lingua.

L'inglese che si parla negli aereoporti, semplificato e flessibile, deformato e mescolato, ne è l'esempio più diffuso.

Per estremizzare possiamo dire che ogni flusso linguistico è un pidgin, un idioletto che si rende comprensibile in rapporto ad un contesto pragmatico e nomadico, un linguaggio che è comprensibile soltanto all'interno di una situazione.

Nel processo di globalizzazione e nell'intrecciarsi delle diaspore, tende a svilupparsi un processo di generale pidginizzazione che si aggrega intorno alla lingua inglese, lingua di derivazione, di avvicinamento ed allontanamento dai flussi instabili di comunicazione.

Come mai l'inglese ha sviluppato un ruolo egemone di lingua franca planetaria, di base universale dei pidgins nomadici?

Si tende a pensare che questa egemonia linguistica sia legata al ruolo politico ed economico centrale che il mondo anglo-americano ha sviluppato nel corso dell'epoca moderna.

Ma le cose non stanno così; semmai è vero il contrario, e cioè che il mondo anglofono ha conquistato una posizione dominante sul piano politico ed economico grazie alla plasticità; alla flessibilità e alla invasività della lingua.

L'inglese nasce come lingua di contaminazione, come mescolanza di elementi sassoni, elementi normanni e di elementi latini. La contaminazione linguistica produce un effetto di semplificazione delle strutture sintattiche e di flessibilità della fonetica. La plasticità dell'inglese deriva dalla struttura semplificata, dalla duttilità lessicale di quella lingua. La capacità di adattamento culturale, la modularità e la adesività della cultura anglo-americana è funzione essenziale del suo successo economico e politico. L'egemonia dell'inglese è tutt'uno con la sua plasticità.

L'inglese è lingua semplificata e flessibile, e questo la rende facilmente assimilabile, e soprattutto facilmente adattabile da parte dei parlanti delle aree geografiche più diverse.[5]

Nel processo di deterritorializzazione tardomoderno abbiamo visto nascere uno spazio intimamente deterritorializzato, il ciberspazio.

Internet, che è stato nel decennio novanta il nuovo spazio comunicativo ed economico della colonizzazione, è un luogo infinitamente complesso nel quale le lingue locali sono marginali rispetto alla lingua planetaria, che è un inglese in costante divenire, un inglese mutevole e costantemente ridefinito. A questo proposito McKenzie Wark, in un suo articolo scrive:

> Quando parlanti non inglesi cominciano a scrivere in inglese, elementi della loro grammatica e del loro stile entrano nell'inglese. Questo arricchisce l'inglese enormemente...[6]

Quello che va formandosi è una sorta di Netpidgin che mescola elementi del linguaggio tecnodigitale, elementi del linguaggio underground di provenienza controculturale, per fonderli in un flusso transidiomatico, che sembra realizzare i sogni della lingua perfetta.

E dal momento che si può ritenere che ogni lingua renda possibili alcune strutture concettuali, aprendo così nuove prospettive di pensiero e di immaginazione, è interessante chiedersi quali effetti potrà avere, sul pensiero e sulla immaginazione il rapido costituirsi di un pidgin di rete, questa sorta di magma transidiomatico in perpetuo divenire.

---

[5] H. Bradley, *The Making of English* (London: Macmillan, 1904).

[6] M. Wark, Netlish-English on the Net, <http:// www.mcs.edu.au/Staff/mwark /warchive/Other/netlish,html>.

UN TEATRO PER L'ESTETICA: EDIPO CONTRO FREUD

Carlo Ferrucci

Può farsi, il teatro, strumento, anzi, alla lettera, scena, di una rivitalizzazione della critica d'arte e dell'estetica? È pensabile, cioè, un tipo di rappresentazione teatrale che consista in un'efficace messa a fuoco, non univocamente discorsiva né univocamente performativa perché insieme dialogata e agita, di questo o quel momento emblematico della storia dell'arte e della riflessione estetica ad esso collegabile?

Io sono convinto di sì, e credo di avere cominciato a dimostrarlo con tre lavori teatrali, due dei quali andati in scena a Roma tra il '98 e il '99, sulla figura, il mondo e l'opera di Giacomo Leopardi, Federico Garcia Lorca e Pablo Picasso. Già questi testi, infatti, hanno messo in evidenza come il vantaggio di tentativi del genere risieda innanzitutto nel riuscire a dare corpo e voce alla tensionalità—all'intrinseca teatralità, appunto—di un campo, qual è quello della produzione artistica e dell'espressione estetica, da sempre fecondato da un incontro-scontro particolarmente intenso fra pensiero ed emozione, consapevolezza e corporeità, costruttività e trasgressione.

Da un punto di vista diverso ma complementare, posso affermare che già in questi lavori ha preso vita una sorta di "arte al quadrato" o "estetica militante," se mi passate un'espressione così paurosamente fuori moda, ossia qualcosa come un'alleanza o un patto di mutua assistenza, diciamo, tra poesia (Leopardi e Lorca) e pittura (Picasso), da un lato, e teatro dall'altro; un patto, una complicità, in cui la densità espressiva delle prime alimenta e rilancia l'onnicomprensività del secondo, e questo mette al servizio di quelle il maggior potenziale performativo dei suoi spazi tridimensionali. Nello stesso tempo, gli inevitabili riferimenti ai lati più personali delle vicende biografiche degli artisti oggetto della ricostruzione teatrale gettano una luce più cruda, facendone slittare i confini e rinegoziandone in qualche modo i luoghi, sul rapporto fra arte e realtà vissuta.

Nella misura in cui mi sono apparse plausibilmente, connaturativamente, direi, veicolabili dalla forma del dramma, la specificità e la radicalità di due forme d'arte pur diverse, nei loro più evidenti principii costruttivi, dal teatro come la poesia e la pittura, hanno lasciato venire in luce una loro più riposta—o rimossa, oggi—ma non per questo meno significativa natura pragmatica, argomentativo-performativa, insomma drammatica, appunto, nel senso originario del termine "dramma," di azione sommuovitrice e instauratrice di realtà. Che è poi, certo, o almeno dovrebbe essere, nell'ottica che già lì privilegiavo di un'arte non an-estetica, non subalterna cioè alla logica oggi prevalente della cultura come sapere tuttologico, omologante-rassicurante, una realtà che da quest'agire estetico teatralmente potenziato risultasse, prima che creativamente ri-generata e per poterlo essere, attraversata una volta di più da parte a parte, scossa nelle basi stesse dei suoi assetti costituiti, scomposta e ricomposta nelle sue situazioni-limite e nei suoi aspetti esistenzialmente più pregnanti, tali da mettere maggiormente a repentaglio l'idea di sé e del mondo nutrita dai soggetti in essa implicati.

La mia comunicazione di oggi prende le mosse da questi precedenti per puntare a un obiettivo forse ancora più ambizioso: la valutazione del modo in cui può assumere forma teatrale un'immaginaria "resa di conti" tra Edipo e Freud, ossia tra il "primo attore," in qualche modo, del complesso psichico per antonomasia, quello di Edipo appunto, e colui che questo nome gli ha assegnato dopo averne scoperto l'archetipo nelle vicende del protagonista dell'Edipo re di Sofocle.

Imbeccato dal personaggio dell'Autore del testo, seduto in mezzo al pubblico, e spalleggiato da un giovane spettatore che si presenta come Amleto—per Freud, com'è noto, tardivo alter ego sotto opposte spoglie del sovrano greco—e da una giovane spettatrice che si presenta come

Antigone, Edipo rinfaccia a Freud di aver proiettato su di lui, che invece era tutto preso da un'ossessiva ricerca del potere, il suo personale, morboso attaccamento alla propria madre e la sua inconfessata ostilità nei confronti del proprio padre. Così facendo, incalza l'ex re di Tebe, lo studioso viennese non ha stravolto solo la figura del personaggio di Sofocle, ma anche la natura stessa del teatro, da lui appiattito sulla scena del sogno—innanzitutto quello di un se stesso più edipico di Edipo—piuttosto che messo a fuoco nell'ambivalente complessità dei suoi linguaggi.

A rimescolare ulteriormente le carte di questo vero e proprio contro-processo che il mondo del teatro intenta al padre della psicoanalisi, intervengono poi anche, da un lato, l'irruzione nella rappresentazione della madre di Freud, a tardiva e controproducente difesa delle posizioni del figlio, e dall'altro il problematico innamoramento di Amleto per Antigone. Lasciandosi cadere, alla fine, pur di ottenere il lavoro di cui ha bisogno e sfuggire nello stesso tempo alle attenzioni di Amleto, tra le braccia di suo "padre" Edipo, quest'ultima sembra quasi riportare in equilibrio lo scontro, dando indirettamente ragione alle tesi del loro comune antagonista; e tuttavia, tale quasi-epilogo risulta a sua volta contraddetto da un ultimo colpo di scena, a suggello di un'ottica comunque più sfumata, in cui le ragioni del sesso, del potere e dell'amore si fronteggiano, nell'oscillante spazio reale/irreale del teatro, senza che nessuna di esse prevalga decisamente sull'altra.

Ma procediamo con ordine.

Una prima resistenza, se non una prima vittoria, del teatro, della teatralità, contro la sua troppo semplice, troppo semplificante assunzione a luogo deputato del realizzarsi di un sogno proibito, si manifesta nell'impossibilità per Freud, che incalzato da Edipo vorrebbe scagliarsi sull' Autore seduto in platea, di attraversare l'invisibile parete che separa lo spazio della scena dallo spazio occupato dal pubblico:

FREUD (verso l'AUTORE, sottraendosi alla presa di EDIPO per portarsi carponi sul bordo del palcoscenico) Ma io non voglio, mi spiego, non voglio, io, Freud, che da assolutamente vivo, per ripetere le assurde parole di... di... (accenna a EDIPO), sì, di quell'incredibile individuo, io che da assolutamente vivo ho dialogato da pari a pari, proprio così, con i più grandi autori di tutti i tempi, non voglio per nessuna ragione al mondo parlare e muovermi adesso agli ordini...agli ordini...

EDIPO (fa un passo verso FREUD) Sigismondo...

FREUD (sbotta, indicando l'AUTORE)...Agli ordini di un tizio che nessuno conosce, e che si capisce fin troppo bene che non sarà mai nessuno!

L'AUTORE si alza e, con le braccia conserte e un leggero sorriso sulle labbra, fa segno d EDIPO di andare a riprendersi FREUD. Questi, allora, si lancia verso l'AUTORE, ma giunto alla scaletta che unisce il palcoscenico alla platea viene respinto da un 'muro' invisibile e ricade sbalordito tra le braccia di EDIPO, mentre l'AUTORE si risiede scuotendo leggermente la testa.

EDIPO (prende FREUD per il collo e lo scuote bonariamente) Eh già, mi ero scordato che per te qui (indica il palcoscenico) o lì (indica la platea) era praticamente lo stesso, per cui quello che è successo qui a me, per esempio, cioè di ammazzare mio padre e sposare mia madre, per gli spettatori secondo te è come se fosse successo davvero lì (indica di nuovo la platea), nella realtà, giusto? Invece, hai visto, anche quando tutto farebbe pensare il contrario, qui sopra c'è pur sempre qualcosa che continua a separarci da loro (indica ancora la platea).

FREUD (si scuote di dosso la mano di EDIPO) Ma se non più tardi di un minuto fa, tu stesso hai detto che anche noi, qui, ridiventiamo vivi!

EDIPO Sì, certo, ma di una vita diversa dalla loro, una vita che loro ci fanno vivere...

AUTORE (a FREUD)...Con le parole che io vi faccio dire, e le azioni che io vi faccio compiere...

EDIPO (con un sospiro, indicando la platea)...Che loro, su iniziativa dell'autore...(Un riflettore si spegne all'improvviso, mentre si ode un leggero martellio metallico. Con un nuovo sospiro, guardando verso la cabina di regia)... E col contributo non meno determinante del regista... (Il riflettore si riaccende e il martellio cessa.)

Un secondo punto di svolta della rappresentazione è costituito, come ho già accennato, dall'entrata in scena di una ragazza che dirà di essere Antigone e di un ragazzo che dirà di essere Amleto, i quali, dopo avere interloquito con Freud dalla platea, salgono sul palcoscenico per dare meglio man forte a Edipo nella rivendicazione di quel margine di senso non edipico della sua storia che fa tutt' uno con l'affermazione dell'incoercibile plurisignificanza dell'evento teatrale:

FREUD Eh no, adesso basta... (insieme all'AUTORE, al pubblico e all'invisibile regista) Vi sembra giusto, oltre che logico, scusate, che chiunque la pensa diversamente da me possa salire quassù, mentre a me non è permesso andare giù?

EDIPO (prende FREUD per le spalle) Si vede che non è la stessa cosa, caro mio. E poi, non devono essere spettatori come gli altri, sennò loro (accenna alla cabina di regia e all'AUTORE) non glielo avrebbero sicuramente permesso.

AMLETO Esatto...Ma, ecco, stavo, anzi (invita con una mano ANTIGONE ad avvicinarsi insieme a lui a EDIPO e a FREUD) stavamo dicendo, al mio...(indica FREUD) ehm, se posso anticipare... sì, quasi collega, in un certo senso... Sì, insomma, al nostro implacabile esploratore della psiche, che non ce l'ha, no, ragione, visto che la parte della storia dello sventurato figlio di Laio qui... (EDIPO gli fa segno di stringere) Eh? Ah, sì, certo... Beh, quello che della storia di Edipo più ci coinvolge, a noi del pubblico, e più che mai se abbiamo il pallino del teatro, non è affatto la presunta realizzazione sulla scena dei nostri desideri più proibiti, ma il modo, un vero thrilling, con cui il protagonista arriva a scoprire la sua vera identità. Che è, e su questo non ci piove, quella di un uomo che ha ucciso suo padre e generato…

ANTIGONE (portandosi le mani al viso) Ah! (EDIPO la fissa turbato e inquisitivo.)

AMLETO …E generato figli con sua madre; ma per lo spettatore non è questa, ripeto, la cosa più importante…

ANTIGONE (sostiene con fermezza lo sguardo cieco di EDIPO, poi guarda l'AUTORE) È vero, non lo è.

EDIPO (a AMLETO, dandogli la mano, ma senza distogliere il viso da ANTIGONE) Grazie, amico, chiunque tu sia.

AMLETO Non c'è di che. Dovere.

ANTIGONE (colpita) Dovere?

AMLETO Sì… (indica con un gesto tutt'intorno) Lo faccio per questo, no?, per il teatro… Per il teatro, che (guarda il pubblico) come quasi tutti intuiscono, e (guarda FREUD) chi ancora non l'ha fatto è ora che si decida anche lui, visto che in fondo lo ha bazzicato tanto, il teatro è sempre stato molto di più di uno specchio offerto ai nostri sogni, o incubi che siano.

ANTIGONE (all'AUTORE, indicando AMLETO) Accidenti, ma è bravo…Io invece non lo so, se sarò in grado… (L'AUTORE la rassicura a gesti.)

EDIPO (con una punta di invidia) Eh, sì, va forte, il ragazzo!

FREUD (a AMLETO, sarcastico) Ma perché, allora, visto che è tanto bravo, non finisce di raccontarcelo lei, qui, subito, scusi, signor quasi collega, e senza tanti giri di parole, che cosa sono questa "cosa più importante" e questo "molto di più" che solo io non sarei riuscito a vedere?

AMLETO (fa scorrere lo sguardo dal pubblico a EDIPO a ANTIGONE) Devo? (fa scorrere lo sguardo da ANTIGONE al pubblico a FREUD) No, mi dispiace, ma non posso.

FREUD (C.s.) E perché non può, se è lecito, signor superesperto?

AMLETO Perché...(Si porta, seguito a una certa distanza dagli altri, vicino alle sbarre del fondo, e vi poggia le mani facendo alcune flessioni.) Perché, se riuscissi a spiegarvi... una volta per tutte... con parole davvero appropriate, davvero esaurienti, che cos'è il teatro... queste mie parole esaurirebbero, appunto, ecco, tutto ciò che lo fa essere, e il teatro in quanto tale...

FREUD (spazientito)... Il teatro in quanto tale...?

AMLETO (smette di fare flessioni e torna verso il proscenio) Il teatro in quanto tale, è chiaro, proprio perché esaurito, evidentemente, e quindi esautorato, a quel punto, dalle mie parole di spiegazione, non avrebbe più ragione di esistere.

FREUD Chiaro un accidente! La sua presunta spiegazione, caro il mio giovanotto, è solo un gioco di parole, e neppure tanto brillante!

Un terzo momento significativo della rappresentazione, sempre per quanto riguarda l'aprirsi di varchi di senso alternativi a quello individuato da Freud nella sua analisi dell'Edipo re e di Amleto, è dato dall'emergere della volontà di potere che a detta dei tre personaggi tragici, alleati in questo con la madre di Freud, potrebbe aver costituito il vero sottofondo del suo Edipo:

MADRE Ma possibile che non capisci? Che non vuoi, nemmeno tu, capire?

EDIPO (sarcastico) È una cosa troppo inconscia perfino per lui, si vede.

AMLETO Già, troppo inconscia perfino per il primo della classe! Altro che (cita) "Ma quel che sai di meglio, non lo dire ai tuoi alunni!" (alla MADRE, giratasi verso di lui) Non glielo ha mai sentito dire? Era una delle sue frasi preferite, del suo grande Goethe!

ANTIGONE Magari, non vuole capirlo proprio perché... (tutto d'un fiato) Proprio perché questa cosa fa tutt'uno con quel suo voler essere, di nuovo e (guarda EDIPO) a qualsiasi costo, il primo della classe!

AMLETO (fa un passo verso ANTIGONE, che arretra) Ma sicuro, può essere benissimo così, complimenti! (Guarda EDIPO, che annuisce.)

FREUD (che ha ormai capito, guardando ANTIGONE) A qualsiasi costo, eh, dice?

Pausa. ANTIGONE guarda la MADRE.

MADRE Sì, Sigismondo, sì... (tutto d'un fiato) A qualsiasi costo, anche a quello di desiderare la morte di tuo padre: per questa tua smania di non essere secondo a nessuno, e non per me, per contendermi a lui!

FREUD (con un guizzo di residua incredulità) La morte di mio...? (più rassegnato) Per non essere secondo a nessuno...

EDIPO (in tono di vittoria) Certo, per sentire di poter finalmente diventare quello che sognavi sin da ragazzo, quando ti piaceva tanto identificarti con Annibale, il grande semita vincitore di Roma: il signore incontrastato di un nuovo regno...(prende per un braccio ANTIGONE).

AMLETO (prende per l'altro braccio ANTIGONE)... Fosse pure quello delle tenebre, del male e del dolore...

ANTIGONE (verso il pubblico) "Se non posso smuovere gli dei del cielo, smuoverò quelli di sottoterra," scriveva!

FREUD (ironico) Gli stessi per cui stravedeva Antigone, se non sbaglio...

ANTIGONE Ah, no, non gli stessi! I miei erano più puliti!

FREUD Si vede che non li aveva ancora analizzati a fondo...

EDIPO (frena a stento la sua irritazione)...Il signore incontrastato di un nuovo regno, e non come ti aveva fatto lui, tuo padre, e come, lui vivo, la sua figura continuava, senza saperlo, a volerti: un semplice medico...

MADRE ...Appartenente a una minoranza malvista...

FREUD Senza ragione, e da troppo tempo!

AMLETO ...Derisa...

MADRE Perfino da se stessa!

ANTIGONE ... Esclusa da tutti i posti di comando...

FREUD A dispetto del valore delle sue menti migliori!

EDIPO ...Per questo...

MADRE Solo per questo!

EDIPO ...Hai desiderato, senza mai confessartelo, che il tuo vecchio...

AMLETO ...Che incarnava i limiti della sua nascita...

ANTIGONE (con un sospiro)...E la prigione che era per lei la sua stirpe...

EDIPO Si togliesse di mezzo. E in cuor tuo...

FREUD (con uno scatto d’orgoglio) Molto in fondo! Solo molto in fondo, semmai!

MADRE ...In cuor tuo...(con sforzo) Sì, in cuor tuo, anche se molto in fondo, spero, hai esultato, quando finalmente si è...quando finalmente gli è toccato lasciarci! (Singhiozza.)

Questa vera e propria catarsi imposta al fondatore della psicoanalisi dagli altri personaggi del dramma fa sì che, dopo altri passaggi dello stesso tenore, la rappresentazione si concluda con la messa in scena dell'indecibilità tra le ragioni di Freud, che nel frattempo si è presa la soddisfazione di veder riaffiorare la più inconfessabile delle pulsioni nel rapporto tra Antigone e suo "padre" Edipo, e le ragioni del teatro ovvero di Edipo e – soprattutto – di Amleto, che dopo avere inutilmente tentato di legare a sé Antigone con le armi della poesia assiste, forse, in extremis, da fuori della porta, alla riapparizione della ragazza in veste di sua più o meno legittima compagna di vita:

ANTIGONE Ad Atene, vero?

EDIPO Sì, ad Atene, ad Atene, dove potrò finalmente riposare in pace.

FREUD (fa un passo verso EDIPO e ANTIGONE) Non è che...ehm...potrei venire anch'io? (EDIPO si ferma e lo guarda accigliato.) È che a Roma ci sono stato varie volte, ma ad Atene una sola; (indica la scaletta) e se da quella parte non posso uscire...

EDIPO (a ANTIGONE) Che ne dici? (ANTIGONE alza le spalle.) Su, su, lo so che con un'altra persona vicino ti sentiresti più tranquilla, alla faccia del mio povero Sofocle... (a FREUD) Va bene, vieni, basta però che non sia solo per spiarci, d'accordo? (Va verso l'uscita con ANTIGONE.)

FREUD (ironico, andandogli dietro) Non vorrai mica dire, spero, che qualcuno potrebbe sospettare che chi è andato a letto con sua madre... (EDIPO si ferma e si gira verso di lui.) Per sbaglio, d'accordo, per sbaglio... Possa farlo anche con sua figlia? (EDIPO alza minacciosamente il braccio verso di lui, che fa il gesto di arretrare.) Certo, sempre per sbaglio, naturalmente... Soprattutto se figlia sua lei lo è solo per modo di dire? (EDIPO fa un passo teatralmente minaccioso verso di lui, poi si rigira ed esce.

Ad AMLETO, rimasto immobile col suo foglietto in mano) Bene, giovanotto, conoscerla non è stato esattamente un piacere, ma devo ammettere che lei ha fatto tutto quello che poteva per non rimanere troppo al di sotto del suo grande modello. (Gli dà un buffetto su una guancia.) Via, non se la prenda tanto! Ma come, lei viene qui a parlarmi con tanta sicurezza di potere, e poi non sa quello che sanno tutti, ossia che oggi gli unici poteri rimasti, e non per colpa mia, mi creda, sono quelli del sesso e del denaro? Studia psicologia, ma non sospetta che non riconoscerli, questi poteri, equivale a subirli? Eh? (AMLETO guarda altrove.) Ama tanto il teatro, e non capisce che non mettersi al servizio di nessuno dei due, significa condannarsi al ruolo di comparsa?

AMLETO (guarda verso il punto da cui sono usciti ANTIGONE e EDIPO, inghiotte) Il sesso, potrei anche essere d'accordo... Ma che c'entra ora anche il denaro, scusi?

FREUD Come, che c'entra, benedetto figliolo... Ma davvero, non s'è nemmeno accorto che qui il vero padrone del vapore, di questo (indica tutt'intorno) indegno baraccone, è proprio lui (indica verso dove è uscito EDIPO), lo sciancato, e che andandogli dietro la nostra servizievole crocerossina nonché attrice in erba ha solo seguito l'odore dei soldi, di un, diciamo così...ingaggio? (AMLETO abbassa la testa e la scuote.) Dica la verità, pensava che avesse preso sul serio quei suoi discorsoni sulla religione del teatro, eh? (Gli dà di gomito con un sorrisetto.) E magari anche i suoi accenni all'altra, di religione, quella dell'amore...

AMLETO (con finta condiscendenza) Già, nemmeno fosse stata davvero Ofelia... (piccato, rialzando la testa) Intanto, però, l'altro giorno, era domenica, sono andato a vedere una pièce di Picasso, proprio all'ora della messa, e il teatro era pieno!

FREUD Ah ah ah, questa poi...Ma se lo sanno tutti che la domenica, ormai, come in qualsiasi altra festa, non si fa che ciondolare di qua e di là, attaccandosi a qualsiasi cosa ci capiti sotto mano pur di sentirci un po' più vivi che durante il resto della settimana! È questo che lei intende, per religione? (Gli prende il foglietto dalle mani e lo guarda.) Beh, certo, se lei scrive versi, invece di prendere di petto la prosa della vita...(legge) "Seppellitemi nella mia terra"... Ah, ma allora è proprio un'ossessione, la sua... (Continua a leggere in silenzio.) E la violenza di cui lei parlava prima...Ah, sì, vedo, sarebbe quella fatta ai morti, dice, quando vengono cremati invece che sotterrati... (Restituisce il foglietto a AMLETO.) A essere sincero, mi sembrano versi un po' debolucci, oltre che troppo funebri, per conquistare una ragazza, anche se questa è travestita da quella leccacadaveri di Antigone! E in quanto alla violenza che lei condanna, andiamo, anche un bambino le risponderebbe che è solo un problema pratico, perché di terra ce n'è sempre meno, e quella che rimane serve tutta ai vivi, senza contare che sono gli stessi morituri a chiedere, per le ragioni più diverse, di essere bruciati invece che sepolti, non lo sa? (Va verso l'uscita.) Ma ora la devo proprio salutare...

AMLETO (gli va dietro) Ossia, lei non pensa che la cremazione sia una forma di rimozione della morte, attraverso una... una violenta contrazione del suo tempo e del suo spazio naturali? Che la morte, come l'amore, stia...Sì, stia morendo? (recita, tra sé) "Fratelli, a un tempo stesso, amore e morte/ingenerò la sorte..." Chi l'ha scritto?

FREUD Ancora versi? Se davvero vuole approfondire l'argomento, e glielo dice uno che di teatro forse non capiva proprio tutto però ai poeti gli voleva bene davvero, perché non legge invece il mio *Al di là del principio del piacere,* che parla in modo scientifico e esauriente di eros e...

AMLETO (lo interrompe, amaro) Ma sì, certo, esauriamo, anzi, esautoriamo anche la poesia...

Dal fondo giunge un rumore di macchina che si mette in moto.

EDIPO (da fuori scena) Muoviti, Sigismondo, dai, guarda che non ti aspettiamo!

FREUD (forte, verso il fondo) Arrivo! (a AMLETO) Glielo ripeto, per me non c'è nessuna rimozione o contrazione, è tutto perfettamente trasparente... (scherzoso) Piuttosto, stia attento che qualche mio seguace troppo zelante non le faccia notare che dietro a questo suo desiderio di essere sepolto, si nasconde in realtà la voglia di ricongiungersi con la Terra Madre, ah ah ah! (Fa un gesto di saluto ed esce, mentre AMLETO accenna un gesto di reazione. Da fuori scena) E lasci perdere la poesia, dia retta a me, non sono più tempi! (Si sente sbattere una porta, poi un rumore di macchina che si allontana.)

AMLETO (riguarda il foglietto) Macché terra madre e terra madre... (dopo qualche istante, tra sé) E se invece fosse proprio così? (Getta via il foglietto.) Ma sì, finiamola, una buona volta, con tutti questi fantasmi, e al diavolo anche il teatro e le sue tanto decantate (sarcastico) possibilità! Tanto, per chi non si riconosce in nessun potere, l'impossibile sarà sempre più del possibile. (Scende in fretta dal palcoscenico ed esce dalla porta più vicina. Dopo qualche istante, una porta più esterna sbatterà forte, con un rumore che ricorda uno sparo.)

MADRE (alzandosi, forte e nella direzione in cui è uscito AMLETO) Maleducato! (L'AUTORE la guarda storto.) Eh, ma quando ci vuole, ci vuole! (Si risiede.)

L'AUTORE si alza, sospirando vistosamente all'indirizzo della MADRE, si gira verso la cabina di regia e fa segno di spegnere tutto. Ma mentre le luci cominciano ad attenuarsi, si sente il rumore di una macchina che si avvicina e si ferma, una portiera che sbatte, la macchina che si riallontana; e allora l'AUTORE fa segno al regista di fermarsi. Subito dopo rientra di corsa in scena ANTIGONE, scarmigliata e invecchiata, vi si muove agitata, ansimando fortemente, come alla ricerca di qualcuno o di qualcosa, infine vede il foglietto e lo raccoglie.

ANTIGONE (legge, con voce rotta) Nella mia terra. (pausa) "Seppellitemi nella mia terra.../(ho un rettangolo d'erba, in campagna,/dove corrono lepri gigantesche/ e querce centenarie nutrono/col frutto dei miei giochi di bambino/cinghiali dalla pelle d'acciaio)./ Lascio ad altri/la fredda nicchia in torri di cemento/o la vampa del fuoco, che non ci appartiene:/non c'è che lei, la terra, che possegga, che possa trasmetterci in eterno,/un calore che il nostro ricordi.//Seppellitemi nella mia terra!" (Pausa. Alza gli occhi dal foglio.) Un calore che il nostro ricordi... (Si lancia per scendere dal palcoscenico.) Amico, dove sei, aspettami! (Viene respinta, come in precedenza FREUD, dal 'muro' invisibile, e cade in ginocchio. Più piano, dopo un istante di smarrimento) Aspettami, fratello! (Scorre con le palme aperte sul 'muro', muovendosi sul bordo del palcoscenico. Ogni volta che vi appoggerà con più forza le mani, si sentirà sbattere una porta; finché non è colta da un pensiero improvviso.) Nella mia terra... (Si china e 'scava' freneticamente con le mani sotto il 'muro' fino ad aprirsi un 'varco' che le permette di scavalcare strisciando il bordo del palcoscenico e di lasciarsi cadere dall'altra parte, dove avanza in direzione della porta da cui è uscito AMLETO rimanendo carponi e con i gesti faticosi di chi si fa largo in uno stretto cunicolo, mentre a un ultimo gesto dell'AUTORE le luci finiscono lentamente di spegnersi.) Amore, dove sei? Dove sei, amore? Dove sei?

SIPARIO

1789-1989:
ROMANTICISM, LIBERALISM, AND THE END OF HISTORY?

Gary Kelly

Following the collapse in 1989 of the Berlin Wall and what it symbolized, there were claims that the end of history had been reached—end as termination, goal, fulfillment.[1] This end, it has been claimed, is the universal triumph of the modern liberal state. The coincidence of this proclaimed world-historical event with the bicentennial anniversary of a major predecessor—the outbreak of the French Revolution—is highly suggestive. Immanuel Wallerstein and others have argued that the French Revolution, together with its aftermath in the culture that later came to be called Romanticism, signaled the inauguration of a process of political, economic, social, and cultural transformation that eventuated in the modern liberal state and that reached another major turning point with the events of 1989.[2] In this paper I develop part of that claim by examining the role in that process of Romanticism, as a set of parallel and often related movements throughout Europe and its colonies and former colonies.

First it is necessary to describe, at least briefly, the complex relationship between the French Revolution and its contemporary, sympathetic, and successor movements. In the past few decades, various historical and cultural studies have suggested a close relationship between Enlightenment ideas of economic, social, cultural, and political modernization and civil society, based on economic individualism, and the French Revolution, with its collateral and dependent movements.[3] To a large extent, and very broadly, this modernization aimed at the radical alteration, if not abolition, of the intertwined systems of patronage, pater-

[1] See Fukuyama.
[2] See Wallerstein.
[3] See the summary in Sanderson, Chapter 6.

nalism, and patriarchy that had long sustained court monarchies and their empires. Some social historians suggest that modernization was led predominantly by the progressive and revolutionary elements of the middle classes and particularly the professional bourgeoisie, with their allies in other classes, especially the landed class and the artisans, in various combinations in different countries and regions, depending on circumstances there.[4] Movements for modernization were also sustained by an ideology of individual identity based on personal autonomy and self-determination, as distinct from and opposed to historic and customary identities based on social rank and relations that were thought to be sustained by and to sustain the historic systems of patronage, paternalism, and patriarchy.[5] Increasingly, the new practices of individualism were constructed in and learned from the literature and culture of Sensibility. This culture, in which nobility of soul, or subjectivity, displaced and subsumed nobility of birth, rank, and status, would furnish the materials for models of the sovereign subject on which post-Revolutionary, Romantic modern liberal states could be founded.

Sensibility's most striking political manifestation—the French Revolution—had a contradictory impact, however. On the one hand, Sensibility, with its emphasis on sovereign subjectivity and civil society, furnished the ideological and cultural language for economic and political modernization, militantly organized by revolutionary and Napoleonic administrations and their puppets or imitators throughout Europe and its colonies. On the other hand, revolutionary violence and warfare discredited Sensibility as the inspiration claimed by a generation of Revolutionary leaders and their sympathizers throughout Europe. Revolutionary violence and expansionism, together with the supposed embodiment of the Revolution in the absolutist and militarist Napoleonic state and empire, alienated

[4] Schulze, Chapter 6, contains a useful survey.
[5] See the entry for "Individual" in Williams.

many in the actual and potential revolutionary classes and coalitions outside France, as well as within.

Accordingly, reformists in many countries modified—had to modify—central ideas of the culture of Sensibility and related programmes of modernization during the Revolutionary and Napoleonic period and the restoration of old orders of monarchy and patronage after 1815.[6] In Spain, for example, many among the progressive bourgeoisie had adopted predominantly French models for modernization even before the Revolution, were confirmed in these commitments by it, and were accordingly known as *afrancesados*. Revolutionary violence, anti-ecclesiasticism, and disestablishment of the Catholic Church made it difficult for many of these to continue open advocacy of French models, however, and the difficulty was later increased by Napoleon's invasion of Spain and dismissal of its monarchy. Similar disillusionments and difficulties were experienced by many in the revolutionary classes elsewhere, especially such politically divided and externally dominated territories as Italy and Germany, according to local conditions.

Attempts to resolve these disillusionments and difficulties took many discursive forms, from the literary to the constitutional.[7] One literary expression that could be cited among very many is Ugo Foscolo's *Ultime lettere di Jacopo Ortis* (1798-1802), an autobiographical novel which is modeled in part on Goethe's widely read and highly influential pre-Revolutionary novel of Sensibility, *The Sorrows of Werther*, thereby disclosing the link between Romantic and Sentimental poetics and politics. Foscolo's work maintains a reformist, modernizing, and patriotic discourse against Napoleonic expansionism and exploitation of "emancipated" territories, and the discourse is authorized by the representation of sovereign subjectivity in the protagonist-narrator, which is implicitly that of the author. *Ortis* illus-

[6] See Droz; Jardin and Tudesq; Woolf, Parts 3 and 4.
[7] See, for example, Thom.

trates one way in which Romantic literary form could sustain a post-Revolutionary and, in this instance, proleptically post-Napoleonic politics. A significant parallel to *Ortis* in explicitly political and constitutional discourse is the liberal Spanish constitution of 1812.

This constitution was partly modeled on an idealized version of British constitutional monarchy, and would in the following decades become the model for the foundation of modern liberal states throughout Europe and its former colonies. The constitution was designed by so-called Spanish *liberales* in Cadiz while under a state of siege by Napoleonic armies and as an attempt to extract a promissory post-war political contract from the deposed Spanish king. Significantly, it was these *liberales* who gave the term "liberal" in its specifically political meaning to English and other languages.

"Liberal," in the predominant English sense of "free" as in "generous, open, tolerant," had historic associations with upper-class culture, presuming that only those who were independent in the style of the landed class could be truly "free." "Liberal" in the new sense, taken from Spanish, also designated those who were "free," but more particularly in the sense of free from relations of dependency enforced by the historic regimes of patronage, paternalism, and patriarchy. The predominantly professional and middle-class *liberales* claimed to be free in this sense and demanded a state structure that would guarantee such freedom and a political structure of representative democracy, that is, a system of power controlled by those who were free to represent themselves.

The politics and poetics represented by Ortis and the Spanish constitution of 1812 were complicated and cast into crisis, of course, by the restoration of reactionary court monarchies in many parts of Europe and of internal division and external domination to large parts of territories such as Italy. The restoration was guaranteed by a set of international agreements backed with military intervention, and threatened or exercised variously in Spain, Italy, and elsewhere in the succeeding decades. In response, the revolutionary classes had perforce to subsume pre-Revolutionary, Revolutionary, and Napoleonic modernizing programmes in discourses and projects that were at once local and international, and, for some time at least, predominantly cultural and literary. In this respect it is revealing that one answer to the period's parlor game of naming the three most famous people in Europe was Napoleon, Germaine de Staël, and Byron.

"Europe" here would be the educated, predominantly professional middle classes, greater or lesser in number, more or less regionally concentrated, and more or less influential in different countries.

Napoleon had an obvious, even infamous record as forcible modernizer rousing ambivalent responses in this "Europe" of many places and peoples. De Staël was perhaps the most famous exile from what people like her in all these places could regard as Napoleon's betrayal in institutionalizing their revolutionary programme in monarchic and imperialist form. De Staël not only wrote a pioneering manifesto for the relation between a projected liberal society and literature (*De la Littérature considérée dans ses rapports avec les institutions sociales*, 1800); she also produced two diverse, yet parallel and widely influential, texts for European liberalism and Romanticism in her novel *Corinne; ou, l'Italie* (1807) and her essay in what would now be considered cultural studies, *De l'Allemagne* (1810). Byron was not only the most widely read poet of Romantic subjectivity but also the most widely read social and cultural critic in verse of the Old Order of court monarchy, in historic or restored form, and a major inspirer of support for liberal national liberation movements, as in Greece. It is not surprising that during the Spanish liberal revolt of the early 1820s, and while he was in self-imposed exile in Italy, he made connections with the Carbonari and, with others, founded a (short-lived) literary and political periodical called *The Liberal*. Byron's direct contribution to the Greek War of

Independence, costing his life, is well known; more difficult to calculate is the contribution his poems made to rousing Europe-wide sympathy for the Greeks, leading to British and French military intervention that guaranteed Greek victory.

Not long after Byron's death, various Romantic writers, of whom Victor Hugo is the most often cited, were equating Romanticism and liberalism within various and conflicting political agendas. Modern historians affirm a close connection between Romantic writers and liberal movements for replacement of the Old Order of court government and aristocratic hegemony by nation-states with constitutional governments based on representative democracy of liberal "sovereign subjects." Certainly it can be argued that much Romantic literature is devoted to representing—or inventing—sovereign subjectivity for a largely middle-class reading public. It is no coincidence that in the nineteenth and twentieth centuries members of this reading public would become enfranchised by liberal constitutions to comprise the new political nation. It is also, of course, true that it was the adult male members of the reading public who were first enfranchised and other members, notably women, the working classes, the socially marginalized, and colonized peoples, were excluded until some time later—often much later, and in some places even now.

Nevertheless, the steady broadening of the political nation of liberal states through the nineteenth and twentieth centuries seemed to be accompanied or enabled by certain kinds of literature produced by the Romantic movements and imitated into the late twentieth century.

Among these literary kinds, perhaps the most important represent the construction, conflicts, and survival of the sovereign subject, especially in a social, cultural, and economic order dominated by a hegemonic social other. Notable examples range from confessional memoirs to the Gothic romance and their modern epigones. Another major set of literary kinds contributed and contributes to the "invention of tradition" and the representation of "imagined communities" of region, nation, and empire. The major form here is the social-historical novel engineered by Walter Scott from the pioneering work of certain women contemporaries. The Scott form of historical novel was one of the most influential in world-historical terms because it addressed the interests of revolutionary middle-class reading publics wherever it was read, translated, and imitated.[8] Part of this form, but also predominant in other forms ranging from travelogue to topographical verse, is the representation of nature and regional or national topography (including historic monuments and sites) as the material condition for the construction of such subjects and such communities.

A fuller taxonomy of forms would suggest that the sovereign subject was invented and circulated (and continues to circulate) in such forms as the *bildungsroman*, the confessional novel, lyric poetry, biography and autobiography, and melodrama. The imagined community and its natural, topographical conditions were represented (and continue to be represented) in the social-historical novel, the "national tale" in prose and verse, Romantic travelogues of several kinds, topographical poetry, the description novel, and a wide range of literature modelled on the folklore and folk literature that was also avidly collected and appropriated by Romanticists and founders of modern liberal states. Significantly, such forms had had low literary and cultural status in the historic hierarchized discursive order, but by the Romantic period came to be among the most widely read literary forms. Thus a literary-discursive revolution was a major feature of the cultural revolution that in many cases preceded but certainly accompanied and enabled modern state-formation.

Wherever modern liberal states were founded (and continue to be founded), the discursive order created by

---

[8] The notion of "imagined communities" is from Benedict Anderson; see the book of this title.

this cultural revolution was made an institution of state, formalized as canons of the "national" literature, taught through state education in schools and then universities, supported to various extents with state funding, and socially conventionalized as an important displayable knowledge of the professional classes and others who, with them, staffed and continue to staff the apparatuses of state and allied institutions.

I take it that we in the academic community are beneficiaries of this programme, and most, if not all, of us are also functionaries of literature as state and state as literature. Literature as reconstructed in the Romantic discursive revolution is pretty much literature as we still know it. Literature as a regime of compulsory reading is still considered a major gateway to the (now hegemonic) middle classes and the professions and careers they take up. Literature is still a major way in which we are taught to imagine ourselves as sovereign subjects with a capacity for self-representation.

The creation of literature, predominantly in the forms valorized by Romanticism, and especially autobiography and social-historical fiction, continues to be a major way in which otherwise or hitherto subaltern groups identify themselves to the state and to the political nation as such sovereign subjects, who are therefore and thereby entitled to increased self-representation and participation in the modern liberal state's processes of representative democracy. Striking examples in recent decades include women and people of color and, more recently still, certain aboriginal peoples, ethnic minorities, and peoples of subordinated or marginalized regions. Literature of Romantic kinds has even been used increasingly to attribute sovereign subjectivity of a kind to groups still excluded from participation in the modern state, particularly children and non-human animate nature—a fact that may not be unconnected to the steady rise of children's rights and animal rights in the past two centuries. At the same time, to remain outside of or be excluded from literature of Romantic kinds is to remain subordinated and to permit rationalization of such subordination. Yet some groups choose that alternative, or try to use literature for their own purposes and in ways sanctioned by their own ideologies and cultural practices. An example in my own country, Canada, would be the Doukhobors, a religious sect of Ukrainian immigrants with powerful and continuing commitments to communal identity and life; they reject state education and institutions, including, as it seems, literature, though recently they have begun experimenting with a form of collective autobiography, apparently in order to persuade the Canadian political nation and the Canadian state to leave them alone.

Several related questions can be posed not so much to close as to re-open this sketch of the collusion of Romanticism with the founding of modern liberal states. First, do post-modernism, globalism, and the development of the European and other supra-national states mean the end of the Romantic state and the opening of a new phase of history? Second, was the revolutionary potential of Romanticism exhausted with its collusion in the founding of the modern liberal state? Third, can re-opening the history of that collusion also lead us beyond that state? Finally, the example of the Doukhobors provokes us to ask if there may be other valid identities that the state and its still largely Romantic literature do not enable us to imagine, and if literature, perhaps of other kinds, may not serve other, and preferable, kinds of political and social organization.

WORKS CITED

Anderson, Benedict. *Imagined Communities: Reflections on the Origin and Spread of Nationalism*. Revised ed. London and New York: Verso, 1991.

Droz, Jacques. *Europe Between Revolutions 1815-1848*. Trans. Robert Baldick. London: Fontana, 1967.

Fukuyama, Francis. *The End of History and the Last Man.* New York: Free Press, 1992.

Jardin, André, and André-jean Tudesq. *The Cambridge History of Modern France: Restoration and Reaction 1815-1848.* Trans. Elborg Forster. Cambridge: Cambridge University Press, 1983.

Sanderson, Stephen K. *Social Transformations: A General Theory of Historical Development.* Oxford and Cambridge, MA: Blackwell, 1995.

Schulze, Hagen. *States, Nations and Nationalism: From the Middle Ages to the Present.* Trans. William E. Yuill. Oxford and Malden: Blackwell, 1998.

Thom, Martin. *Republics, Nations and Tribes.* London and New York: Verso, 1995.

Wallerstein, Immanuel. "The French Revolution as World-Historical Event." *The French Revolution and the Birth of Modernity.* Ed. Ferenc Fehér. Berkeley: University of California Press, 1990. 117-30.

Williams, Raymond. *Keywords: A Vocabulary of Culture and Society.* Glasgow: Fontana, 1976.

Woolf, Stuart. *A History of Italy 1700-1860: The Social Constraints of Political Change.* London and New York: Routledge, 1979.

CAPITAL FLOWS THROUGH LANGUAGE
Market English and the World Bank

J. Paul Narkunas

In 1997 the World Bank Group[1] published in English one of its many country studies, entitled *Vietnam: Education Financing*. Its goal was to measure "what changes in educational policies will ensure that students who pass through the system today will acquire the knowledge, skills and attitudes needed for Vietnam to complete the transition successfully from a planned to a market economy?"[2] Skills, knowledge and attitude designate for the Bank the successfully "educated" Vietnamese national subject. The educational "system" performs, therefore, a disciplinary function by using the technologies of the nation-state to cultivate productive humans—measured by technical expertise and computer and business skills—for transnational companies who do business in the region. Certain attributes, however, bring excellent returns:

---

[1] The World Bank Group includes the International Bank for Reconstruction and Development, the International Development Corporation, the Multilateral Investment Guarantee Agency (MIGA) and the International Center for Settlement of Investment Disputes. The World Bank is actually comprised of the IBRD and IDA, which serve different clients. The IDA is the development organ of the most impoverished countries of the world that are suspect in their creditworthiness due in part to a below-acceptable per capita income level. Higher per capita countries qualify for IBRD grants. They share the same offices, strictures and staff, but merely mark two different tiers of financing. The International Finance Corporation was created in 1956 to lend and invest in private companies in developing countries that cannot attract private funding. The Bank instigated the IFC because of the threat that the United Nations would start a competing development organization. It has become an increasingly powerful tool of the Bank as its mandate for ubiquitous privatization has increased over time. MIGA, founded in 1988, offers insurance to private investors in developing countries to protect investors in the event of political upheaval. ICSID has moderated disputes between governments and private investors since its creation in 1966. See Catherine Caufield's magisterial study of the Bank in *Masters of Illusion: The World Bank and the Poverty of Nations* (New York: Henry Holt, 1996).

[2] See *Vietnam: Education Financing* (Washington, DC: World Bank, 1997), xiii.

> Many foreign languages have been imposed on Vietnam over the centuries—Chinese, French, and Russian. Today, English has emerged as the dominant language for business in the East Asian region, and there is considerable incentive for Vietnamese to learn English, especially as Vietnam joins Association Southeast Asian Nation (ASEAN) and the economy opens up. According to preliminary HEGTS (Higher Education Graduate Tracer Study) results, those graduates with more than elementary proficiency in the English language earn 8 percent more than do others. English language training will increase the lifetime earnings of recent graduates enough to yield a rate of return of between five and eight percent on the individuals' investments.[3]

The World Bank ignores England's and the United States' colonial and imperial legacies in the world, particularly in Southeast Asia. Instead, English proliferates "naturally" for the Bank because it is an effect of inhuman complex forces—of the market, capital, and their system. Unlike the colonial ventures of France and China, where there is willful force orchestrated in the sovereign interests of specific nation-states, the flow of English happens due to the "spontaneous" organization of market forces. Learning English as a primary, secondary, or tertiary language indicates that one is integrated into the global market or, as the Bank suggests, consents to the "right" attitude.

In this essay, I will address what the Bank's mechanical rationalism and economism take for granted about English. Thinking of English within the center of the humanist tradition as a sign of a national history, literature, and

[3] Ibid., 109. Other reported factors include that men earn 8% more than women, that knowledge of spreadsheets was important, and that computer programming was a lucrative profession. All of this information seems to presume a subject from heavily industrialized countries with massive wealth accumulation, rather than an impoverished country like Vietnam, where, despite a highly-educated work force, the preservation of life is still a struggle due to famine, basic health concerns, and massive unemployment due, ironically, to wage compression and the massive auctioning of state industries per World Bank loan conditionalities.

culture has fallen apart, and fails to think English's increasing role as a language of the global market, flowing as capital. Yet considering English outside the humanist tradition of cultural formation does not unleash mere anarchy upon the world, but forces reflection on how English functions more as a commodity, a mechanism, and a device. The transformation of English from signifier of national culture to commodity announces emerging relations of force and power other than the sovereign exercise of force. I will discuss how English operates as a form of what philosopher Michel Foucault calls bio-power. Bio-power produces and manages a "population" that can exist indeterminately from geography, or from such technologies of the nation-state as language, culture, and history.[4] In other words, the population is the primary locus of organized "biopolitics," not the state, nation, or people. Bio-power names dynamic networks of relations that construct the human as a technical system—in other words, as a matrix or locus where force and power relations are exercised. Consequently, I will use the term "Market English" below to emphasize that the language is not connected to a specific nation-state, culture, or national history, and to draw attention to the virtual universalization of neo-liberalist (laissez-faire capitalist) discourses, the waning sovereignty of nation-states, as well as the flow of forms of intelligence or agency that do not have the production of citizen subjects or national subjects as their function.[5]

The World Bank and the International Monetary Fund (IMF) form the Bretton Woods Institutions, and were created in 1945 as economic regulatory mechanisms to fore-

[4] See Michel Foucault, *The History of Sexuality, Vol. 1*, trans. Robert Hurley (New York: Pantheon, 1978), particularly Part Five: "Right of Death and Power Over Life," 135-59.

[5] I focus on the World Bank because of its institutionalization of development discourses, often overlooked in the post-World War II moment by many scholars of cultural studies and postcolonial studies who emphasize decolonization. However, the discourse of development ironically has become the common sense of the global system as decolonizing nations measure the vitality of newly emerging "postcolonial" sovereign nation-states.

stall potential economic crises lurking in the global economic system. The Bank's auspicious history began as the International Bank for Reconstruction and Development (IBRD) to help rebuild Europe after WWII, but soon branched out into making loans for the impoverished world.[6] Although it is technically an umbrella organization of the United Nations, the World Bank has since grown to become the wealthiest and foremost development institution of the world. The Bank holds 11 percent of public and private debt in the impoverished world, and its loans often pave the way for foreign direct investment from private companies.[7] Nation-states form partnerships with the Bretton Woods institutions because they need an infusion of capital and have no other options. Yet there is an obvious uneven relationship because of the structure of debt.

Structural Adjustment Loans (SALs), introduced in 1979 by then President of the World Bank Robert McNamara, mark a turn in the Bank's history, toward intervening in spaces that were previously the domain of national sovereignty. (Incidentally, McNamara was the Secretary of Defense during the Kennedy and Johnson administrations and was responsible for much of the military escalation of the US during the Vietnam War, earning him the moniker of the "Butcher of Hanoi" during the late 60's.) Designed as quick disbursing loans to thwart an existing or impending "balance of payment" loan crisis, SALs represent a shift in the Bank's emphasis from lending only for specific projects—say, the building of a dam—to policy-based lending that carries specific provisions to which countries that take these loans must adhere. Indeed, programs of "structural adjustment" invariably require currency devaluation; trade liberalization; privatization of state industries; a reduced role for government, including reduced social spending; high interest rates; and a compression of

---

[6] The Bank is situated in Washington, DC, at 1818 H Street, ironically in a former State Department building, and its language of business is English.

[7] Caufield, 2.

wages.[8] These tactics interfere in the economic policy of autonomous nation-states by obligating them to shift resources from production for the domestic economy to export in the global market.[9] Furthermore, when debt payments come due, more funds are forthcoming to service the outstanding debts, creating endless cycles of loan disbursement and debt servicing. Indeed, only Barbados (1993) and South Korea (1995) have "graduated" from the Bank's cycle of loans and debt servicing. Failure to fulfill debt obligations accrues further debt from the World Bank or the IMF, and increases the Bank's intervention and prescriptive mandates. The Bank has even been involved in the crafting of constitutional amendments for sovereign countries to remove restrictions that would keep them from taking out loans with the Bank.[10] The endless drain of capital, people, and resources to service debts to the World Bank and its creditors makes it impossible, however, to realize the economic benefits and freedoms offered by World Bank strictures. In this capacity, debt operates as a system of management and control, a hybrid form of hegemony and incorporation into the global market. In other words, debt functions as a complex matrix of power and management techniques that challenges the sovereign power of nation-states through fluid and dynamic "open" systems of control. This begs the question how debt to the World Bank performs as statist forms of control—*étatisation* in Foucault's parlance—in an array of intellectual, po-

[8] See Susan George and Fabrizio Sabelli's *Faith and Credit: The World Bank's Secular Empire* (Boulder, CO: Westview Press, 1994) for further details.

[9] According to Richard Feinberg, the World Bank can "influence [...] Third World Countries and [...] international capital markets. Desperate for help, debtors and creditors alike are willing to devolve a portion of previously guarded management prerogatives to a capable international agency, and the Bank alone is fit for the task." See Richard Feinberg, et al., *Between Two Worlds: The World Bank's Next Decade* (New Brunswick, NJ: Transaction Books, 1986), 3.

[10] Caufield discusses how this practice occurred in Mexico. The amendment that was instituted entailed the privatization of communal farms, which resulted in large fiefdoms held by single landlords. The Zapatista movement actually arose from these "policies," and has been an outspoken critic of these formations.

litical, economic, and cultural formations that usurp the sovereign force of the nation-state.[11]

Vietnam's "partnership" with the World Bank portrays, for example, how nation-states auction their sovereignty to global institutions. In 1986 the government of Vietnam instigated a program of *doi moi*, "renovation," that sanctioned a program of market liberalization. At the time of "renovation" Vietnam's statist technologies were on the verge of bankruptcy, in part due to prolonged wars with France, Japan, the United States, Cambodia, and China, and also due to the financial instability of the Soviet Union, its primary trading partner and patron at the time. Although Vietnam's strong nationalist tradition has repelled every single invading military force, virtually nonstop warfare between 1945 and 1989 has left it one of the poorest countries in the world, leading to a form of "economic colonizaton" by the Bretton Woods institutions.[12] According to economist Michel Chossudovsky, the Vietnamese government repeatedly devalued the *dong* against the dollar between 1984 and 1985 per an IMF suggestion as a way to curb inflation and generate liquidity for the government's industries.[13] Poverty subsequently intensified, and the government was forced to obtain extensive loans with the IMF and World Bank.[14] The World Bank required

---

[11] It is for this reason that Foucault would suggest that the state merely serves to represent "as mythicized abstractions" forces of control and management that he called "governmentality." See his essay "Governmentality," in *The Foucault Effect*, ed. Graham Burchell, et al. (Chicago: University of Chicago Press, 1991), 87-104.

[12] After reunification of North and South Vietnam in 1976, Vietnam's entire economy still remained mobilized for warfare due to its occupation of Cambodia (1978-1989), which spawned tensions with China culminating in China's invasion of Vietnam in 1979. Outfitting a standing army of one million troops drained needed liquidity and resources because 40% of GNP routinely went to defense. See Nigel Thrift and Dean Forbes' *The Price of War: Urbanization in Vietnam – 1954-1985* (London: Allen & Unwin, 1986), 60.

[13] See Chapter 8, "The Post War Economic Destruction of Vietnam," in *The Globalization of Poverty: Impacts of IMF and World Bank Reforms* (London: Zed Books, 1997), 149-153.

[14] Since Vietnam's movement to a market economy began, the dollar has become the store of value and, in effect, a safer mechanism of exchange than the local

severe macroeconomic reforms in Vietnam, including the privatization of Vietnam's heavy industries, its agricultural production, and its education and health systems. The results were disastrous. According to Chossudovsky, using the World Bank's own statistics: "[F]ive thousand (out of a total of 12,000) state enterprises have been driven into bankruptcy [by 1994], [and] more than a million workers and some 200,000 public employees [by 1992], including thousands of teachers and health workers, have been laid off."[15]

The Vietnamese nation-state does not provide a mode of resistance to financial or global capital in this configuration. This has become especially apparent in light of the World Bank's initiatives on education in Vietnam. The Bank pledged over $83.3 million by 1997 to implement programs of "coherence, flexibility, accountability, efficiency and transparency" for Vietnam's education system. Due to these sizable loans, the Vietnamese state's oversight of projects in education depends upon the imperatives and loan agreements of the World Bank. The World Bank, in concert with other supra-national organizations and non-governmental institutions like the United Nations Educational, Scientific, and Cultural Organization (UNESCO), increasingly affects educational policies that were once the exclusive domain of the state.[16] In the process, a hegemonic set of codes and procedures appears throughout the world, facilitating the efficiency of this system for transnational corporations. By having potential workers with the same technical skills—such as English and computer knowl-

currency, the *dong*. In other words, Vietnam's economy is tied to the fluctuations of the American dollar.

[15] Ibid., 147. The government, through "decision no. 111," planned to lay off another 100,000 workers by 1994 to cut the civil service a further 20%. Ibid., 151.

[16] The World Bank shares a similar mission to UNESCO, but it does not share the latter's pretense to maintaining cultural heritage, or working with the nation-state to maintain an international system of national and cultural states. The Bank's foremost operating principle, it seems, is lending, which has often led to hastily prepared projects that are never actually followed to measure their success.

edge—anywhere in the world, a corporation can move where it likes and use locals to gain entrance to other markets, a luxury that citizens in nation-states cannot afford. In effect, the government of Vietnam merely heightens the efficiency of the global system by mobilizing people within Vietnam for the global market.

HUMAN CAPITAL

The World Bank has increasingly focused on education as part of its "human capital" development initiatives throughout the '90s,[17] demonstrating that it is no longer merely the tool of infrastructure building. The escalation of investment in education by the World Bank is part of its "poverty reduction" mandate because it has recognized that humans are technical resources that can be refined for productivity.[18] Affecting education policy is very impor-

---

[17] The eminent Nobel Prize-winning economist Theodore Schultz championed the idea of human capital in 1960. Humans were resources overlooked by nation-states and corporations that could be cultivated to improve efficiency, capital accumulation and flow. Schultz suggested that the investment in human capital would produce enormous benefits to remove disparities between social classes. Education would permeate society because human beings could never stop refining themselves along the path of evolution and development. Schultz thought education would produce enormous benefits in the Third World. Consequently, Schultz's article provides the incentive behind the World Bank's "Investing in People" series. For Schultz, there was a direct correspondence between education and the systematic extirpation of poverty: "Some growth of course can be had from the increase in more conventional capital even though the labor that is available is lacking both in skill and knowledge. But the rate of growth will be severely limited....It is simply not possible to have the fruits of a modern agriculture and the abundance of modern industry without making large investments in human beings." In "Investment in Human Capital," *The American Economic Review Vol.* 51: 1 (March 1961): 16. Schultz has provided the mantra for the World Bank's emphasis on human capital. (Indeed, it is still cited even in the Vietnam document of 1997.) Education was to be one tool in alleviating poverty in the third world, and for helping to put this unrecognized labor-power to work. These tendencies persist, as the World Bank has spent considerable money directing funds to women's health care and education as a mechanism to forestall overpopulation. Development through the alleviation of poverty would create a more secure and organized world without economic or social differences.

[18] Robert McNamara initiated this program in the early 1970s. The Bank's focus on education has increased substantially because health and education are two of the most prominent sectors that nation-states must sacrifice when selling off state

tant for the Bank because of the historical importance of education as a domain of the nation-state, and its lasting impact on the future.[19] The Bank plays a singularly important role in international lending for education because it is armed with endless reserves of capital, an army of consultants, and a mission to perfect: "The World Bank's experiences and the policy implications of those experiences carry particularly significant weight in how educational development and lending proceeds worldwide. With more than US $4 billion flowing to developing countries annually for education and training, the World Bank will have an important impact on educational change—hence economic development—in the coming decade."[20] Moreover, the Bank has a new consensus that education loans have a high rate of return on investment, and can successfully produce the policies that the Bank wants. The Bank loans $2 billion dollars a year for education, which makes up nine percent of its annual budget.[21]

Nation-states have historically fostered their legitimacy through citizens. Education plays the primary role for state forces in the production of citizen-subjects. Language and national literatures have played an essential part in the creation and sanctioning of culture in the West to define the history of human experience through subject formation. The organic model of culture that unites the "authentic" cultural subject with a language comes from the Ger-

---

assets as a requirement for structural adjustment loans. The Bank has also been remaking itself more and more throughout the Nineties as a knowledge-based research institution. It spends $100 million a year on research for country-clients, as well as providing larger theoretical papers on "global" strategies. Since then, the Bank has become increasingly interested in education financing and the production of education initiatives, due to its virtually unparalleled wealth and ability to enact programs.

[19] In particular, the Bank argues unironically that educating women is extremely important because educated women have fewer children and can work more productively. Such a policy demonstrates, it claims, its commitment to feminist politics.

[20] *Vietnam: Education Financing*, 37.

[21] Since the 1970s the World Bank has been the single largest provider of external funding for its programs of educational development, providing approximately 15 percent of all official external aid to education.

man idealist tradition of Friedrich Schleiermacher and Johann Fichte, and, most synthetically, Alexander von Humboldt. (Humboldt, it should be recalled, is responsible for the organization of the University of Berlin in 1807 and 1810 that serves still as the structure of the university for much of Europe and Japan.) The learning process includes accumulating knowledge over time [*Wissenschaft*], expertise in language, national history, and a set of identities by which to recognize the community and its differences from other communities. Training, or *bildung*, forms the character and morality of individuals as reflections of that culture, or in other words, as subjects of the state.[22] Indeed, technologies of the state codify culture and histories to produce continuity between generations and ascribe a culture to territory; in the process, they circulate an ideal and guiding principle of what its citizens are supposed to embody. Departing from this conception, writing, national language, and literature presume, therefore, a state-form in order to standardize and arrange their structures of expression through a grammar, phonetic matrix, and symbolic regime.[23] Inclusion within a language marks an individual's acculturation, the success of culture as marking the human and national subject, which has a consciousness, can reflect critically, and thus participate as a citizen-subject of the state.[24] In other words, the *langage d'etat* re-

---

[22] This entire paragraph owes a debt to Bill Readings' *The University in Ruins* (Cambridge, MA: Harvard University Press, 1997) and to Giorgio Agamben's *Infancy and History: Reflections on the Destruction of Experience* (London: Verso, 1991).

[23] See Gilles Deleuze and Felix Guattari, *A Thousand Plateaus: Capitalism and Schizophrenia*, trans. Brian Massumi (Minneapolis: University of Minnesota Press, 1987), chapters entitled "The War Machine" (351-423) and "Apparatus of Capture" (424-473).

[24] A subject with an identity can be recognized, disciplined, and simultaneously protected by the law. See Giorgio Agamben, *Homo Sacer: Sovereign Power and Bare Life*, trans. Daniel Heller-Roazen (Stanford: Stanford University Press, 1998), particularly the following: "In exactly the same way only language as the pure potentiality to signify, withdrawing itself from every concrete instance of speech, divides the linguistic from the nonlinguistic and allows for the opening of areas of meaningful speech in which certain terms correspond to certain denotations. Language is the sovereign who, in a permanent state of exception, declares that

quires the nation-state's funding and codification. (For example, elites and then institutions of the British government funded scholars for over sixty years to create the first volume of the *Oxford English Dictionary*.) What happens when funding of education shifts from sovereign nation-states to techno-bureaucratic institutions like the World Bank that do not need to produce citizens to foster their legitimacy?

The World Bank has little use for the nation-state system's tools of national culture, national history, and a national language. Such a notion of education substantially differs from humanist and Enlightenment concepts of education, which envision the human subject as the central agent of the world. The Bank institutes the German idealist's development model of *bildung* formation by development over time, but deviates in its goals. Utility is both the origin and final goal (telos) of the Bank's education policies. It has no need for something like the human condition, or a concept of culture as resistant and redemptive, as is pervasive in some US cultural studies circles. Indeed, the study of culture is of no use to the World Bank, save as a commodity to facilitate the tourist industries. Tourism is one of the Bank's main prescriptions for sustaining economic development, and such industries need a raw material like culture to multiply difference and facilitate the production and extension of new sites of capital accumulation.[25]

The Bank's deployment of culture as a commodity suggests a need for cultural critics to think further on how cultural practices and their intellectual arguments can be quickly incorporated into a discourse that works contrary

---

there is nothing outside language and that language is always beyond itself. The particular structure of law has its foundation in this presuppositional structure of human language. It expresses the bond of inclusive exclusion to which a thing is subject because of the fact of being in language, of being named. To speak is, in this sense, always to 'speak the law,' *ius dicere*" (21).

[25] See Jean-Francois Lyotard's highly ironic "Marie Goes to Japan," in *Postmodern Fables*, trans. Géorges Van Den Abbeele (Minneapolis: University of Minnesota Press, 1997).

to their intentions. In some area of US cultural studies, for example, transnational analysis is gaining ground as a tool of resistance to globalization; however, the Bank deems transnational analysis cost-effective for creating regional trade and intellectual blocs. According to the Bank, "There is considerable room for making universities more cost-effective by regionalizing certain expensive specialties and by developing alternatives to traditional, European-style university education....This requires more, not less, investment in higher education and research, but in a more cost-effective manner and one that probably transcends national boundaries."[26] The Bank has no need for citizen subjects, so critical to modernity's organization of knowledge and the nation-state. Instead, money is spent on training and skills acquisition. Human practices, such as the humanities, are streamlined because they are not efficient. Education does not guarantee, in other words, the production of subjects with wills who think and make rational choices, often associated with the subject of the nation-state. Rather, education produces total quality managers who can perpetually acquire new skills and consume mechanized and easily fungible knowledge.[27] These new managers efficiently plug into the network to manipulate forces, but avoid disrupting the efficiency of the system. They operate as conduits of and for information—like living databases—which have the capacity to act in a number of fluid situations. In short, humans in this capacity are capital.

---

[26] Wadi Haddad, Martin Carnoy, Rosemary Rinaldi, and Omporn Regel, *Education and Development: Evidence for New Priorities* (Washington, DC: The World Bank, 1990), 61.

[27] See Jean-Marie Guéhenno's *La fin de la démocratie* (Paris: Flammarion, 1994), in English as *The End of the Nation-State*, trans. Victoria Elliot (Minneapolis: University of Minnesota Press, 1996). See also the work of Gilles Deleuze, Michel Foucault, Jean-François Lyotard, and Giorgio Agamben for elaborations and articulations of this line of thinking.

MARKET ENGLISH

Market English is a skill or tool that expedites the efficiency of the global system.[28] English maintains hegemony in the publication of global intellectual production with particular significance in medicine, science, and economics. According to UNESCO statistics, 1.3 billion out of the 4.5 billion humans in the world have some familiarity with English.[29] Fifty percent of all translations in the world are into English, while only 6% of the world's intellectual production is translated from another language into English.[30] This is not to suggest that English is being standardized—far from it, if one considers Singapore English (Singlish), Konglish, Jamaican English, or the multiple forms of linguistic expression in every country where English is spoken. Rather language as constitutive of a particular national tradition is losing its critical force. Even in countries where English is the so-called native language, like the US, literacy requirements are barely fulfilled even after years of schooling. I want to emphasize that English does not function as a universal global language, but as an instrumental language conducive to international commerce,

---

[28] In Europe, for example, the European Union frequently uses English as a relay language to cut the costs of translators between, say, Finnish and Italian. According to the European Bureau of Lesser Used Languages, 42% of European Union citizens indicated that they could converse in English, compared to 31% German and 29% French. For more information on English's pervasiveness, see David Crystal, *English as a Global Language* (Cambridge: Cambridge University Press,1997, 82. Crystal's insidious text received funding from the "English-only movement" in the United States, which is trying to constitutionally mandate English as the language of state in the US.

[29] Wlad Godzich, in his "Global English: English and the Future," offered this statistic in his paper presented at the University of Pittsburgh, April 15, 1998.

[30] See the UNESCO website section for translation statistics in "Index Translationum: Did you Know? English Dominates," at http://www.unesco.org/culture/xtrans/html_engl/index6.htm. As UNESCO acknowledges: "Certain publishing houses tend to use the difficulty of finding good translators as an excuse to hide their reluctance to pay translation rights....This is perhaps one way of controlling the market and maintaining the cultural dominance of English and the market is controlled through what is on offer, through the availability of products sold by the industry of culture—whether it is music, or films, or books."

tourism, and international governance technologies. For example, it is the official language of the Association of Southeast Asian Nations (ASEAN) and Asia-Pacific Economic Council (APEC), customs declarations, air-traffic controllers, maritime agreements, and international contracts.

Although English's ubiquity does mark the trace of an imperial legacy of the United States and Britain in Asia, principally during the Cold War and especially the Vietnam War, and during transformations in the global economy such as the economic rise in Asia of Singapore and Hong Kong, many perceive English as a language that does not belong to any specific nation-state of Asia. It is "neutral" only in the sense that it no longer bears the mark of a colonial or imperial center, but rather indicates a tool to achieve economic development.[31] In fact, English language training is frequently left to private companies. An effect of this formation is that English language programs teach "Basic English" or "tourist English," which merely provide a series of English-language scripts of various client contexts that can be rehearsed. However, any use of

[31] The Vietnamese nation-state's role transformed from the moment it instigated *doi moi*, but perhaps even earlier with its implementation of the notion of development. Development is not only an economic, historical, or biological idea. Instead, it names a non-teleological conceptual matrix premised on indeterminate unfolding without finality and without reference. Jean-François Lyotard in his "Introduction: About the Human" in *The Inhuman: Reflections on Time*, trans. Geoff Bennington and Rachel Bowlby (Stanford, CA: Stanford University, 1991), 6-7 is important here for describing what he calls the "metaphysics of development," a "negative entrop[ic] system of complexity." This delineates development as chaotic and indeterminate differentiation, and yet simultaneously mediation and systematization in order to save time and energy. The "metaphysics of development" has no end for humans: "the interest of humans is subordinate in this to that of the survival of complexity" (6). The limitless extension of development disintegrates the adequation of an idea attached to the human, "like that of the emancipation of reason and of human freedoms"(7). Indeed, as Lyotard describes, development operates as quanta of force with the capacity of infinite extension; it also names permutating networks that are made intelligible or stratified, which perennially connect and organize disparate practices and forms in the world. Nonetheless, development disciplines chaotic and divergent forces into a structure of unfolding or evolution. In this capacity, development channels forces, but lives off them in a fluid or parasitic manner.

English outside of the script exceeds the limits of this mechanized or transparent English. The US and Britain are, therefore, not selling culture or a specific way of life with its language, but rather a commodity that facilitates market integration and the cash-nexus. Needless to say, this system is being fostered to help companies from the US and Britain to penetrate and gain leverage in markets throughout the world.

Market English flows with transnational capital, seeming to belong to everyone and no one, much like the market. Market English transforms continuously from its standardized or grammatical form, for much of it derives from televisual media, music, and movies. In this formation English is oral and visual, not textual and symbolic, or the domain of the law and technique of state. The language is therefore more likely inflected by the lyrics of the Spice Girls than Charles Dickens or William Shakespeare. Consequently, new formations of humans emerge who can rehearse the song lyrics of 'N-Sync or Rage Against the Machine with impeccable American accents, but cannot understand what they are saying. In this situation we have an articulation without reference, a statement without reference. A language divorced from reference, national history, and state formation indicates an interesting facet of Market English's circulation. English increasingly operates as a vehicle of communication detached from the notion of a bond between a state, national identity or culture, historical tradition, and geographical territory that has guided modernity and the technology of the European nation-state. It does not need to be formally funded by the state organization, and therefore does not follow the same acculturation technologies as colonialism and imperialism.

Access to, and knowledge of, English may facilitate the production of new forms of life: a "global human" who gains advantage through knowledge of the market and the possibility of becoming freed from the determinate horizon of the nation. Let me offer an example. Vietnam has one of the highest literacy rates in the world. UNESCO awarded Vietnam a literacy award in 1998 for its commitment to literacy because more than 93% of its population can read and write Vietnamese.[32] The Vietnamese nation adhered to humanist and Enlightenment conceptions of culture by allocating money to maintain the language as the bearer of the culture, as part of repeated government mandates on language acquisition in the aftermath of its 1975 victory over US-backed South Vietnam. In this regard, Vietnam demonstrates an often-repeated move by countries in the wake of decolonization. By preserving the language, national history and culture are unshackled or reborn at the moment of decolonization. In this capacity, the condition of "Vietnameseness" is marked as the ability to speak and be literate in the language.

Since moving to market reforms, however, the level of those who are "functionally literate" has not dropped. Nonetheless, the number of students forced to leave school because of newly instituted fees has risen dramatically. The state has so quickly divested itself of education that it now requires fees for every level of schooling. Access to education has ceased to be a universal right of citizenship, but is connected to the accumulation of wealth. At the same time, an increasing number of literate Vietnamese subjects do not have the necessary skills to work with transnational corporations because they do not speak English. They have become, in the language of commerce, redundant. Literate Vietnamese merely become unnecessary or stores of culture that have no value in the market. Culture conceived as reflection of linguistic expression or as vehicle of knowledge does not seem to have a future in this brave new world.

Developing into authentic market subjects for the World Bank (and in the process transcending the disciplinary mechanisms of the nation-state) requires learning English. The World Bank does not need, however, to pro-

[32] See *Vietnam News*, the official statement of the Vietnamese consulate in the US, at http://www.viam.com.

mote English in its curriculum reform, nor does it need to attach it as one of its loan requirements. Moreover, the World Bank does not represent sovereign or institutional power insofar as it does not fund or create institutions of governance, education, or language training for the production of literate subject-citizens. Rather, it fosters a fluid system that creates and regulates subjects into a floating population of managers, who assess risk to avoid general crises to the system on the order of economic collapse or revolution. In short, the World Bank tries to define the limit of what was previously the sovereign decision, namely, what life is "worth living." The sovereign decision of who or what can be a citizen gives way to defining what a human is and can be. The control of the very definition of the human through the management of life is what Foucault calls bio-power. Bio-power in this emerging formation is a form of life that follows the discourses of market liberalization and economic development—in other words, the production of human capital. Language acquisition is not the right of entry for citizenship, but can help define life that is worth living in the impoverished world, as exemplified by Vietnam. Those who speak English have a comparative advantage; others are considered redundant and relegated to the black hole of poverty, which is no longer confined solely to specific geographies.

With the waning sovereignty of nation-states over their people and the increased role of transcultural and parastatal organizations like the World Bank, I am suggesting that we need different conceptual tools for thinking about the emerging systems of complexity and development. If the human can only be conceived as capital by the World Bank and nation-states, we must imagine nothing less than an inhuman form of agency that does not have the human as its referent or object. We ought to begin by acknowledging that no predetermined language of the national subject exists: language is not the bearer of knowledge or the human. It may, however, function as bio-power, and determine the limits of what forms of life are worth living.

Market English forces reflection on inchoate formations of society, and on what forms society and community. Language must be thought of differently—in other words, no longer as an organic structure of being and identity. Organic formations of language codify the different forms of enunciation that exist within each language to engender a codified national subject who speaks a language. Languages, conceived as organic forms, put other languages into relation and mark their differences. They gain coherence for the state only when articulated next to other languages. In other words, language becomes standardized communication and information precisely when other people do not understand it. Culture and its relation to expression, however, will not redeem us in this global formation, which ascribes an economic value to every form of human expression. We see this paradox in the so-called "subversive" work in US cultural studies circles that frequently relies on a concept of culture's redemptive abilities and the capacity of nation-states to challenge economic forces. At the same time, they find themselves being slowly phased out because they cannot defend how they add value.

Recognizing the indeterminacy of semiotic regimes problematizes the organic notions of language and reference that we see proliferating in heinous acts of ethnic violence, where language and ethnicity are collapsed into being. Instead, language must be addressed as a coalescence of several coexisting regimes of signs that do not add up to a predetermined register of writing, or have a corresponding referent. We need to acknowledge that every sign is merely a sign of another sign; the referent does not hold. There is utterance without reference.

As Michel Foucault suggests, language must be a thinking that simultaneously provokes the "outside of thought"—in other words, unraveling the limits of nation, people, and aggregates of identities. Language functions for Foucault as an indeterminate matter, a "collective assemblage of enunciation" that does not have the human as an object.[33] Through non-linguistic or nonrepresentational aspects of language, we may find some ways to struggle with such fluid organizations as the World Bank. In short, conceiving language as chaotic and fluid relations of force, as always exceeding our grasp or attempts to structure it as culture, is nothing less than to think language physically and mathematically. In short, it is to think language not as pre-given, but as relations of forces, energy, and molecules that forces of power try to discipline, domesticate, make national or native. Considering language as fluctuating matter and function may provide some lines of flight for thinking's potential in the emerging global system. Otherwise, we may sit waiting for a debt to be repaid by language's redemptive qualities, and the immaculate return of state sovereignty and cultural resistance. But the debt we think is only a state of emergency is the rule.

[33] "The Thought of the Outside," in *Aesthetics, Method, and Epistemology*, ed. James Faubian (New York: Free Press, 1998), 151.

IL MURO DI GUTENBERG

Grazia Sotis

In un discorso di globalizzazione culturale, nel suo nuovo romanzo, *Il muro di Gutenbeng*, Giuseppe Cassieri raggiunge una sintesi storica e culturale. I rapporti interdisciplinari, dati dalla presenza di studiosi di varie materie riunitisi sull'isola di Ventotene, per discutere di temi nuovi per il convegno europeo di Anversa, ne evidenziano la natura e la mutazione di valori. Il concetto di globalizzazione implica una conflittualità che esiste anche nel titolo del romanzo. Johann Gutenberg usò nuovi strumenti per la fabbricazione degli specchi, così erano chiamati allora quei libretti, manoscritti, o xilografici, che si vendevano nelle sagre e nei mercati, quindi di ampia diffusione. Oggi Internet permette la diffusione globale e universale, ma è anch'essa un motivo di dibattito. Giorgio Bocca dice che (*L'Espresso*, 17 febbraio, 2000) "assistiamo al formarsi di una nuova casta, con i suoi linguaggi ermetici, le sue corrispondenze e i suoi rapporti elitari." In fondo è il concetto di cultura ad essere messo in discussione, così come avviene nel libro di Cassieri. Uno dei personaggi, Mauro Sparagna, è il sostenitore che "che tutto deve andare a tutti" e in ciò "vede la mirabile corsa a un futuro senza recinti e senza scarti, senza privilegi e senza analfabeti" (67). Una cultura che abbatte qualunque tipo di barriera. D'altro canto c'è la presa di posizione di un altro partecipante, Fabio Gerace, che riassume la teoria anticonflittuale dell'uguaglianza e della diversità. Possiamo riportare quanto affermato da Furio Colombo a proposito di Bill Gates, dell'uomo senza cultura: Gates abbandona gli studi per fare "cose utili." In tutto ciò, continua Colombo, "non c'è nulla di culturale. Non lascia spazio alla dignità o anche solo alla legittimità della cultura. Ogni attività teorica e riflessiva viene screditata. Il compito delle avanguardie è assorbito dalla tecnica" (156). Una tecnica che tende a livellare perfino la scrittura in un processo di globalizzazione, possiamo aggiungere noi, stilistica, per dare vita a una creazione di un linguaggio virtuale privo della componente trascendentale ed utopica che esso dovrebbe avere.

La scrittura è l'espressione di un processo intellettuale tale da considerarla una metafora che contraddistingue l'identità anagrafica, storica e culturale di ogni scrittore. Secondo Wolf Lepenies "... il processo intellettuale e morale consiste in una storia fatta di metafore più efficaci e non nell'aumento della nostra conoscenza su come sono veramente le cose" (82). Scrittura intesa metaforicamente quindi è ciò che permette lo slittamento di confini sia territoriali sia culturali.

Nel romanzo Cassieri valica i confini regionali e per regionali intendiamo sia quelli pugliesi, la Puglia essendo la sua terra d'origine, sia italiani. La territorialità dello scrittore è di fatto un recupero della tradizione storica della sua terra. Ciò lo porta ad assimilarla e a viverla in un contesto di vita moderna non necessariamente italiano. È utile definire lo scrittore attraverso i suoi personaggi, e per questo prenderemo in considerazione altri suoi due romanzi precedenti, *I festeggiamenti* e *Diario di un convertito,* ai quali faremo riferimento durante lo svolgimento del lavoro. Ad essi aggiungiamo l'apporto di una cultura "bassa," se per bassa intendiamo quella non ufficiale delle favole e racconti popolari. Sarà proprio la sua traduzione interpretativa delle favole pugliesi dal dialetto a una considerazione de *Il muro di Gutenberg* di una favola moderna o mito, tale da prescindere da qualunque configurazione territoriale e temporale.

Nel romanzo Willy è la voce dell'autore. Egli esprime il significato di che cosa sia la letteratura, pur essendo un antropologo che "...non inventa...non conosce rapimenti...rielabora magari impreziosisce vecchi manufatti, toglie qualche crosta, segnala guasti e vizi di forma sotto gli stucchi e li tramanda corretti" (11). Non è di certo una "confusione di generi," lui si avvale della sua esperienza per recuperare una dimensione della storia e della società che altrimenti andrebbe perduta, al punto che lo potremmo porre come una forza e prova contrastante all'affermazione di Lepenies che "l'arte, che a lungo tempo ha compensato la scomparsa della dimensione magica e mitica del mondo, deve ora fare i conti con la probabile fine di esso. L'arte ci deve offrire sorprese e alternative, deve ricordarci il passato e convincerci che ci potrà essere un futuro." Cassieri, con Willy, propone un personaggio che fra l'altro è uno studioso di miti e leggende, volto al recupero di storie che sono alla base delle trasformazioni della vita dell'uomo, della società e dei valori. Willy è l'eccipiente culturale, congiunge o sintetizza posizioni divergenti come quella di un Vito Basile, l'intellettuale cosmopolita, sostenitore della tecnologia nel mondo umanistico: ha studiato a Londra, a New York, in società di formazione culturale anglosassone dove l'apporto della tecnologia sembra assumere, per le materie letterarie, un valore di primaria importanza, e fa sì che lui si scontri con un personaggio come Mauro Sparagna sostenitore del solo mondo cartaceo. Entrambi si muovono su posizioni irriducibili. A contrastarli c'è la coppia Bressan, esperti di cucina, beniamini di un vasto pubblico di sostenitori della loro materia. Ciò è sufficiente a fare di loro dei personaggi di primo piano. Certo non hanno nulla a che vedere con lo spessore e sintesi storica e culturale del libro di un Pellegrino Artusi, che raccoglie duemila anni di storia dell'arte del mangiare. Il volume dell'Artusi certamente testimonia le trasformazioni avvenute nella società! Quindi cucina come metafora. Fabio Gerace è l'ideatore della metafora del bosco, della coesistenza dell'uguaglianza e delle diversità culturali, e dell'adeguarsi della letteratura ai nuovi tempi. Un libro come questo di Cassieri non a caso ha suscitato l'interesse di studiosi di sociologia: ne è testimonianza l'attenzione datagli da Franco Ferrarotti, da Ulderico Bernardi, e la dedica fatta dall'autore allo studioso Alfonso di Nola. Questo rafforza la posizione di Lepenies quando sottolinea l'importanza della letteratura di come essa sia (stata) la migliore delle sociologie.

Nell'universo dei personaggi cassieriani non poteva certo mancare un paranoico come Fabio. La sua paranoia è il risultato di uno scontro fra la sua volontà di superare i "muri" culturali, in questo caso, la conflittualità scaturita da una vita vissuta a Nord, e l'affievolirsi del suo accento che invece lo avrebbe definito non solo territorialmente, ma anche culturalmente. L'appartenenza e, nello stesso tempo, l'allontanamento dalla sua regione sono sviluppati in un modo molto sottile da Cassieri, il punto di osmosi fra i due, superamento e asserzione, è dato dal suo santo protettore, legato a un ricordo che il flusso dei secoli tende ad offuscare, San Nilo di Rossano di Calabria.

San Nilo definisce quindi il territorio anagrafico del personaggio. Il santo è stato costretto a lasciare i suoi luoghi per emigrare in un territorio più sicuro in seguito alle incursioni saracene. San Nilo era un monaco basiliano fondatore del monastero a Grottaferrata, un monastero dove vigeva il rito greco proprio alle porte di Roma. Il riferimento agli affreschi del Domenichino sulla vita del santo opera da parte di Cassieri una sintesi e un superamento di confini più profondi. Non è solo il riferimento alla coesistenza (e non confusione!) delle varie arti e generi, e Domenico Zampieri ne è l'esempio con il rapporto che lui stabilisce fra le varie arti e discipline, pittura, architettura, musica, matematica, come testimonia l'affresco dell'incontro del Santo con Otto III nell'anno Mille, al passaggio nel nuovo millennio, ma è prendere ad esempio il Barocco come espressione di una sintesi delle varie arti o di rapporti interdisciplinari, di estensione e raggiungimento delle altre province d'Europa, ma non senza aver prima asserito l'identità, e, in secondo luogo, il superamento e l'arricchimento. Questo è l'aspetto che Cassieri stabilisce fra Fabio Gerace e il suo santo che fra l'altro va anche collegato a un filone di fiabe e leggende, che tratteremo in seguito.

Conflittualità esiste nei personaggi anche nel tentativo di caratterizzarli nella loro indefinitezza e imperfezione, ed in ciò è la forza della loro universalità tale da renderli sempre nuovi ed antichi. La componente antica prevale infine su tutti i personaggi di questo romanzo. È nella definizione di antico che vige la coesistenza della loro identità culturale e territoriale, ed è dopo averla rafforzata che possiamo parlare di superamento. La necessità di identificare Sparagna e Gerace con la costa ionica degli antichi greci con i quali i due uomini conservano e perpetuano tratti somatici simili, è un arricchimento caratteriale universale, tale da farci riscoprire gli antichi Eurialo e Niso nella loro complementarità.

Le origini umili di uno come Sparagna attaccato al mondo cartaceo del Novecento lo rendono cauto ai cambiamenti che invece rafforzano la posizione di un Fabio Gerace. "Un decennio bianco che non sappia alimentare una concezione utopica della storia che Decennio è?" Per quest'ultimo la letteratura deve creare o perpetuare valori, quali quello etico ed estetico, quest'ultimo anche sotto forma di scrittura che assurge a una nuova forma di trascendenza. È utile tener presente il titolo del romanzo. "Muro" va inteso come la forza della scrittura che viene a mancare come elemento unificante e diversificante, creando invece barriere e mancanze di utopie o valori che hanno dato prova di vita etica ed estetica. Infatti, per Gerace la metafora del bosco diventa la capacità, attraverso la scrittura, di immaginare e creare una realtà migliore, grazie alla forza del pensiero e della parola. Nell'universo dei personaggi cassieriani Federico Nardò raccoglie e rappresenta una conoscenza enciclopedica e l'importanza che lui dà alla finzione che mette in moto la realtà e ne determina la consistenza. Anche di questo personaggio Cassieri mette in evidenza la dimensione mitica attraverso la scelta semantica di selenitico.

Il personaggio che esula da una definizione tipo è Eva Gherardi, che si astiene da ogni tipo di discussione e per questo motivo diventa elusiva. Lei è ciò che ognuno vuole vedere. Lei è poetessa, "distillatrice di angosce cosmiche, rigorosa e soave: perfetta." Lei è poesia. Per questo personaggio la forza della scrittura permette la coesistenza dell' antico e del nuovo e all'autore di vestirsi di una serenità espressiva che agisce anche sull'ambiente circostante come indicatore del tempo, dell'ora del giorno, ma anche di assenza del tempo, che agevola uno slittamento verso una considerazione antica dei personaggi e della stessa isola come luogo di incontro di culture diverse nel passato e nel presente. L'isola si pone in un continuum intellettuale fra il passato, il presente e il futuro del convegno di Anversa. In questa fluidità svanisce la componente temporale per asserire valori di valicamento ed estensione di ogni tipo di culture. Eva si pone in questo flusso. Lei dà un significato essenziale a ciò che era, è, sarà la letteratura o scrittura, nonostante le forze estranianti ed alienanti del mondo.

Precedentemente ne *I festeggiamenti* Cassieri, attraverso la figura del professor Redi, difende la sua dignità professionale pur avvalendosi degli apporti della tecnologia, nonostante già allora lo stato di allarme di Jean Starobinski per il quale "il baccano diffuso, la distrazione permanente, l'ingombro di troppe cose e fatti sembrano allontanarci dalla nostra vita più intima e quindi dalla poesia." Oppure da quanto affermato da Francois-Regis Bastide, a proposito dei mass media quando sono al servizio della letteratura "… la danneggiano .... D'altra parte si allargherà sempre più fatalmente una produzione letteraria che ubbidirà alle esigenze dei media, rinunziando ad un vero impegno creativo, radio e televisione, … tenderanno a soppiantare il libro, l'orecchiabilità, e la comunicabilità a sostituire la mediazione."

Gli argomenti di facile consumo diventano il semplice elemento narrativo, e, a livello psicologico, di crisi nevrotiche e agiscono sullo scrittore come motivo di barriera fra la sua creatività e l'identità stilistica, ed aumenta il timore dello studioso, del professor Redi de *I festeggiamenti*, timore che si traduce in incubo "… l'improvvisa sensazione di non poter più articolare le falangi della destra … e guardav(a) disperato la (sua) Ardea 2 cm. sullo scrittoio ..." (108). L'uomo esprime il legame profondo che ha con la letteratura sentita come "antica vita" (109). La letteratura mette l'uomo in un intimo rapporto con se stesso: "La penna non gratta sul foglio, ma vi soffia sopra come greco spirito, come pneuma" (54). Attraverso la sua materia il professor Redi stabilisce un rapporto più profondo e sensuale con i suoni e le lettere, ritornando agli albori del "mito" delle parole e del pensiero. La chirografia rappresenta più un legame con il passato che con il futuro e fino ad oggi essa ha avuto un cammino difficile, pieno di equivoci, "chirografo per chiromante è lapsus quotidiano" (17). Il professor Redi sente la scrittura come poesia. Purtroppo egli rimane uno studioso e un artista isolato e incompreso. Il duemila avrebbe perpetuato gli aspetti negativi del precedente. Il simbolismo di "transito con le mie catene" si trasforma in una mutazione grafica di "mie" minuscola in maiuscola.

Ne *Il muro di Gutenberg* Cassieri raggiunge un livello di serena contemplazione. Il romanzo si apre sotto gli auspici di un settembre di "antiche stagioni." L'isola diventa soporifera. Lo stesso personaggio di Willy diventa più caldo e aperto a superare ogni conflittualità. A differenza del professor Redi, qui Cassieri-Willy attraverso Eva recupera una dimensione della scrittura tale da far rivivere l'antico mito/leggenda della favola di Saffo. Eva è interpretazione e tramite di nuova e antica poesia. Ciò che la spinge al suicidio è la volontà di un riscatto di se stessa e di ciò che lei rappresenta, e gli eventi che l'hanno portata ad appartarsi dalle discussioni. Per l'autore l'abilità di superare la specificità della vita stessa della donna, cioè tutto ciò che l'hanno segnata profondamente, lo aiutano a definirla simbolicamente. Nel riproporre la figura di Saffo, scopre l'essenza della donna e riprende il mito del Paradiso in terra, un mondo utopico che può essere visto come l'estensione del paradiso dell'isola di Ventotene.

Il risalire agli antichi nomi dell'isola, e di prediligere Bentilem, termine saraceno, per associazione sonora è possibile collegare il luogo con lo studio di Willy sui tre re magi e a Betlemme, così l'isola si pone come un richiamo di paradisi mediorientali anticipati in *Diario di un convertito*. Questo romanzo rappresenta un ritorno alle radici primordiali, non ancora intaccati da "precetti balordi." Lo scrittore attraverso la figura del professor Taris, studioso di arte cristiana del periodo iconoclasta, va alla ricerca di una patria antica, più genuina in spirito, ciò che era alla base della sua terra natia e che, col sovrapporsi dei secoli era andato perduto. Ma è una forte componente pagana che l'autore sembra cercare in Turchia dove vige una spiritualità che avvicina di più la gente a Dio, anche se con profondi dubbi, che rasentano a volte il comico, da parte dello studioso. *Diario di un convertito* si pone come un tentativo di uno slancio metafisico da parte di Cassieri, solamente un tentativo perché molti sono i richiami all'erotismo e molte le descrizioni-simbolo dell'era nuova.

Già in questo romanzo l'uomo cerca di superare le restrizioni di una cultura nel tentativo di comprenderne un'altra, esprime il desiderio e la volontà di valicare i propri confini percepiti nella loro contrapposizione ed estensione sia fisica che intellettuale. I preparativi della conversione del Professor Taris, per poi poter sposare una donna di cultura diversa, quella musulmana, sono soprattutto indice di una smania intellettuale e conoscitiva, sono l'auto da fé di un uomo insofferente ai problemi della sua società, di un uomo che è alla ricerca di altri valori. Per il professor Taris, Fatma, la donna che lui vuole sposare, è l'odalisca, l'antitesi della donna occidentale, diventa figura arcana, sacerdotessa e vestale di un periodo passato, è tradizione, elemento essenziale nella cultura musulmana.

Se da un lato Fatma è libera dalle impurità del mondo occidentale, pur rappresentando una via d'uscita per il professor Taris, è anche incarnazione di un vecchio mondo, del paradiso in Terra, in termine persiano, e lo studioso sembrerebbe andare alla ricerca di questo tipo di felicità. Tuttavia anche in Cappadocia c'è presenza della nuova età; infatti, quando il professor Taris lascia un sito archeologico e rientra in città, "implacabili affiorano i flash sincronizzati della paranoia" (89).

Il mondo di Fatma è possibile solo in uno stato di dormiveglia e nei giardini in cui esistono "i prati di amaranti e papaveri, i gialli cigdem e i minuscoli igde dal profumo miracoloso dedicato nei libri mitologici ad Afrodite e motivo di fascino non secondario per Elena di Troia" (89). Cassieri qui crea un certo indugio nella descrizione paesaggistica prolungata dalla presenza costante del suono *m* per la sua innata estensione sonora nelle scelte semantiche di *amaranti, cigdem, minuscoli, profumo, miracoloso, mitologici*. Inoltre, parole quali *cigdem* ed *igde*, che forse a prima vista potrebbero apparire estranee dal punto di vista linguistico, sono invece portatrici di un ritmo cadenzato, come se l'autore avesse voluto echeggiare il canto dei muezzin. Ancor di più, esse non si sostituiscono alla lingua italiana, ma sostituiscono un mondo, dietro queste parole avviene un cambiamento di ambienti. Non è solo quindi un richiamo al mondo musulmano già presente storicamente nella terra di Cassieri, ma anche alle radici più profonde, che determina un'attrazione mentale al luogo da parte dell'autore.

È utile prendere in considerazione il lavoro di traduttore fatto da Cassieri delle fiabe pugliesi per la Mondadori (1983) che ha dedicato una collana alle fiabe regionali italiane testimoniando un grande interesse per il folklore e la cultura popolare come espressione di identità territoriale. Nella favola tradotta in una prosa popolare d'arte, la personalità e la regionalità del traduttore-scrittore si trasmette attraverso la lingua, che testimonia il suo bagaglio culturale. Infatti, un personaggio del mondo fiabesco può operare un recupero del valore e significato insito in quello di Eva.

Abbiamo già accennato che Cassieri nel proporre Eva riprende il motivo di Saffo. I versi inediti che la donna cassieriana dona a Willy—"Ultime rive di settembre/ lisce di ricordi/ il mare ci assapora/ con insolenza/ di morte"—chiama in causa la millenaria presenza del mare e ciò porta l'autore ad andare oltre l'esperienza della musulmana Fatma. Egli ripropone la poesia come fonte di vita e di civiltà mediterranea, allontanandosi dal mondo della donna musulmana che vive la sua vita in accordo con tutto ciò che la circonda. Eva non riesce a conciliare il suo mondo con la realtà esterna al punto da lasciarsi andare al mare che, sulla scia montaliana, è l'antico padre e maestro di poesia. La poesia non muore né con Eva, né con Saffo, ma continua ad essere.

"Il pensiero è la fonte della vita dell'uomo che mette in moto la realtà e ne determina la consistenza" (26). Questa è anche la posizione di Fabio Gerace, "con le finitudini e i limiti imposti tornerebbero a farci soffrire la sete dell'ineffabile" (89). Eva è l'ineffabile: "...a vederla in sogno, nuda e casta nella folla dei redivivi, è stato ...fiabesco" (125). Fatma non è fiabesca!

La presenza di alcuni versi creati dallo stesso Cassieri sulla scia di una poesia araba che Willy recita è un modo per l'uomo di isolarsi dal cicaleccio del mondo al punto da soffocare il suo cellulare in un cassetto dello scrittoio per non interrompere il momento magico creato da quei versi: "Io il pruno e tu la melagrana/ io il lucignolo e tu la lumiera/ io la morte e tu l'acqua chiara" (130).

In questa poesia dal tono cadenzato di stampo, oserei dire, biblico e contrappuntuale allo stesso tempo per via delle immagini, avviene il passaggio, anche osmosi di complementarità, fra il mitico e il fiabesco. In una favola tradotta da Cassieri *Redelia* è personaggio femminile che collega Eva mitica al fiabesco. Cassieri, con Eva, sembra ricalcare il mondo della favola di *Redelia*. Già l'eco sonora con redimere/redentrice, e il suo valore semantico, stabilisce il rapporto. Redelia è la figlia di un mago. Lei gli disubbidisce per aiutare un giovane, di cui poi s'innamora, a superare le difficili prove. Per sfuggire alla furia paterna, con l'aiuto di un anello magico, i due giovani si trasformano "lei in orto e lui in ortolano" e in seguito "lei in fiume e lui in pesce." Questa sequenza ritmica-immagistica riecheggia i versi della poesia araba che possiamo così continuare: "io l'orto e tu l'ortolano/ io il fiume e tu il pesce."

La correlazione interna dei lavori di Cassieri ci permette di mettere in rapporto la poesia con la favola, o la figura di Eva con Redelia. Entrambe le donne si sottopongono a un rituale di purificazione per poi rinascere rinnovate, create o ricreate. Eva si abbandona al mare e Redelia e il giovane, per vanificare la sentenza del genitore crudele che li condannava a una eterna tristezza, per liberarsi da questo incantesimo, devono sottoporsi al rito attraverso le fiamme. Ne usciranno più freschi che se fossero stati immersi nel mare! *L'Orfeo in fiamme* è ciò che Eva regala a Willy prima di suicidarsi. Eva morendo afferma la sua rinascita e universalità. Eva, la poesia e la scrittura sono l'ineffabile che trascende le finitudini e i limiti territoriali, mentali e culturali.

WORKS CITED

Cassieri, Giuseppe. *Diario di un convertito.* Milano: Mondadori, 1986.

_______. *I festeggiamenti.* Milano: Rizzoli, 1989.

_______, trans. *Fiabe pugliesi.* A cura di Giovanni Battista Bronzini. Milano: Mondadori, 1983.

_______. *Il muro di Gutenberg.* Venezia: Marsilio, 1999.

Colombo, Furio. *La vita imperfetta.* Milano: Rizzoli, 1999.

Lepenies, Wolf. *Ascesa e declino degli intellettuali in Europa.* Roma-Bari: Laterza, 1998.

Closing Address

Una notte a Internet

Paola Colaiacomo

Accendo il computer, anche stasera, e mi metto a navigare su *Altavista*. Da qualche tempo per me, lettrice notturna, c'è questa nuova lettura prima dell'altra. Questo leggere che più che altro è un guardare, uno scegliere tra differenti opzioni, un puntare l'indice e cliccare. Un muoversi tra "informazioni," tra notizie impacchettate, compatte come pillole. All'Inghilterra elisabettiana tutto il mondo si presentava sotto forma di palcoscenico, a Internet la recita è sempre già una replica. Il replicante assume le fattezze della notizia; del *piece of news*, come dice l'inglese, sottolineando come l'informazione che mi viene data non sia che un "pezzo" di un unico, inarrestabile flusso informativo. Tra me e le parole verso le quali faccio vela si interpone, a differenza di quanto avveniva col libro, un misterioso garante, un intermediario: forse un lontano discendente di quel famiglio di Montaigne il quale, avendo soggiornato a lungo nella Francia Antartica, poteva veridicamente riferire al proprio padrone delle usanze dei popoli cannibali che si trovano laggiù. Per me ora è Internet l'intermediario, il famiglio che si incarica di far sì che le singole notizie si raccordino sotto i miei occhi nella tonalità del racconto. O meglio, del racconto nel racconto.

È un curioso slittamento, questo per cui la notizia si fa immediatamente racconto, e il racconto, a propria volta, perde forza, e decade a resoconto. Ma racconto di chi, e a chi? Ma questi sono problemi troppo difficili. Non posso certo concentrarmici sopra adesso che sto navigando. Devo invece star bene attenta a predispormi dei punti d'appoggio che mi consentano il recupero e il salvataggio degli occasionali relitti ancora utilizzabili che trovo sparsi sul mio percorso. Apro perciò, sotto la pagina di *Altavista*, un mio *file* personale, che denomino "Scarti." Do a Scarti un formato eccedente rispetto alla pagina Internet, in modo da poterlo agganciare facilmente, ogni volta che ho una preda da depositare: un particolare modo di dire, l'indice di una rivista, una piccola posta curiosa.

Formattato in stile Internet, anche l'invito a pronunciarmi con un sì o con un no sul personaggio di un serial televisivo, mi immette in un ciclo narrativo. Costruisco pian piano, come un magazzino di curiosità, il mio racconto, mescolandolo di riflessioni mie, e di notizie che mi riporta l'intermediario. Agisco con "taglia e incolla": il collage crea un corto circuito tra parola e cosa, quale si verifica nell'opera di Rauschenberg così denominata (*Short Circuit*, del 1955). La decisione se buttare o conservare devo prenderla istantaneamente: so infatti che se perdo quella per me interessante tra le infinite schegge di narrazione in cui mi imbatto, non la recupererò mai più. Do dunque alla macchina i comandi necessari, senza la minima pretesa di ordinare, di schedare il mio materiale. Tutte operazioni superate una volta compiuto l'innesto del mio leggere/scrivere sul sistema web/computer.

L'esperienza della lettura, a Internet, è assolutamente immateriale, e casuale. *Randomized*: dato che è pressoché impossibile tornare sui propri passi. A prima vista sembra che non debba essere così perché, a differenza che con un film, o con un programma televisivo (che però può facilmente essere registrato), qui lo strumento di lettura lo teniamo in mano. Il PowerBook come dice la parola è un libro potenziato. Forse perché privo di pagine. L'antico esercizio di memoria visiva—in alto/in basso, a destra/a sinistra—che mi aiuta da tutta la vita a ritrovare sulla pagina quello che so di averci letto, ora mi è impedito dalla natura del mezzo.

Su Internet imparo dunque a non voltarmi indietro. Certo, la macchina mi dice quali sono le pagine che via via ho aperto: tuttavia non riesco a stabilire quel tanto di distanza che mi faccia desiderare di ritornare sulla me stessa anche solo di un attimo fa. Estroflessa dal corpo, non più dentro di noi, ma intorno a noi, nelle nostre mani, nel nostro tatto, la memoria diventa irriconoscibile. Diventa una memoria incapace di conservare: è dunque l'operazione stessa della memoria studiosa—ordinare, classificare, schedare—a perdere valore. Il tatto, il tocco delle dita, è molto meno addestrato a ricordare che non l'occhio. Perciò: *cut and paste*, e mi ritrovo una pagina composita e variegata di frammenti prestampati, un po' in italiano e un po' in inglese, mescolati alle mie annotazioni, caratteri e "giustificazione" ogni volta diversi.

Di nuovo affiora il ricordo della pagina di Montaigne, coi suoi tagli, le sue spezzature, i suoi virgolettati: il francese continuamente interrotto dal latino delle citazioni. Perché la lettura/scrittura, a Internet, è tutt'altro che un'esperienza superficiale, anche se la sensazione è quella di scivolare su un'unica superficie, fatta di tanti moduli equivalenti, irriducibili, tra i quali non si stabilisce gerarchia. Diventa palpabile quella certa "torbidità del pensiero" di cui parlava il *land artist* Robert Smithson negli anni '70. Quella certa sua resistenza alla simmetria, alla trasparenza degli schemi.

Una quarantina d'anni fa Samuel Beckett ci ha regalato, in *Krapp's Last Tape*, l'immagine dell'uomo anziano che ascolta la memoria di se stesso giovane depositata nei nastri magnetici. Si trattava di uno straordinario esperimento di resa verbale di quello stesso processo di esternalizzazione della memoria che oggi riaffiora nel nostro abitare Internet. La memoria lì era *detta* nel suo farsi tatto, pressione del dito sul pulsante, e subito dopo udito: sonorità non interiore, nè organica, e tuttavia ancora dominata dalle immagini della registrazione e della traccia.

Dominante restava il paradigma della conoscenza come frontalizzazione: paradigma visivo, quale che sia il senso di volta in volta impegnato. Conoscere era ancora un mettersi di fronte alla cosa da conoscere. A Internet, invece, è proprio l'immagine del faccia a faccia a non tenere. La memoria non è più una "piega" dell'io. Rinuncio dunque a ordinare, a schedare, poiché so che la mia memoria si è spostata fuori di me. E tutto quello che posso fare per recuperarla da tale ambiguo "fuori" è un'operazione, appunto, di *retrieving*. Io non contengo, non sono la mia memoria. Vi entro dentro: mi aggiro nelle sue stanze, ma sono stanze che non mi appartengono. È davvero un'inedita arte della memoria, quella che sperimento questa notte a Internet.

Non si tratta di semplice inversione dello sguardo, da guardare ad essere guardati. Certo qualcosa da guardare c'è, a voler essere letterali, altrimenti non potrei nemmeno scrivere queste righe; ma ciò che voglio dire è che nella mia testa non si forma visione d'assieme, panorama prospettico. È per questo, in realtà, che non riesco a ricostruire i luoghi attraverso i quali sono passata. Ritornare indietro diventa un gesto senza senso, ben diversamente da quanto accade con la pagina stampata. Non basta infatti che lo strumento sia in grado di farmi rifare il percorso a ritroso: sono io che non posso riprendermi il tempo che ho investito nelle operazioni di selezione, apertura e attraversamento dei siti. Tutti i tempi morti della macchina, durante i quali la mia vita continuava a scorrere, alla velocità che le è connaturata, e intanto si intrecciava all'elettricità della lettura. Sicché ora, al contrario di Krapp, non potrei più riavvolgere la bobina su se stessa.

Al confronto, il tempo di lettura del libro è invisibile, insensibile. Si mimetizza con la velocità stessa del pensiero e si dissolve senza residui inelaborati. A Internet, invece, il libro non sta propriamente nè dentro nè fuori di me: è una striscia di Moebius, in cui dentro e fuori, vicino e lontano, trasmutano l'uno nell'altro, impossibili da disgiungere eppure ben distinti nella mia mente. Internet mi diventa così, letteralmente, *ambiente*. Si fa habitat. *Environment* completo: che io uso, indubbiamente; ma che a propria volta, proprio in quanto suo "user," mi contiene e mi comprende.

Quello che si produce è un disturbo della distanza. Un turbamento della prospettiva, che con la distanza ha il compito di venire a patti, "scorciandola" e dominandola. La prospettiva è stata il modo classico, dal Quattrocento in poi, per ordinare lo spazio e orientarvisi: stabilito un punto d'osservazione, la Terra e il Cosmo si aprono lungo geometriche linee di fuga. La fiducia nel possesso ordinato dello spazio apre la strada alle scoperte di Colombo, Copernico, Galileo, Keplero. Ma il mondo era già stato prospetticamente raffigurato infinite volte, quando dalle colonne d'Ercole, come da un gigantesco arco di proscenio, si era spalancato l'Oceano. Prospettiva spaventosa, sulla quale ben poterono avventurarsi quanti già si erano allenati sul *trompe l'oeil* della distanza prospettica: la sola capace, scrive Argan, di "assorbire e dissolvere la materia della quale la cosa è composta in un sistema di relazioni proporzionali."[1] Mentre oggi ciò che Internet mi riporta a galla è, paradossalmente, l'irriducibilità di certe distanze, che non si lasciano mettere in prospettiva. Che non è più nemmeno corretto denominare distanze.

È interessante interrogare questa caduta d'aura della distanza spaziale. Questa perdita di sfondo, da parte della parola e dell'immagine. Robert Smithson, nella *Spiral Jetty*, schiacciava l'opera d'arte sulla Terra, affinché risultasse quasi indistinguibile dalla superficie o tutt'al più appena visibile, come per un affioramento oltre la crosta della tettonica del profondo. E la docilità con cui la Spirale è sprofondata nel terreno e poi ne è riemersa, nelle alterne vicende dei suoi ormai trent'anni di vita, sta a dimostrare quanto perfettamente sia riuscito l'innesto della struttura man-made sulla superficie terrestre. Altro che lontananza, altro che fuga prospettica!

Ma non è questo dell'incollatura dell'occhio sull'oggetto, fino ad accecarlo per la troppa vicinanza, il metodo seguito da Montaigne in *Des cannibales*? Non si potrebbe forse leggere anche quel grande *essai* come un precoce saggio di resistenza alla regola dell'omologazione prospettica, peraltro così fortemente promossa dalla contemporanea congiuntura storica delle scoperte geografiche e dei primi insediamenti coloniali? Creatura antipodica, circondata di mistero e di leggenda eppure concretamente

[1] G. C. Argan, "The Architecture of Brunelleschi and the Origins of Perspective Theory in the Fifteenth Century," in *Journal of the Warburg and Courtauld Institutes* 1 (1946): 142.

dimostratasi presente su questa terra, il Cannibale—grado zero dell'umano, e figura della costitutiva torbidità del pensiero—diventa per la cultura del tardo Rinascimento l'emblema del nodo insolubile—resistente cioè a qualsiasi scioglimento in prospettiva, anche in prospettiva di salvezza—che stringe l'anima al corpo. È per questo, si pensa, che va salvaguardato.

Nella *Tempesta* di Shakespeare, Caliban, replica anagrammatica del Cannibale montaignano, è sia *savage* che *salvage*: "selvaggio" e "relitto" insieme. Radice ed esito dell'umano. Materia, "cosa," di tenebra, impossibile da annientare nella luce della prospettiva. Ma vi sono, nella letteratura inglese del Rinascimento, altre tracce di resistenza all'omologazione prospettica. Penso per esempio all'episodio della "Casa di Alma" (II, ix) nel poema cavalleresco *The Faerie Queene*, nel quale Spenser disordina in profondità uno spazio che è insieme domestico, e coincidente con quello del Castello. Interno ed esterno: e allora proprio la nitidezza del confine deve essere annebbiata. Domina il canto una spazialità aprospettica, tarda sopravvivenza di una sensibilità allo spazio di origine medievale e saggio di resistenza al prospettivismo pittorico da Spenser studiato, se non altro per quanto riguarda la rappresentazione del corpo femminile, sulle copie della *Primavera* e della *Nascita di Venere* di Botticelli, ampiamente circolanti in Inghilterra.

Per quanto asessuato, o magari bisessuato, il Castello di Alma è ben riconoscibilmente corpo: ma è anche "bellissimo castello" assediato da nemici crudeli. Dopo averlo liberato, il Principe e il Cavaliere, che si trovano a passare di là, chiedono alla damigella di farglielo visitare. Incomincia così l'esplorazione della Casa-corpo: dall'esterno verso l'interno. Veniamo immessi in uno spazio architettonico fortemente antropomorfizzato, secondo un percorso che va dalle mura di cinta alle stanze interne. E dal basso delle gambe verso l'alto della testa, "torre di mirabile struttura, alta sulla massa terrestre, che domina" (II, ix, 45). Nel leggere, siamo sorpresi ogni volta che scopriamo la possibile applicazione anatomica del singolo elemento architettonico.

La forma umana qui è "paradigmatica,"[2] ma non nel senso in cui lo è la tavola anatomica nel modello leonardesco. Più che di una figurazione astratta ed allegorica del corpo umano, visto attraverso la perfetta armonia geometrica e numerologica del cerchio, del quadrato e del triangolo (II, ix, 22), il Castello assume ora la funzione di un plastico in grandezza più che naturale. Di mappa, modellino, *maquette,* di quello spazio irriducibile che è il Corpo di Alma. In molti giochi elettronici l'utente è incoraggiato a percepire se stesso come l'inventore e il dominatore di una griglia spaziale: preme un tasto ed entra in "narrazioni" che sono insieme di scoperta, di creazione e di esplorazione. Quella di cui si rende padrone giocando è una pratica cartografica.

Si può credere che una carta geografica ci dia la rappresentazione letterale, esente da metafore, delle proprietà reali e preesistenti della porzione di territorio terrestre lì "geo-graficamente" trascritta, secondo determinati principi cartografici. In realtà la carta ci mette sotto gli occhi una metafora complessa; un tropismo, che chiama in causa molteplici livelli di decifrazione. La mappa è già un intervento abitativo sul mondo. Ci si cade dentro, così come si cade nel gioco elettronico. Non si ha mai visione d'assieme del suo spazio, alla distanza: ci si limita a muoversi nel suo interno. Ma anche il castello-corpo di Alma lo conosciamo per la via endoscopica.

La pianta topografica della città mi riporta a un luogo reale, o ritenuto tale, ma il legame che con esso mi fa stabilire è tutt'altro che univoco: per questo non finirei mai di guardarla, specie se la città è conosciuta. Vengono in mente i *mesurages* di Orlan: performances nelle quali l'artista "misurava" il proprio corpo contro spazi architettonici famosi, come il Centre Pompidou di Parigi o il Mu-

[2] C. Paglia, *Sexual Personae: Art and Decadence from Nefertiti to Emily Dickinson* (New York: Vintage, 1991), 176.

seo Guggenheim di New York. Corpo ed edificio, messi l'uno contro l'altro, confermavano la loro natura problematica di oggetti provvisti di un dentro e di un fuori, secondo l'apprensione ordinaria dello spazio edificato, ma anche di punti d'emersione, e cause efficienti, di quella distinzione dentro-fuori che non esisterebbe se essi stessi—corpo ed edificio, cioè—non la promulgassero con tanta violenza.

Forse questa capacità del corpo-casa di Alma di darsi come cosa insieme esterna, perfettamente conchiusa in se stessa, ma conosciuta solo nel momento in cui viene percorsa dall'interno, ecografata più che fotografata, è un po' la consumazione di quella qualità che aveva in mente Virginia Woolf quando, a proposito del poema di Spenser notava come suo tratto caratteristico fosse la qualità spaziale, il suo sapersi offrire come spazio "da abitare." Leggendo, "viviamo come in un'immensa bolla di sapone, soffiata dal cervello del poeta," scrive, e il poeta, a propria volta, è posseduto da un'intrepidezza, da una semplicità, "che sono l'esatto equivalente dei movimenti di un selvaggio nudo."[3]

L'attraversamento del corpo-casa, nell'episodio di Alma, diventa l'equivalente della, del resto coeva, penetrazione in profondità nei territori vergini della "wilderness" americana. Allo sguardo nutrito di lontananza, nutrito di prospettiva, la "wilderness" oppone una sfida insormontabile: per definizione, non si lascia distanziare, nè relativizzare. Lo spazio della wilderness lo si conosce solo entrandovi. In questo è "wild." Spazio pazzo. Quando lo sguardo da lontano si arresta sulla cosa di tenebra, allora entra in scena, assieme al famiglio di Montaigne e al Caliban shakespeariano, anche l'Alma di Spenser. Figure intermediarie che con un gusto della contaminazione spaziale davvero inusitato adempiono all'ufficio, più che di avvicinare il lontano, di abolire il senso della distanza *tout*

[3] Cit. in H. MacLean, A. L. Prescott, ed., *Edmund Spenser's Poetry* (London: Norton, 1993), 674-75.

court: nel nome di luoghi che, come Atlantide, l'Isola e il Castello, occupano, rispetto al mondo conosciuto, la doppia posizione del lontano e del vicino. Dello sconfinato e del circoscritto.

Sono pensieri che tornano oggi che Internet ci sospinge con sempre maggior decisione verso una forma di conoscenza non geometrica. Non chiara. Non limpida. Ma anzi nebulosa, o nuvolosa. L'antica e fondamentale connessione di "terra" e "misura," quale risulta appunto dalla parola, "geometria," che designava la più oggettiva e impersonale delle forme di conoscenza—*more geometrico,* appunto—tende ora ad oscurarsi. Man mano che il tempo si fa "reale," è la realtà dello spazio a non essere più sentita come decisiva: entra in crisi il sistema delle distanze relative, delle simmetrie, delle sezioni auree, delle angolature corrispondenti.

A Internet sta di casa Calibano, il Cannibale. Nel mondo del tempo reale, cosa mai può contare una maggiore o minore distanza? E soprattutto distanza da che, e come misurata? Di sicuro è un mondo sempre più piccolo, quello che l'arte lavora, senza bisogno di alcun compensatorio allargamento ideale. Lo faceva notare Beckett molti anni fa: "Art tends not to make bigger," diceva, "but to shrink."

CONTRIBUTORS

BRENT ADKINS is an Assistant Professor of Philosophy at Roanoke College in Salem, Virginia.

FRANCO BERARDI, known as "Bifo," is a writer affiliated with the Università di Bologna.

MASSIMO CANEVACCI is a Professor in the Department of Cultural Anthropology at the Università di Roma "La Sapienza."

JOHN CASEY, translator of Professor Perniola's opening address, teaches Philosophy at Coe College in Cedar Rapids, Iowa.

PAOLA COLAIACOMO is a Professor in the Department of English Language and Literature at the Università di Roma "La Sapienza."

ANTHONY ELLIS, a doctoral candidate in English at Loyola University Chicago, teaches in the Writing Program at the University of California, Santa Barbara.

BARBARA FAEDDA is a Professor in the Department of Cultural Anthropology at the Università di Roma "La Sapienza."

CARLO FERRUCCI is a Professor in the Department of Aesthetics at the Università di Roma "Tor Vergata."

LAURA HENGEHOLD is an Assistant Professor of Philosophy at Case Western Reserve University in Cleveland, Ohio.

MARCO JACQUEMET is an Assistant Professor in the Department of Communication Studies at the University of San Francisco.

GARY KELLY holds a Canada Research Chair in Literature and Language in Society at the University of Alberta.

ZEYNEP MENNAN is a Professor in the Department of Architecture at Middle Eastern Technical University in Ankara, Turkey.

J. PAUL NARKUNAS is an Assistant Professor of English and Humanities at the Pratt Institute in New York City.

KYRIAKI PAPAGEORGIOU is a graduate student in Anthropology at the University of California, Irvine.

MARIO PERNIOLA is a Professor in the Department of Aesthetics at the Università di Roma "Tor Vergata."

RACHEL POULSEN, a doctoral candidate in English at Loyola University Chicago, teaches in the English Department at the University of Illinois at Chicago.

Patrocinio P. Schweickart is a Professor of English and Women's Studies at Purdue University in West Lafayette, Indiana.

Grazia Sotis is a Professor in the Department of Italian Literature at Loyola University Chicago (Rome Center).

Isabella Vincentini is an editorial consultant in Rome.

Anne Wingenter recently completed her doctorate in History at Loyola University Chicago.

INDEX

Acker, Kathy, 45
Aeneas, 84
Agamben, Giorgio, 88, 198-200
Amsterdam Treaty (1999), 121
Anchises, 84
Anderson, Benedict, 113, 119, 185
Antarctica, 221
Antigone, 167, 169-176, 178
Aphrodite, 216
Appadurai, Arjun, 58, 114-115, 125, 127, 160
Archimedes, 69
Argan, Giulio Carlo, 225
Artusi, Pellegrino, 210
Asia-Pacific Economic Council (APEC), 202
Association of Southeast Asian Nations (ASEAN), 202
Atlantis, 229
Augustine, Saint 25
Augustus, 84

Balkan States, 11, 59-61
Bangladesh, 133
Barbados, 193
Barthes, Roland, 88-89
Bartky, Sandra Lee, 55
Basques, 118, 124
Baudelaire, Charles, 47-48, 87
Baudrillard, Jean, 18, 42, 44
Beckett, Samuel, 229
    Krapp's Last Tape, 223-224
Belgium, 126
Benjamin, Walter
    "The Work of Art in the Age of Mechanical Reproduction," 16-18, 21
Berger, Suzanne, 117
Berlin Wall, 179
Bernardi, Ulderico, 210
Bernstein, R. J., 69, 74-75
Beuys, Joseph, 18
Blackwoord, Evelyn, 136
Blanchot, Maurice, 88-89
Bloch, Marc, 50-51
Bloom, Harold, 89
Blumenberg, Hans, 88
Bobbitt, Lorena, 137
Bocca, Giorgio, 208
Boltanski, Christian, 18
Boltanski, Luc, 24-27
Bonnefoy, Yves, 89
Borges, Jorge Luis, 92
Bossuet, Jacques Bénigne, 25
Botticelli, Sandro, 226
Bourdieu, Pierre, 17
Bové, Paul A., 88
Bradley, Henry, 164
Braudel, Fernand, 50-51
Bravo, L. Ferrari, 109
Bridenthal, Renate, 147
Brittany, 4-5, 117-128
Brunelleschi, Filippo, 225
Bullmann, Udo, 121, 125
Byron, George Gordon, Lord, 183-184

Cacciari, Massimo, 89
Caliban, 7, 226, 228-229

Calvet, Pierre, 159
Calvino, Italo, 89
Cambodia, 194
Camus, Albert, 92
Canada
  Aboriginal Justice Strategy, 101
  Doukhobors, 187
  Native Law Centre, 98, 100, 103, 107
  Office of Native Claims, 100
  and substate groups, 5, 97-110
Canevacci, Massimo, 37
Canuti, Giovanna, 146, 151
Carnoy, Martin, 200
Cassieri, Giuseppe, 5, 208-218
Castoriadis, Cornelius, 18
Catalonia, 119, 126
Catholic Church, 132, 152, 181
Caufield, Catherine, 189, 192-193
Céline, Louis-Ferdinand, 92
Char, René, 89
China, 190, 194
Chossudovsky, Michel, 59, 194-195
Christo, 18
Clifford, James, 37
Cold War, 202
Colombo, Furio, 218
Columbus, Christopher, 225
Condillac, Étienne Bonnot de, 113
Copernicus, Nicolaus, 225
Crabb, Michael, 117
Crystal, David, 113, 201
Daddabbo, Leonardo, 48-49
Dammeyer, Manfred, 123
Debord, Guy, 18
De Felice, Renzo, 142-144
De Grazia, Victoria, 150, 152, 154
De Jacobis, Giustino, 143
Deleuze, Gilles, 60, 67, 88-89, 198, 200
De Man, Paul, 88
Derrida, Jacques, 77, 88
Descartes, René, 69-70
De Staël, Germaine, 183
Diaz-Andreu, Margarita, 119
Dickens, Charles, 203
Didi-Huberman, Georges, 17
Di Nola, Alfonso, 210
Dogliani, Patrizia, 149
Droz, Jacques, 181
Duchamp, Marcel, 18
Duns Scotus, 50
Durkheim, Émile, 41

Eco, Umberto, 1, 89
Elena, Queen of Savoy, 148, 150, 153
Eliot, T. S., 87
Engels, Friedrich, 118
England, 190
  Elizabethan, 221, 226-229
Enlightenment, 6, 47-56, 61-62, 113, 116, 179, 199, 204
Esman, Milton J., 118
Ethiopia
  and the Italo-Ethiopian War, 142-155
European Union

and Brittany, 117-128
and Canada, 5, 97-110
and the Committee of the Regions, 4-5, 118, 120-125, 127-128
and economic unification, 98
and English, 201
Ewald, François, 55, 58-59

Fallacara, Antonietta, 143
Farge, Arlette, 50, 52
Fascism, Italian, 142-155
Febvre, Lucien, 50-51
Federman, J., 43
Feinberg, Richard, 193
Ferguson, James, 126
Ferrarotti, Franco, 210
Fichte, Johann, 198
Fischer, Michael M. J., 36
Fish, Stanley, 73-74, 77
Flake, Macella Monk, 106
Fontana, Lucio, 18
Forbes, Dean, 194
Forgacs, David, 1
Fortier, David H., 118
Foscolo, Ugo, 181-182
Foucault, Michel, 47-62, 66, 88, 193-194, 200
The Archeology of Knowledge, 51
biopower, 4, 191, 205-207
Discipline and Punish, 48, 52, 55-56
"Nietzsche, Genealogy, History," 49-52
The Politics of Truth, 47-48
France, 190, 194
and contemporary theory, 65-85
and the Revolution, 119, 179-183
and substate groups, 4-5, 105, 117-128
Freud, Sigmund, 165-178
Frow, John, 23
Fukuyama, Francis, 179

Gadacz, Rene, 98
Gal, Susan, 113
Galilei, Galileo, 225
Ganuza, José María Munoa, 124
Garcia Lorca, Federico, 165
Gargani, Aldo Giogio, 89
Gates, Bill, 208
Geertz, Clifford, 7, 34
George, Susan, 193
Germany, 107, 121, 126, 147, 179, 181, 198-199
Gnoli, Antonio, 91
Godzich, Wlad, 201
Goethe, Johann Wolfgang von, 172, 181
Goodman, Ellen, 133
Gowan, Peter, 59
Gradev, Vladimir, 59
Gramsci, Antonio, 2
Great Britain, 182, 184, 202-203
Greece
ancient, 9, 84, 93, 111
War of Independence, 183-184
Griggs, Richard A., 122, 126
Grossman, Atina, 147
"Gruppo 63," 88
"Gruppo 93," 88
Gruzinski, Serge, 116

Guattari, Felix, 88, 160, 198
Guéhenno, Jean-Marie, 200
Guggenheim Museum, 227-228
Gupta, Akhil, 126
Gutenberg, Johann, 208
Gutierrez, Navidad, 126
Gypsies, 109

Habermas, Jurgen, 53, 70-73, 77
Haddad, Wadi, 200
Hall, Stuart, 2
Hamlet, 166-167, 169-178
Hannibal, 172
Hardie, Frank, 143-145
Hegel, George, 11, 59
Heidegger, Martin, 79
Heinich, Nathalie, 18-23, 26
Helen of Troy, 216
Hercules, 225
Herder, Johann Gottfried von, 113
Hill, Anita, 130
Hillman, James, 93
Hobbes, Thomas, 25
Hoebel, E. Adamson, 99
Hoggart, Richard, 2
Hong Kong, 202
Hugo, Victor, 184
Husserl, Edmund, 75

India, 133
International Monetary Fund, 191-194
Internet, 208
    and language, 6-7, 164
    and literature, 7, 221-229
    and time, 56
    and visual culture, 7, 33-45
Inuit, 99-100, 109
Italo-Abyssinian War (1896), 144
Italo-Ethiopian War (1935-1936), 142-155
Italy, 111, 115, 181-183
    and cultural studies, 1-3, 7
    and the *Giornata della "fede"* (1935), 142-155

Jabes, Edmond, 89
Jacquard, Albert, 124
Jameson, Frederic, 65-66
Japan, 59, 194, 198
Jardin, André, 1810
Johnson, Lyndon, 192
Junger, Ernst, 91, 93

Kafka, Franz, 92
Kant, Immanuel, 75
    Critique of Pure Reason, 9-10
    "What is Enlightenment?", 47, 52-53, 56
Kaplan, Marion, 147
Keating, Michael, 119
Kellner, Douglas, 2-5
Kennedy, John F., 192
Kepler, Johann, 225
Kojève, Alexandre, 58-59
Koonz, Claudia, 147
Kymlicka, Will, 98

Lacan, Jacques, 67, 88
Lateran Agreements (1929, 1936), 143
Lawton, Ben, 1-2

League of Nations, 142, 145, 147, 153
Le Coadic, Ronan, 127
Leduc, Jean, 50
Lega Nord, 119
Leopardi, Giacomo, 87, 165
Lepenies, Wolf, 209-211
Lessona, Alessandro, 144
Levi, Carlo, 154
Lévinas, Emmanuel, 89
Levi Strauss, Claude, 89
Llobera, Joseph R., 118
Losano, Mario G., 100
Loughlin, John, 121
Ludwig, Emil, 142
Lumley, Robert, 1
Lyotard, Jean-François, 89, 199-200, 202

Maastricht Treaty, 122
Macciocchi, Maria Antonietta, 143
MacDonald, Sharon, 119
Mack Smith, Denis, 143-144
Magris, Claudio, 89
Makiling, Maria, 133
Malkki, Lisa, 127
Mallarmé, Stéphane, 87
Mann, Thomas, 87
Marcus, George E., 36
Mars, 84
Mazzini, Giuseppe, 144
McNamara, Robert, 192, 196
Mead, Margaret, 36
Mexico, 193
Milanesi, E. Moavero, 109
Minangkabau (West Sumatra), 136
Mirzoeff, Nicholas, 43
Montaigne, Michel de
    "Of Cannibals," 7, 221, 223, 225-226, 228
Moroncini, Bruno, 48, 58-59
Motta, Riccardo, 97-98
Mugerauer, Robert, 79, 83
Mussolini, Benito, 142-147

Nader, Laura, 98
Napoleon Bonaparte, 180-183
Negri, Ada, 151-152
Newhouse, John, 125-126
Newman, Charles, 161
Nietzsche, Friedrich, 49, 51-52, 79, 92
    Human, All Too Human, 20, 24
'N-Synch, 203
Nunamiut, 99

Oedipus, 165-178
Onestini, Cesare, 120-121
Ophelia, 175
Oreja, Marcelino, 124-125
Orlan, 227
Otto III, 211
Oxford English Dictionary, 199

Padania, 119-120
Paglia, Camille, 227
Pakistan, 133
Parati, Graziella, 1-2
Philippines
    and sexual harassment, 129-141
Picasso, Pablo, 165, 175
Pickering-Iazzi, Robin, 143
Pizzorno, Alessandro, 54-56
Plato, 71

Pomian, Krzysztof, 57-58, 60-61
Pompidou Center, 227
Pospisil, Leopold, 99
Poster, Mark, 55
Procacci, Giovanna, 54
Propp, Vladimir, 89
Prosperini, F., 146

Rage Against the Machine, 203
Ramirez, Juan de Dios, 124
Ransom, John S., 54
Rauschenberg, Robert, 222
Readings, Bill, 198
Regel, Omporn, 200
Remotti, Francesco, 99
Rhea Silvia, 84
Rimbaud, Arthur, 87
Rinaldi, Rosemary, 200
Risorgimento, 144
Romanticism, 6, 113, 179-188
Rome
    foundation myth of, 84
    and the *Giornata della "fede"* (1935), 142-155
Romulus and Remus, 84
Rosaldo, Renato, 35-36
Rouland, Norbert, 97-98, 105
Rousseau, Jean Jacques, 25

Sabelli, Fabrizio, 193
Sachs, Jeffrey, 59
Saint-Simon, Count de, 25
Samonte, Elena, 136
Sanderson, Stephen K., 179
Sappho, 214, 216-217
Sartre, Jean Paul, 66
Schierup, Carl-Ulrich, 58-61
Schleiermacher, Friedrich, 198
Schultz, Theodore, 196
Schulze, Hagen, 180
Scotland, 119
Scott, Walter, 185
Sen, Amartya, 133
Shakespeare, William, 203
    The Tempest, 7, 226, 228
Singapore, 202
Smith, Adam, 25
Smithson, Robert, 223, 225
Socrates, 92
Sophocles, 166-167, 174
South Korea, 193
Soviet Union, 53, 59-60, 194
Spain, 121, 123-124, 126, 132, 181-183
Spanos, William V., 88
Spengler, Oswald, 87
Spenser, Edmund
    The Fairie Queene, 7, 226-229
Spice Girls, 203
Stampino, Maria Galli, 1-2
Stuard, Susan, 147
Sukenick, Ronald, 44

Tallberg, Christina, 124
Thayer, John A., 144
Thévenot, Laurent, 24-27
Thom, Martin, 181
Thomas, Clarence, 130
Thrift, Nigel, 194
Tito, Marshal, 59
Troy, 84
Tudesq, André-jean, 181
Turkey, 111

United Nations, 107, 112, 115-116, 189, 192
United Nations Educational, Scientific, and Cultural Organization (UNESCO), 195, 201, 203-204
United States
and Japanese-Americans, 105-106
and refugees, 107
and sexual harassment, 129-141
and substate groups, 98-99
and the World Bank, 189-207

Vattimo, Gianni, 21, 24
Venus, 84
Veyne, Paul, 50
Vietnam, 189-190, 192, 194-197, 202-205
Vietnam War, 192, 202, 204
Virgil, 84
Virilio, Paul, 42
Volpi, Franco, 91
Von Humboldt, Alexander, 198

Wallerstein, Immanuel, 179
Warhol, Andy, 18
Wark, McKenzie, 164
West Sumatra, 136
Williams, Raymond, 2, 180
Winterson, Jeanette, 94
Wittgenstein, Ludwig, 66
Woolf, Stuart, 181
Woolf, Virginia, 228
World Bank, 4, 189-207
World War I, 144, 146-147, 154
World War II, 191-192

Yazzie, Robert, 103-104

Zangrandi, Ruggero, 143
Zanker, Paul, 84
Zanzotto, Andrea, 89
Zapatista movement, 193
Zizek, Slavoj, 60

VIA FOLIOS

A refereed book series dedicated to Italian studies and the culture of Italian Americans in North America.

GEORGE GUIDA
Low Italian
Vol. 41, Poetry, forthcoming

RUGGERO STEFANINI
Marriage with Tenure
Vol. 40, Play, forthcoming

DANIELA GIOSEFFI
Blood Autumn/Autunno di sangue
Vol. 39, Poetry, $15.00

FRED MISURELLA
Lies to Live by
Vol. 38, Stories, $15.00

STEVEN BELLUSCIO
Constructing a Bibliography
Vol. 37

ANTHONY JULIAN TAMBURRI, ED.
Italian Cultural Studies 2002
Vol. 36, Essays, $18.00

BEA TUSIANI
con amore
Vol. 35, Memoir, $19.00

FLAVIA BRIZIO-SKOV, ED.
Reconstructing Societies in the Aftermath of War
Vol. 34, History/Cultural Stud., $30.00

A.J. TAMBURRI, M.S. RUTHENBERG, G. PARATI, AND B. LAWTON, EDS.
Italian Cultural Studies 2001
Vol. 33, Essays, $18.00

ELIZABETH GIOVANNA MESSINA, ED.
In Our Own Voices
Vol. 32, Ital. Amer. Studies, $25.00

STANISLAO G. PUGLIESE
Desperate Inscriptions
Vol. 31, History, $12.00

ANNA CAMAITI HOSTERT & ANTHONY JULIAN TAMBURRI, EDS.
Screening Ethnicity
Vol. 30, Ital. Amer. Culture, $25.00

G. PARATI & B. LAWTON, EDS.
Italian Cultural Studies
Vol. 29, Essays, $18.00

HELEN BAROLINI
More Italian Hours & Other Stories
Vol. 28, Fiction, $16.00

FRANCO NASI, A CURA DI
Intorno alla Via Emilia
Vol. 27, Culture, $16.00

ARTHUR L. CLEMENTS
The Book of Madness and Love
Vol. 26, Poetry, $10.00

JOHN CASEY, ET. AL
Imagining Humanity
Immagini dell'umanità
Vol. 25, Interdisciplinary Studies, $18.00

ROBERT LIMA
Sardinia • Sardegna
Vol. 24, Poetry, $10.00

DANIELA GIOSEFFI
Going On
Vol. 23, Poetry, $10.00

ROSS TALARICO
The Journey Home
Vol. 22, Poetry, $12.00

EMANUEL DI PASQUALE
The Silver Lake Love Poems
Vol. 21, Poetry, $7.00

JOSEPH TUSIANI
Ethnicity
Vol. 20, Selected Poetry, $12.00

JENNIFER LAGIER
Second Class Citizen
Vol. 19, Poetry, $8.00

FELIX STEFANILE
The Country of Absence
Vol. 18, Poetry, $9.00

PHILIP CANNISTRARO
Blackshirts
Vol. 17, History, $12.00

LUIGI RUSTICHELLI, ED.
Seminario sul racconto
Vol. 16, Narrativa, $10.00

LEWIS TURCO
Shaking the Family Tree
Vol. 15, Poetry, $9.00

LUIGI RUSTICHELLI, ED.
Seminario sulla drammaturgia
Vol. 14, Theater/Essays, $10.00

Fred L. Gardaphè
Moustache Pete is Dead!
Long Live Moustache Pete!
Vol. 13, Oral literature, $10.00

JONE GAILLARD CORSI
Il libretto d'autore, 1860–1930
Vol. 12, Criticism, $17.00

HELEN BAROLINI
Chiaroscuro: Essays of Identity
Vol. 11, Essays, $15.00

T. PICARAZZI AND W. FEINSTEIN, EDS.
An African Harlequin in Milan
Vol. 10, Theater/Essays, $15.00

JOSEPH RICAPITO
Florentine Streets and Other Poems
Vol. 9, Poetry, $9.00

FRED MISURELLA
Short Time
Vol. 8, Novella, $7.00

NED CONDINI
Quartettsatz
Vol. 7, Poetry, $7.00

ANTHONY JULIAN TAMBURRI, ED.
MARY JO BONA, INTROD.
Fuori: Essays by Italian/American Lesbians and Gays
Vol. 6, Essays, $10.00

ANTONIO GRAMSCI
PASQUALE VERDICCHIO,
TRANS. & INTROD.
The Southern Question
Vol. 5, Social Criticism, $5.00

DANIELA GIOSEFFI
Word Wounds and Water Flowers
Vol. 4, Poetry, $8.00

WILEY FEINSTEIN
Humility's Deceit: Calvino Reading Ariosto Reading Calvino
Vol. 3, Criticism, $10.00

PAOLO A. GIORDANO, ED.
Joseph Tusiani: Poet, Translator, Humanist
Vol. 2, Criticism, $25.00

ROBERT VISCUSI
Oration Upon the Most Recent Death of Christopher Columbus
Vol. 1, Poetry, $3.00

Published by BORDIGHERA, INC., an independently owned not-for-profit scholarly organization that has no legal affiliation to the University of Central Florida, Florida Atlantic University, or State University of New York—Stony Brook.

www.ingramcontent.com/pod-product-compliance
Lightning Source LLC
Chambersburg PA
CBHW031151270326
41931CB00006B/234
9781884419829